The Fighter Command War Diaries

Volume One

*This book is dedicated to the memory of the
pilots, navigators and air gunners of
RAF Fighter Command,
Air Defence of Great Britain,
Second Tactical Air Force
and No.100 (Bomber Support) Group
who died in the aerial defence of the United Kingdom
and in the offensive aerial campaign over
northwest Europe 1939-45*

The Fighter Command War Diaries

The operational history of Fighter Command,
Second Tactical Air Force, 100 Group and
Air Defence of Great Britain fighters 1939-45

by

John Foreman

Air Research Publications

First published 1996
This edition 2002 by
Air Research Publications
PO Box 223, Walton-on-Thames,
Surrey, KT12 3YQ
England

© John Foreman 1996

All Rights Reserved.
No part of this publication
may be reproduced, stored
in any form of retrieval
system, or transmitted
in any form or by any
means without prior
permission in writing
from the publishers.

Typeset in Great Britain by
A.C.E.Services,
Radlett, Herts, WD7 8LU

Printed and bound by
Antony Rowe Ltd, Eastbourne

ISBN 1-871187-44-3

CONTENTS

Introduction		7
Notes		8
Sources		10
Acknowledgements		10
Photo Credits		10
Chapter One	Beginnings	11
Chapter Two	The Phoney War	17
Chapter Three	The Waiting Game	31
Chapter Four	Blitzkrieg in the West	45
Chapter Five	The Battle of the Channel	97
Chapter Six	The Battle of the Airfields	139
Summary		203
Index		209

Introduction

Like so many of my contemporaries, my fascination with fighter aircraft and fighter pilots began after reading Pierre Clostermann's magnificent book *The Big Show*. That fascination has never waned.

Over twenty-five years ago I began researching into Fighter Command operations over northwest Europe. This was initially to discover what happened following the Battle of Britain and how the great 'change-around' from defensive to offensive operations came about. And it 'snowballed'. The more I discovered, the more I wanted to know until I found that my records stretched from 1939 to 1945!

Much has been published on the operations of Bomber Command in recent years, yet for Fighter Command, apart from biographies and many, many versions of the Battle of Britain, there is little to show of the daily operations that cost this country the lives of so many of young men. Therefore I decided that this omission should be rectified, at least as far as was practicable. A few years ago Martin Middlebrook produced 'The Bomber Command War Diaries', which has proved such an invaluable work of reference and so, in the much the same style, but with, I hope, more detailed content, comes 'The Fighter Command War Diary'. This is a day-by-day record of the achievements and sacrifices of those young men whose contribution to the eventual Allied victory over Germany has never been sufficiently recorded or recognised.

- *John Foreman*
Radlett,
July 1996

Notes

Format of the Book

The format of this book is a straightfoward diary. In the early part - the 'Phoney War' - not too much was happening on a daily basis and so the essential information is contained within the text. From the Battle of France, however, daily actions were heavy and I have decided to present the information on claims and losses in a tabulated form as shown below:

			BEF France Hurricanes					
Unit	Dest	P.D.	Dam	MIA	Cat E	KIA	MIA	WIA
1 Sqn	3	2	1	1	3	1	1	1

The example above shows that No.1 Squadron, flying Hurricanes with the British Expeditionary Force in France, claimed three enemy aircraft destroyed, two probably destroyed and one damaged. They suffered four aircraft casualties, one reported missing in action and three Category E (write-offs). Pilot casualties amounted to four; one killed, one missing and one safe but wounded. Footnotes are added as necessary. There is a summary for each month, showing the total air victories claimed in the normally accepted form 50:22:17 i.e. fifty confirmed, twenty-two probably destroyed and seventeen damaged. There will also be squadron notes giving movements, changes of equipment etc. Also in the text I have included Combat Report transcripts, biographies of notable pilots, information on the aircraft types and 'events', where particular operations have been analysed in greater detail. All of this, I hope, will serve to give a greater understanding of the rôle of the fighter pilot in World War Two.

Claims and Losses

The reported claims fall into three categories:
 1) Destroyed - where an aircraft was seen to be on fire, or to crash, or where the pilot was seen to parachute.
 2) Probably destroyed. Where an aircraft was left so severely damaged that, in the opinion of the RAF fighter pilot, it was unlikely to have reached its base.
 3) Damaged. Self-explanatory.

There was, however, a fourth category; this was 'destroyed unconfirmed' a contradiction in terms and which, in all respects, was identical to 'probably destroyed'. Indeed, the Air Ministry agreed and, in 1941, such claims were retrospectively downgraded to 'probables'. This annoyed the pilots of some squadrons intensely; at a stroke they had been removed from the top of the high-scoring table and placed some way down the list. Thus the term 'destroyed unconfirmed' will always be referred to as 'probably destroyed', except in some of the 'Event Narratives'.

Claims themselves have always been a problem, since people seem to regard them as 'shoot-downs', which they were not. They should be regarded as simply claims, and should be used as a general guide to the level of combat. It is now well known that heavy overclaiming took place in the heat of battle. Indeed, for the entire war, the heavier the action the greater the overclaim rate. But this is no reflection on the fighter pilots involved. Claims were made in good faith in an environment swarming with aircraft and then, seconds later, empty sky. Events frequently moved too fast for the eye and brain to follow and the eyes played tricks. For the entire war the 'norm' seems to have been three claims to two actual losses and this includes the period from 1941 onward when RAF fighters carried cameras as standard. Thus even the cameras sometimes lied.

The losses are given as missing in action (MIA), which is self-explanatory, or Category E. This may indicate an aircraft lost at sea, but from which the pilot is saved, or an aircraft shot down or crashed on mainland UK. Sometimes it refers to an aircraft that was flown back to base but was found to be damaged beyond repair.

Sources

The prime sources for this book are to be found at the Public Record Office Kew, the basis being Fighter Command Combats and Casualties (AIR16/960), which provided much of the basic framework. The individual squadron diaries (AIR27 series) and the Combat Reports (AIR50 series) provided the detail.

Apart from official sources, the only published works used were: *Twelve Days in May*: Brian Cull, Bruce Lander & Heinrich Weiss, which provided hitherto unknown detail about the British Expeditionary Force Hurricane squadrons in France, The Fledgling Eagles, by Chris Shores, Chris Ehrengardt, Heinrich Weiss, Bjorn Olsen and myself, and the huge *The Blitz Then and Now, Vols 1-3*. All comments and conclusions are necessarily my own.

Acknowledgments

To Simon Parry, for his help and support with this project, and to Simon, Chris Goss, David Brocklehurst, Dilip Sarker, Chris Ellis, Herbert Scholl, and Brian Cull for their assistance with photographs. My thanks also go to Julia Munro of Lloyd's Bank for her help and enthusisatic support through often troubled times and finally, but by no means last in importance...

.....to my wife Pam, for putting up with everything!

Photo Credits Not Credited Elsewhere

Dave Brocklehurst P.25, 26, 34, 79, 80, 82, 100; Brian Cull P.88, 174, 198; Chris Ellis P.58, 89, 122, 180; Simon Parry P.103; Dilip Sarkar P.38, 42, 63, 83, 118, 130, 165.

Chapter One.
Beginnings

As has so often been seen in history, the period following the successful prosecution of a war frequently leads to a time of calm, where the victor fondly believes that the horrors of warfare 'can never happen again', with the inevitable relaxation that attitude implies. So it was with the Royal Air Force following World War One, which was popularly supposed to have been 'The war to end all wars'. By the early 1920s the massive air force which, together with that of the French Allies, had contributed so much toward the defeat of Germany, had all but disappeared; a handful of direct support units - insufficient for the task - and practically no air defence at all apart from guns, balloons and stored equipment. This situation was exacerbated by a growing mistrust of Britain's former ally, France. Voices were raised in protest against the massive run-down of the Royal Air Force, notable among them that of Air Chief Marshal Hugh Trenchard, the man remembered as the 'Father of the Royal Air Force'.

Thus by 1922 an awareness of Britain's military air deficiencies was growing. Against these were raised the voices proclaiming that Germany was finished as a military nation. Her air force disbanded under the Versailles Treaty of 1920, which restricted German aviation to gliding, plus a handful of permitted civilian aircraft to be operated by *Lufthansa*, the German airline. Indeed, Germany was expressly forbidden to build or import any aircraft or any type of aero-engine, a rule that was amended in April 1922 to allow light aircraft to be built. Four months later the British government announced the 'Twenty-three Squadron Expansion Plan', to protect the British Isles against attack by three hundred bombers. This actually provided for just fourteen squadrons with a nominal strength of 158 aircraft! However, by the end of 1922, the mistrust of France had given the British a new potential enemy. The French, always realists and with a frontier bordering Germany, had not fallen into the complacency of their allies. They possessed a strong and well-equipped air force that now outclassed the British forces to such an extent that the Air Staff had become greatly concerned. The disparity in air power between Britain and France had, in their eyes, reached 'menacing' proportions, which resulted in a new air expansion plan, announced on 20th June 1923. This was intended to bring the Royal Air Force to a strength of 52 squadrons amounting to 394 bombers and 204 fighters. The Auxiliary Air Force was formed a year later and was planned to comprise twenty squadrons, supplementing the original 52 regular units. However, by 1925, (when Britain's defences were coalesced into Air Defence of Great Britain under Air Marshal Sir John Salmond) only some 25 squadrons were in place, the fighter units equipped with aircraft that were only marginally superior to the Camels and SE5As of the 1914-18 conflict.

On the continent however, moves were afoot that would ultimately plunge the world into another World War against Germany. Russia and Germany had signed a treaty on April 16th 1922, which amplified an earlier trade agreement in 1921. This, known as the Rapallo Treaty, led to close rapport and collaboration between the German *Reichswehr* and the Red Army, which was eventually to allow the establishment of secret training bases in the Soviet Union to provide the cadre for a new German Air Force - the *Luftwaffe*.

In late 1925 a blow was dealt to the slowly expanding RAF, when a new climate of friendship between Britain and France allowed a slow-down of the expansion. Although the 'Fifty-two Squadron Plan' was retained, it was felt that it could now safely be slowed down by several years. Thus by 1928, RAF strength stood at only 31 squadrons, increased in the next four years by eleven more, ten less than the planned number.

Developments in Germany had proceeded with some speed. A training base had been established at Lipezk where, from 1924 onwards, German cadets were trained in the use of the most modern aircraft, such training including extensive schooling in fighter tactics and close support operations. When in 1933 the National Socialist Party, led by Adolf Hitler, was swept to power in Germany on a wave of popular support, the die was finally and irrevocably cast. At that time however, Britain did not regard Germany as a potential enemy, feeling that any quarrel that Hitler might provoke would be mainly directed against France. As soon as Hitler's power was confirmed, the Russian training bases were immediately disbanded and personnel and aircraft transported to the Reich. This included several types, ostensibly designed as civilian aircraft, but actually first-line combat aircraft such as the Dornier 17P, Heinkel 51 and Arado 65, all of which which had been clandestinely tried and tested in Russia. On May 15th 1933, the fledgeling German Air Force was placed under command of the German Air Ministry, **controlled by Hermann Goering**. Two years later, in March 1935, the German Air Force was brought into the open when the existence of the *Luftwaffe* was announced. At that time the *Luftwaffe* possessed a strength of sixteen front-line squadrons but by August 1935 had expanded to an astonishing 48 squadrons. A year earlier a tender for a new fighter had been put out to the German aviation industry, with the result that Willi Messerschmitt's Bf109 was tested and chosen for the *Luftwaffe* following flight trials in October 1935.

In Britain also the search for a new fighter aircraft was underway. Private tenders were issued early in 1935 which resulted in the prototype Hawker Hurricane (flying in November 1935) and the private venture Supermairine Spitfire in March of the following year. Two more fighters were under development. The Boulton-Paul Defiant first flew in August 1937 and the Westland Whirlwind in October 1938. The Royal Air Force was in no doubt as to its priorities, for an order for 600 Hurricanes and 310 Spitfires was placed between 1936 and 1937, a decision which would, within three years, prove to be one of the most decisive factors of the Second World War.

Meanwhile, on 14th July 1936, Air Defence of Great Britain had been disbanded and replaced by four separate Commands; Fighter, Bomber, Coastal and Training. The new AOC in C Fighter Command, Air Marshal H.T.Dowding, had earlier served on the Air Council as Member for Supply and Research. It was he who had proposed the private tenders to the Hawker and Supermarine companies following the successful Schneider Trophy attempt in 1931. Dowding's office had then been relieved of supply duties in January 1935 in order to concentrate on the problem of radio detection of incoming aircraft (RDF - later to become known as radar). When in 1936 approval was obtained for the establishment of twenty such detection stations, this visionary and courageous man moved on to Fighter Command. Dowding had been largely responsible for the main factors which were to play such a decisive part in the events just a few years hence - the Hurricane, the Spitfire and RDF.

On establishment, Fighter Command comprised eighteen squadrons, all equipped with obsolescent aircraft; four with Bristol Bulldogs, five with Hawker Demons, six with Gloster Gauntlets and three with Hawker Furies. By the time of the Munich Agreement (August 1938) there were 29 squadrons, still mainly equipped with biplanes (only five had received Hurricanes). Fighter Command was still outmatched by the strength of the rapidly expanding *Luftwaffe*, both in quality and numbers. Indeed by this time German first line strength stood at over 3,000 combat aircraft serviceable, including over one thousand bombers. With the prospect of conflict with the belligerent Germany becoming a distinct possibility, the government cast caution to the winds. The announcement of 'Scheme L' commanded the Air Ministry to procure as many first line aircraft as possible, with the intention of equipping 38 squadrons by the spring of 1940. This was quickly superceded by 'Scheme M' to provide a total of 50 fighter squadrons. Within a year (August 1939) 38 squadrons existed, 17 with Hurricanes, ten with Spitfires, seven with Blenheims, two with Gladiators and a single Gauntlet squadron.

Thus on 3rd September 1939, when war was officially declared, the strength and dispositions of Fighter Command was as follows:

Order Of Battle 3rd September 1939		
1 Squadron	Hurricane I	Tangmere
3 Squadron	Hurricane I	Croydon
17 Squadron	Hurricane I	Croydon
19 Squadron	Spitfire I	Duxford
23 Squadron	Blenheim IF	Wittering
25 Squadron	Blenheim IF	Northolt
29 Squadron	Blenheim IF	Debden
32 Squadron	Hurricane I	Biggin Hill
41 Squadron	Spitfire I	Catterick
43 Squadron	Hurricane I	Tangmere

46 Squadron	Hurricane I	Digby
54 Squadron	Spitfire I	Hornchurch
56 Squadron	Hurricane I	North Weald
64 Squadron	Blenheim IF	Church Fenton
65 Squadron	Spitfire I	Hornchurch
66 Squadron	Spitfire I	Duxford
72 Squadron	Spitfire I	Church Fenton
73 Squadron	Hurricane I	Digby
74 Squadron	Spitfire I	Hornchurch
79 Squadron	Hurricane I	Biggin Hill
85 Squadron	Hurricane I	Debden
87 Squadron	Hurricane I	Debden
111 Squadron	Hurricane I	Northolt
151 Squadron	Hurricane I	North Weald, det Martlesham Heath
213 Squadron	Hurricane I	Wittering
501 Squadron	Hurricane I	Filton
504 Squadron	Hurricane I	Digby
600 Squadron	Blenheim IF	Northolt
601 Squadron	Blenheim IF	Biggin Hill
602 Squadron	Spitfire I	Abbotsinch
603 Squadron	Gladiator II/ Spitfire I	Turnhouse
604 Squadron	Blenheim I	North Weald, det Martlesham Heath
605 Squadron	Gladiator I, Hurricane I	Tangmere
607 Squadron	Gladiator I	Usworth
609 Squadron	Spitfire I	Catterick
610 Squadron	Hurricane I	Hooton Park*
611 Squadron	Spitfire I	Duxford
615 Squadron	Gauntlet II, Gladiator I/II	Croydon
616 Squadron	Battle, Gauntlet II	Leconfield*

* Non-operational

Chapter Two
The 'Phoney War'

September 1939

3rd - 5th September 1939
- nil -

6th September 1939
UK:- Two 56 Squadron Hurricanes were shot down in error over Tilbury by Spitfires of 74 Squadron (see inset).

> **6th September 1939 "The Battle of Barking Creek".**
> This unfortunate incident took place when a hostile raid was plotted approaching from the east (due to the limitations of the fledgling RDF sets, this was actually a friendly aircraft to the west). Hurricanes of 56 Sqn were scrambled to intercept, and were themselves plotted as hostile, causing a scramble of 74 Sqn Spitfires, which bounced two 56 Sqn aircraft between Gravesend and Ipswich. Farce turned to tragedy when both were shot down; P/O Hulton-Harrop was killed and P/O Rose force-landed uninjured.
>
> *Pilot Officer Hulton-Harrap of 56 Sqn was the first of many RAF fighter pilots to be killed by 'Friendly Fire'* (D.Brocklehurst)

9th - 30th September 1939
- nil -

Summary September 1939

Air Combat Claims:
>nil

Missing/destroyed aircraft:
>2 Hurricanes. 1 pilot killed.

Notes:

1 Sqn	(Hurricane I) transferred to BEF France.
73 Sqn	(Hurricane I) transferred to BEF France.
85 Sqn	(Hurricane I) transferred to BEF France.
87 Sqn	(Hurricane I) transferred to BEF France.

October 1939

1st - 15th October 1939
>- nil -

16th October 1939
UK:- German aircraft intruded over and around Scotland, Spitfire pilots of 602 Squadron claiming an He111 damaged in the morning. Later Ju88s, sent out to attack the battlecruiser *Hood* in the Firth of Forth, were engaged by Spitfires. Pilots from 602 Squadron claimed one Ju88 shot down, one 'shared destroyed' and a 'probable', while 603 Squadron pilots claimed another bomber destroyed. (see inset).

16th October 1940 'First Blood'

Following a successful reconnaissance over the Firth of Forth by a lone He111, fifteen Ju88s of *I./KG 30* set out to attack the warships sighted there, including the battlecruiser HMS *Hood*. Several sections of 602 and 603 Squadron Spitfires scrambled to engage the bombers, one certainly being shot down by Flight Lieutenant G. Pinkerton and Flying Officer P.A. Webb. It was also possibly engaged by Squadron Leader A.D. Farquhar, all of 602 Squadron. Another Ju88 was almost certainly attacked by several 603 Squadron pilots and 'finished off' by Flight Lieutenant A.Gifford. These two bombers, the first victories claimed by Fighter Command, fell into the sea, from which four men were rescued to become prisoners. A third Junkers reached German territory in a badly shot-up condition. Two British warships were damaged in the attack.

17th October 1939
UK:- Scapa Flow was raided by He111s. A lone Gladiator of the Scapa Defence Flight engaged the bomber, but was shot down by crossfire. A Do18 of *K.Fl.Gr.606* was shot down by Gladiators of 607 Squadron and an He111 of *KG 26* by Spitfires of 41 Squadron, both over the North Sea.

18th - 20th October 1939
- nil -

21st October 1939
UK:- A Convoy was attacked off Yorkshire by He115s, which were intercepted by Spitfires of 72 Squadron and Hurricanes of 46 Squadron, pilots claiming seven destroyed. *Luftwaffe* losses were four aircraft missing.

22nd October 1939
UK:- Spitfires of 603 Squadron intercepted and shot down an He111.

23rd - 26th October 1939
- nil -

27th October 1939
UK:- Another error of recognition took place when Hurricanes of 46 Squadron attacked and shot down an Anson of 608 Squadron off the Humber. One man was rescued.

28th October 1939
UK:- Sections of Spitfires from 602 and 603 Squadrons engaged an He111, shooting it down near Kidlaw - the first *Luftwaffe* aircraft to be shot down by Fighter Command pilots over Britain.

29th October 1939
- nil -

30th October 1939
BEF:- A Do17P reconnaissance aircraft was engaged by 1 Squadron Hurricanes and was shot down near Toul by Pilot Officer P.W.O.Mould, the first victory in France for the RAF Hurricane units.

The Hawker Hurricane I (S.Parry)

28th October 1940. The First Of the Many

During the morning of 28th October, a lone German aircraft was plotted approaching the Firth of Forth. Sections of Spitfires from 602 and 603 Squadrons were scrambled to intercept and found an He111 from *Stab./KG 26* (1H+JA) at 14,000 feet. Flight Lieutenant Archie McKellar led the 602 Squadron Spitfires into the attack, quickly followed by Flight Lieutenant A. Gifford, Pilot Officer C. Robertson and Pilot Officer George 'Sheep' Gilroy of 603 Squadron.. The Heinkel was very badly damaged. *Leutnant* Rolf Niehoff was wounded by gunfire and brought the bomber down to low level seeking to forceland. After circling a bus, the German aircraft made a creditable crashlanding in open country near Kidlaw, the first German aircraft to be downed by fighters on British soil. Two of the crew were killed in the attack. The bomber was found to be completely riddled by .303 machine-gun bullets.

The Hawker Hurricane I.
Basic Specifications
Type: Single-seat, single engined low wing monoplane fighter.
Span: 40 feet. **Length:** 32 feet. **Height:** 13 feet 1 inch
Power Plant: Rolls-Royce Merlin II in-line liquid-cooled engine
Armament: Eight Browning .303 inch calibre machine guns
Performance
Max Speed: 318 mph at 16,200 feet. **Initial climb:** 2,520 ft/min
Service History

Developed from the long stable of Hawker biplane fighters, the Hurricane was to be the first monoplane design from Sir Sydney Camm, chief designer. The idea began life as the Fury monoplane project, which in 1934 was modified to accept the Rolls-Royce PV-12 engine (later to become known as the Merlin). An Air Ministry Specifiation, F.5/34, issued late in 1934 further modified it, now requiring eight guns to be fitted. A totally new design was then prepared by Hawkers, but the older project seemed superior and was encompassed by AM Spec. F.35/34, issued on 4th September 1934. A mock-up was built and, on 21st February 1935, the Air Ministry issued a contract for one prototype, which was ready in October and made its maiden flight on the 23rd.

Following trials at Martlesham Heath, an official order was placed for 600 aircraft on 3rd June 1936, the name Hurricane being approved some three weeks later. Shortly after production began however, the Merlin I engine was replaced by the Merlin II

The first deliveries went to 111 Squadron in late 1937 and, by the outbreak of war, nearly five hundred Hurricanes were on RAF strength. The aircraft was to bear the brunt of all air fighting in 1939-40 and by July 1940, when the Battle of Britain is judged to have commenced, equipped thirty fighter squadrons.

Although inferior in several ways to its companion the Spitfire, the Hurricane possessed several advantages. The high useage of fabric covering allowed it to accept greater punishment and was easier to repair than all-metal fighters; its wide-track undercarriage allowed operations under conditions that the Spitfire, with its narrow track and comparitively flimsy undercarriage could not have accepted; the close-mounted guns offered a greater concentration of fire-power and this, with its greater stability, gave greater destructive capability and it had better all-round visibility.

By the time the last Hurricane was delivered in 1944, some 14,000 machines had been produced.

The Fighter Command War Diaries

31st October 1939

- nil -

Summary - October 1939

Air Combat Claims:
  16:1:1
Missing/destroyed aircraft:
  1 Gladiator.

Notes:

92 Sqn	formed at Tangmere with Blenheim IFs on 10th.
141 Sqn	formed at Turnhouse with Gladiator Is on 4th.
145 Sqn	formed at Croydon with Blenheim IFs on 10th.
152 Sqn	formed at Acklington with Gladiator I/IIs on 2nd.
219 Sqn	formed at Catterick with Blenheim IFs on 4th.
229 Sqn	formed at Digby with Blenheim IFs on 4th.
234 Sqn	formed at Leconfield with Gauntlet Is (until December), Battles and Blenheim IFs on 30th.
242 Sqn	formed at Church Fenton on 30th to equip with Blenheim IFs and Battle Is in December.
245 Sqn	formed at Leconfield on 30th to equip with Blenheim IFs.
253 Sqn	formed at Manston on 30th, to equip with Battles in December.
263 Sqn	formed at Filton with Gladiator I/IIs on 2nd.
264 Sqn	formed at Sutton Bridge on 30th, to equip with Defiant Is in December.
266 Sqn	formed at Sutton Bridge on 30th, to equip with Battles in December.
615 Sqn	replaced Gladiator Is with Gladiator IIs.
616 Sqn	received Spitfire Is, retaining Battles and Gauntlet IIs.

November 1939

1st November 1939
- nil -

2nd November 1939
BEF:- An He111 was destroyed at Hazebrouck by 87 Squadron Hurricanes. Another He111 was engaged by this unit, but escaped damaged after hitting two Hurricanes with return fire.

3rd - 7th November 1939
- nil -

8th November 1939
BEF:- A Do17 was destroyed by 73 Squadron Hurricanes. One Hurricane force-landed in Luxembourg and the pilot, Pilot Officer R.E.Martin was interned. Martin escaped on December 26th by simply walking away from his guards whilst on exercise on a foggy night, returning to France and his unit.

9th November 1939
BEF:- One 87 Squadron Hurricane force-landed in Belgium where the pilot was interned.

10th - 12th November 1939
- nil -

13th November 1939
UK:- Ju88s bombed the Sullom Voe seaplane base, dropping the first bombs on British soil. A Do18 coastal aircraft, plotted along the east coast, was engaged and damaged by Hurricanes from 56 Squadron.

14th November 1939
BEF:- Another two 87 Squadron Hurricanes forcelanded in Belgium, where their pilots were interned. The three pilots held there, Pilot Officer R.E.Martin, Flying Officer R.L.Glyde and Squadron Leader W.E.Coope, escaped on November 27th, subsequently returning to their unit in France.

Squadron Leader Archie Ashmore McKellar DSO DFC*

Joined the Auxiliary Air Force and commissioned in 602 Squadron in 1938. Posted to 605 Hurricane Squadron in 1940 as a Flight Commander, rising to command the unit during the Battle of Britain. He was killed in action on 1st November 1940 during combat with Bf109s of *JG 27* near Maidstone.

Victory List

28.10.39	He111	shd destroyed	15.9.40	Bf109	destroyed
15.8.40	He111	destroyed	15.9.40	Do17	destroyed
15.8.40	He111	destroyed	15.9.40	He111	prob destroyed
15.8.40	He111	destroyed	15.9.40	He111	destroyed (night)
15.8.40	He111	prob destroyed	7.10.40	Bf109	destroyed
9.9.40	He111	destroyed	7.10.40	Bf109	destroyed
9.9.40	He111	destroyed	7.10.40	Bf109	destroyed
9.9.40	He111	destroyed	7.10.40	Bf109	destroyed
9.9.40	Bf109	destroyed	7.10.40	Bf109	destroyed
11.9.40	He111	shd destroyed	7.10.40	Bf109	damaged
11.9.40	He111	prob destroyed	27.10.40	Bf109	destroyed
15.9.40	Bf109	destroyed			

***Note** 'shd' indicates 'shared'*

15th - 19th November 1939

- nil -

20th November 1939

UK:- A Do17 reconnaissance aircraft was pursued by 74 Squadron Spitfires and was shot down off Southend.

21st November 1939

UK:- Two Hurricanes of 79 Squadron were scrambled from Biggin Hill and engaged a Do17, which was shot down into the Channel.

Flying Officer Edgar James Kain DFC

The New Zealand born 'Cobber' Kain scored the first victory for 73 Sqn on 8th November 1939 by bringing down a Do17P reconnaissance aircraft of *1.(F)/123* at Lubey, France. Kain was to become the first 'ace' of the RAF when, on 26th March 1940, he claimed two Bf109s destroyed, the second while his own aircraft was on fire. He fought throughout the Battle of France, claiming a further twelve victories before being posted home on leave. As he was leaving for England on 6th June, he attempted a low level 'beat-up' by performing high speed rolls across the airfield. On the third roll his wingtip hit the ground. He crashed and was killed instantly.

Victory List

8.11.40	Do17	destroyed	12.5.40	Hs126	destroyed
23.11.40	Do17	destroyed	14.5.40	Bf109	destroyed
3.3.40	Bf109	destroyed	15.5.40	Do17	destroyed
26.3.40	Bf109	destroyed	19.5.40	Ju88	destroyed
26.3.40	Bf109	destroyed	19.5.40	Do17	destroyed
23.4.40	Bf110	damaged	19.5.40	Bf110	destroyed
10.5.40	Do17	destroyed	25.5.40	Do17	destroyed
11.5.40	Do17	destroyed	26.5.40	Hs126	destroyed
11.5.40	Bf109	destroyed	27.5.40	Do17	destroyed

BEF:- An He111 was destroyed off Cap Griz Nez by Flight Lieutenant R.H.A.Lee, an 85 Squadron Hurricane pilot.

22nd November 1939

- nil -

23rd November 1939

BEF:- Two Do17s were destroyed over France by 73 Squadron Hurricanes. Two Dorniers and an He111 were shot down by 1 Squadron, the latter shared with French Hawk 75As. A further claim for an He111 destroyed was submitted by 73 Squadron pilots, but no details are known.

24th - 25th November 1939
- nil -

26th November 1939
UK:- Blenheim fighters from 25 Squadron flew an offensive sweep, making an abortive attack upon the Borkum seaplane.

27th November 1939
- nil -

28th November 1939
UK:- Another offensive sweep was flown to Borkum. Six Blenheims each from 25 and 601 Squadrons attacked the seaplane base, crews

---

Flt Lt Richard Hugh Anthony Lee DSO DFC
A regular officer and Cranwell graduate, Lee was serving with 85 Squadron at the outbreak of war and was posted to France with the BEF. On 11 May 1940 he was shot down by *Flak*, captured, escaped, and returned to his unit. Posted to 56 Squadron when 85 returned to Britain to reform, but returned to his old unit as Flight Commander for the beginning of the Battle of Britain. Reported missing in action on 18th August 1940, last seen chasing a pair of Ju88s out to sea. His combat tally was at least nine, with others unconfirmed, but due to the confusion of the fighting in France and the loss of so many records, it has not proved possible to establish a definitive victory list for this pilot.

Victory List

Date	Aircraft	Result	Date	Aircraft	Result
21.11.39	He111	destroyed	13.5.40	He111	possible
10.5.40	Hs126	destroyed	13.5.40	He111	possible
10.5.40	Ju88	shd prob. dest.	14.5.40	He111	destroyed
10.5.40	Ju88	shd destroyed	14.5.40	He111	destroyed
11.5.40	Do17	shd destroyed	15.5.40	He111	destroyed
11.5.40	Do17	destroyed	16.5.40	He111	destroyed

claiming to have shot-up five seaplanes. Two German aircraft sustained slight damage.

29th November 1939
UK:- Hurricanes of 111 Squadron were scrambled to engage an Heinkel off the east coast. This aircraft, from *Stab./KG 26*, was shot down.

30th November 1939
- nil -

Summary - November 1939

Air Combat Claims:
9:0:1

Missing/destroyed aircraft:
    4 Hurricanes. Pilots interned and later escaped.

Notes:

141 Sqn	received Blenheim IFs, retaining Gladiator Is until April 1940.
600 Sqn	received Blenheim IVFs, retaining Blenheim IFs.
605 Sqn	relinquished Gladiator Is, retaining Hurricane Is.
616 Sqn	relinquished Battles, retaining Spitfire Is and Gauntlet IIs.

December 1939

1st - 6th December 1939
- nil -

7th December 1939
UK:- He111s set out to attack a convoy off the Scottish coast and were plotted by radar shortly after midday. Spitfires from 72 and 603 Squadrons intercepted, engaging simultaneously and three bombers were claimed damaged by 603 and three more by 72. Two of the Heinkels subsequently ditched. One RAF pilot was wounded during this combat.

8th - 16th December 1939
- nil -

17th December 1939
UK:- A *KG 26* He111 was damaged off eastern England by a 46 Squadron Hurricane pilot.

18th - 20th December 1939
- nil -

21st December 1939
UK:- 602 and 603 Squadron Spitfires scrambled from Drem to intercept a reported incoming raid. The 'raid' was actually a flight of Hampdens from 44 Squadron, two of which were attacked over the Firth of Forth. Two Hampdens were shot down.
BEF:- Another error of identification resulted in a French Potez 637 being shot down by a 73 Squadron Hurricane pilot.

22nd December 1939
UK:- Two Ju88s - erroneously identified as He115s - were attacked by 602 Squadron Spitfires near Crail. No claim was made but the unit was subsequently credited with one 'confirmed'.
BEF:- The first clash between Bf109Es and Hurricanes resulted in a claim for one Messerschmitt destroyed being submitted by 73 Squadron for the loss of two aircraft, both British pilots being killed (See inset).

23rd - 31st December 1939
- nil -

22nd December 1939 Hurricane vs Bf109E

In the early afternoon three 73 Squadron Hurricanes - Plt Off Waller leading Sgts R.M.Perry and J.Winn - patrolled near Saarbrucken, seeking reconnaissance Do17s. Bf109s of *III./JG 53* were also airborne, covering the Dorniers. The German pilots spotted the three British fighters below and dived to attack. Two of the Hurricanes were shot down in flames, one by *Hauptmann* Werner Molders and the second by *Oberleutnant* Hans von Hahn. Both Sergeants Perry and Winn were killed. Waller claimed a Bf109 destroyed, but none were actually lost. Molders, had become the top-scoring German fighter pilot of the Spanish Civil War and had demonstrated the tactics that he had perfected during that campaign - hit and run. Never stay to dogfight more agile aircraft. This philosophy was to become a great problem for the RAF during the next year. Another problem was the estimation of success by British pilots facing Messerschmitts; the Daimler DB601 engine of the Bf109 was prone to emit plumes of black exhaust smoke under full power, which would give rise to very many erroneous claims for '109s destroyed and damaged, since the standard evasion technique for the Germans was a full-power vertical dive. When accompanied by black smoke it is not difficult to understand how over-claiming occurred.

Summary - December 1939

Air Combat Claims:
    4:0:7

Missing/destroyed aircraft:
    2 Hurricanes. Both pilots killed.
    1 pilot wounded.

Notes:

152 Sqn	replaced Gladiator I/IIs with Spitfire Is.
242 Sqn	kept Blenheim Is for only a few weeks, retained Battles.
616 Sqn	relinquished Gauntlet IIs, retaining Spitfire Is.

Chapter Three
The Waiting Game

The opening few months of the war had begun, for both Fighter Command and for the Hurricane units of the BEF, in a relatively quiet fashion. Spitfire and Hurricane units had proved themselves against unescorted bombers, minelayers and reconnaissance aircraft in the defence of the United Kingdom and, while the new radar system had shown early teething troubles, the coverage appeared to be working well. Of rather less worth was the general standard of aircraft recognition among pilots. Of particular note must be the action leading to the loss of two Hurricanes on 6th September. They were identified as Bf109s, yet no '109 had the range to reach England. Over France however, the outlook was less sanguine. Hurricanes had at last met the German single seat fighters and here the greater experience and superior tactics of the German pilots had won the day. Although a Bf109 had been claimed destroyed, none was even hit. The only losses were two RAF pilots, both killed. This was to be a grim portent for the future. In the meantime the waiting game continued. No-one was in any doubt that the Germans would strike hard in the west, but when?

At 1st January 1940, the strength of the British fighter force was as follows:

Order of Battle 1st January 1940		
1 Squadron	Hurricane I	Vassincourt, det Rouvres (BEF)
3 Squadron	Hurricane I	Croydon, det Kenley
17 Squadron	Hurricane I	Martlesham Heath
19 Squadron	Spitfire I	Duxford
23 Squadron	Blenheim IF	Wittering
25 Squadron	Blenheim IF	Northolt, det

Squadron	Aircraft	Base
29 Squadron	Blenheim IF	Debden, det Martlesham Heath
32 Squadron	Hurricane I	Biggin Hill
41 Squadron	Spitfire I	Catterick
43 Squadron	Hurricane I	Acklington
54 Squadron	Spitfire I	Hornchurch
56 Squadron	Hurricane I	Martlesham Heath, det North Weald
64 Squadron	Blenheim IF	Church Fenton, dets Evanton, Leconfield & Catterick
65 Squadron	Spitfire I	Northolt
66 Squadron	Spitfire I	Duxford
72 Squadron	Spitfire I	Drem
73 Squadron	Hurricane I	Rouvres (BEF)
74 Squadron	Spitfire I	Rochford
79 Squadron	Hurricane I	Manston
85 Squadron	Hurricane I	Lille/Seclin, dets Le Touquet & St Inglevert (BEF)
87 Squadron	Hurricane I	Lille/Seclin, det Le Touquet (BEF)
92 Squadron	Blenheim IF	Croydon, det Gatwick
111 Squadron	Hurricane I	Drem
141 Squadron	Gladiator I, Blenheim IF	Grangemouth
145 Squadron	Blenheim IF	Croydon
151 Squadron	Hurricane I	North Weald, det Martlesham Heath
152 Squadron	Gladiator I, II, Spitfire I	Acklington. dets Leconfield & Sumburgh
213 Squadron	Hurricane I	Wittering
219 Squadron	Blenheim IF	Catterick. Dets Scorton, Leeming & Redhill
222 Squadron	Blenheim IF	Duxford
229 Squadron	Blenheim IF	Digby, dets Biggin Hill & Kenley
234 Squadron	Battle, Blenheim IF	Leconfield

238 Squadron	Hurricane I	Chilbolton
242 Squadron	Battle	Church Fenton
245 Squadron	Blenheim IF	Leconfield
253 Squadron	Battle	Manston
263 Squadron	Gladiator I/II	Filton
264 Squadron	Defiant I	Martlesham Heath, det Wittering
266 Squadron	Battle	Sutton Bridge
501 Squadron	Hurricane I	Tangmere
504 Squadron	Hurricane I	Debden
600 Squadron	Blenheim IF/IV	Manston
601 Squadron	Blenheim IF	Tangmere
602 Squadron	Spitfire I	Drem
603 Squadron	Spitfire I	Prestwick
604 Squadron	Blenheim I	North Weald, det Martlesham Heath
605 Squadron	Hurricane I	Tangmere
607 Squadron	Gladiator I	Vitry-en-Artois, dets Abbeville & St Inglevert
609 Squadron	Spitfire I	Kinloss
610 Squadron	Spitfire I	Wittering
611 Squadron	Spitfire I	Digby, dets North Coates, & Ternhill
615 Squadron	Gauntlet II, Gladiator II	Vitry-en-Artois, det St Inglevert
616 Squadron	Spitfire I	Leconfield
Fighter Flight	Gladiator I	Sullom Voe

January 1940

1st January 1940

UK:- Gladiator pilots of the Sullom Voe Fighter Flight claimed two Ju88s shot down during an attack on shipping between Scapa Flow and the Shetlands, but only one was credited.

2nd - 10th January 1940

- nil -

11th January 1940

UK:- An He111 was attacked by 66 Squadron Spitfires off Cromer and crashed into the North Sea on the return flight.

Air Commodore Roy Gilbert Dutton CBE DSO DFC*

Roy Dutton was a regular RAF officer with 111 Squadron at the outbreak of war. His first engagement came on 13th January 1940 when, with two others from the squadron he 'finished off' a Heinkel previously attacked by 602 Squadron. Before the *Blitzkrieg* began he was posted to 145 Squadron and fought during the Battle of France, claiming seven victories. Still with 145 he fought through the early part of the Battle of Britain and then, in early 1941, took command of 452 (RAAF) Sqn, later commanding 19 Squadron. In 1942 he flew as a Flight Commander with 141 Squadron, flying Beaufighters at night. At the end of the year left to occupy various staff positions, finally commanding 512 (Glider Tug) Squadron and led the gliders across the Rhine in March 1945. He remained with the RAF after the war, retiring in 1970 and has recently died.

Victory List

13.1.40	He111	shd destroyed	17.7.40	Ju88	damaged
8.3.40	He111	destroyed	19.7.40	He111	shd destroyed
18.5.40	He111	destroyed	1.8.40	Ju88	damaged
18.5.40	He111	shd destroyed	8.8.40	Ju87	prob destroyed
19.5.40	He111	destroyed	8.8.40	Ju87	prob destroyed
22.5.40	He111	destroyed	8.8.40	Ju87	prob destroyed
31.5.40	Bf109	destroyed	8.8.40	Bf110	damaged
31.5.40	Bf109	shd destroyed	11.8.40	Bf110	prob destroyed
1.6.40	Bf109	destroyed	11.8.40	Bf110	prob destroyed
1.6.40	Bf109	destroyed	11.8.40	Bf110	damaged
1.6.40	Bf110	destroyed	11.8.40	Bf110	damaged
1.7.40	Do17	shd destroyed	12.8.40	Ju88	destroyed
10.7.40	Do17	shd destroyed	23.6.41	Bf109	damaged
11.7.40	He111	destroyed			

12th January 1940

- nil -

13th January 1940

UK:- He111s had operated off the northeast coast on 12th, attacking British shipping without hindrance from the RAF. However a lone reconnaissance He111 was plotted off East

Anglia on 13th and was destroyed near Farne Island by 602 Squadron Spitfires and 111 Squadron Hurricanes.

14th January 1940
UK:- Two 43 Squadron Hurricanes were lost to a mid-air collision on patrol. Both pilots were killed.

15th - 18th January 1940
- nil -

19th January 1940
UK:- A lone He111 was destroyed off the Firth of Forth by 603 Squadron Spitfires.

20th - 28th January 1940
- nil -

29th January 1940
UK:- Three marauding He111s were engaged by Hurricanes, Spitfires and Gladiators. No claims were submitted, although two bombers were damaged.

30th January 1940
UK:- Two separate anti-shipping raids were engaged off the east coast, one He111 of *4./KG 26* being caught and shot down by defending 43 Squadron Hurricane pilots.

31st January 1940
- nil -

Summary - January 1940
Air Combat Claims:
  6:0:0
Missing/destroyed aircraft:
  2 Hurricanes lost to accident
Notes:
266 Sqn received Spitfire Is, retaining Battles until May.

There were no engagements involving BEF fighter units in France during January.

February 1940

1st - 2nd February 1940
- nil -

3rd February 1940
UK:- During interceptions off the east coast, three He111s were credited as destroyed and one damaged by 43 Squadron Hurricanes, one was credited as destroyed to 152 Squadron Gladiators, one damaged by 46 Squadron Hurricanes. One Hurricane of 46 Squadron was reported missing, but the pilot was rescued. (See Inset)

4th - 8th February 1940
- nil -

9th February 1940
UK:- An He111 was destroyed by 602 Squadron Spitfires off Scotland. 43 Squadron engaged two He111s without success, but lost one Hurricane into the sea, from which the pilot was rescued.

10th - 12th February 1940
- nil -

13th February 1940
UK:- Spitfires of 54 Squadron, flying a convoy patrol, intercepted an He111 of *K.Gr.100*, shooting it down off Manston.

14th - 20th February 1940
- nil -

21st February 1940
UK:- Two RAF fighters were lost; a 43 Squadron pilot was injured when his Hurricane crashed on take-off for convoy patrol, and a 616 Squadron Spitfire dived into the sea off Hornsea, killing the pilot.

22nd February 1940
UK:- An He111 of *FAG O.b.d.L* was brought down on land near St Abbs Head by 602 Squadron Spitfires, one (L1007) was

3rd February 1940 - Defending the Shipping

During the morning the Luftwaffe sent twenty-six bombers out to attack British shipping off the coast between the Orkneys and East Anglia. These were plotted on radar and many fighter patrols were scrambled to intercept. The first engagement took place at approximately the same time. Flying Officers J.W.C.Simpson and J.D.Edwards of 43 Squadron found two He111s attacking shipping near Farne Island. They attacked one, claiming a 'probable', and this was subsequently and erroneously confirmed by intelligence. 43 Squadron gained further success a short while later when Flight Lieutenant Peter Townsend led Flying Officer Folkes and Sergeant J.H.Hallowes on a patrol off Whitby, where they caught another KG26 Heinkel - 1H+FM of *4 Staffel* - which was badly shot-up and turned towards the English coast. *Feldwebel* Helmut Wilms crash-landed his aircraft on Banniel Flat Farm, near Whitby, with two of the crew dead and a third injured.

Later in the morning 43 Squadron was again in action. Flight Lieutenant C.B.Hull led Flying Officer Carswell and Pilot Officer North off to patrol over Farne Island, where another Heinkel was discovered. It escaped badly shot-up, the returning pilots claiming a 'damaged'. Shortly after this patrol had taken off, Three Gladiators from 152 Squadron scrambled from Acklington. They sighted yet another of *KG26*'s big Heinkels, a *I Gruppe* machine, over Druridge Bay. Squadron Leader F.W.C.Shute and Pilot Officer J.Falkson delivered several attacks, losing sight of the bomber with black smoke pouring from it and with its undercarriage hanging down. It crashed into the sea and was later confirmed by intelligence.

equipped with 20mm cannons. Another He111 was shot down into the North Sea by 43 Squadron Hurricanes.

BEF:- Three 1 Squadron Hurricanes intercepted an He111 over France, but the freezing conditions caused the Browning guns to fail and the bomber escaped.

23rd - 26th February 1940

- nil -

Group Captain Peter Wooldridge Townsend CVO DSO DFC*

Peter Townsend served first as a Vildebeeste pilot in Singapore, but was posted to 43 Squadron in England, claiming several victories in the 'Phoney War'. In late May 1940 he took command of 85 Squadron in France too late to see any action. He fought through the Battle of Britain, being shot down and wounded on 31st August. He returned to the squadron and converted it from day to night fighting, the unit re-equipping with Havocs in 1941 when, now as a Wing Commander, he left the squadron. He later commanded 605 Squadron and, after holding several administrative posts, became Equerry of Honour to King George VI. He retired from the RAF in 1956 and recently died.

Victory List

3.2.40	He111	destroyed	26.8.40	Do17	shd destroyed
22.2.40	He111	destroyed	28.8.40	Bf109	destroyed
8.4.40	He111	destroyed	29.8.40	Bf109	destroyed
11.8.40	Do17	destroyed	30.8.40	Bf110	damaged
18.8.40	Bf110	destroyed	31.8.40	Bf109	destroyed
18.8.40	Bf109	destroyed	25/26.2.41	Do17	destroyed
18.8.40	Bf109	destroyed	9/10.4.41	Ju88	prob destroyed
26.8.40	Do17	shd destroyed	10/11.4.41	Ju88	damaged

27th February 1940

UK:- He111s flew armed reconnaissance operations off the east coast between Newcastle the Orkneys. Two were shot down by Spitfires, one off St Abbs Head by 609 Squadron, the other one near Farne Island by 152 Squadron.

28th - 29th February 1940

UK:- Two RAF pilots were lost, both at sea. On the 28th a 611 Squadron Spitfire crashed near the East Dudgeon Lightship. Next day one of 152 Squadron, flown by the CO, Squadron Leader F.W.C.Shute, also crashed into the sea. Both pilots were killed.

Summary - February 1940

Air Combat Claims:
9:0:2

Missing/destroyed aircraft:
3 Hurricanes and 3 Spitfires. 2 pilots killed, one injured, two rescued.

Notes:
242 Sqn	replaced Battles with Hurricane Is.
245 Sqn	received Battles, retaining Blenheim IFs.
253 Sqn	received Hurricane Is, retaining with Battles until April.
601 Sqn	replaced Blenheim IFs with Hurricane Is.

March 1940

1st March 1940

- nil -

2nd March 1940

BEF:- A Do17 was engaged near Metz by 1 Squadron Hurricanes. One Hurricane was shot down by return fire, pilot killed. No claim was submitted, but the German aircraft subsequently crashed. 73 Squadron Hurricanes, escorting a French Po63, were attacked by Bf109Es. All four British fighters crash-landed after Flying Officer E.J.Kain had claimed a Messerschmitt shot down in flames.

3rd March 1940

UK:- Yet another recognition error occurred, when a Hudson of the Photgraphic Development Unit was engaged by Spitfires and shot down near Meopham.

BEF:- An He111 was shot down near Forbach by 1 Squadron Hurricane pilots.

4th - 6th March 1940

- nil -

7th March 1940

UK:- A reconnaissance He111 was destroyed by 603 Squadron Spitfire pilots off Scotland.

8th March 1940

UK:- A reconnaissance Ju88 was destroyed near the Orkneys by a 111 Squadron Hurricane while on a sortie to the Scapa Flow naval base.

9th - 16th March 1940

- nil -

17th March 1940

UK:- Spitfires of 603 Squadron fought He111s off Scotland. No claims were made, but one bomber returned damaged.

18th - 21st March 1940

- nil -

22nd March 1940

BEF:- 73 Squadron pilots fought Bf109Es over Bouzonville, one Bf109 being claimed destroyed for the loss of a Hurricane, pilot safe.

23rd March 1940

BEF:- Two 607 Squadron Gladiators were lost to mid-air collision, both pilots being killed.

24th - 25th March 1940

- nil -

26th March 1940

BEF:- Three 73 Squadron Hurricane pilots engaged Bf110s, claiming one damaged. Further 73 Sqn pilots fought Bf109s over Saarlautern, claiming two shot down plus a 'probable'. Flying Officer E.J.Kain was shot down in flames and baled out unhurt. A second fight with Bf109Es brought claims of two destroyed by Flying Officer N.Orton.

27th March 1940

- nil -

28th March 1940

UK:- An He111 was engaged by Hurricanes of 43 and 605 Squadrons and was shot down in flames between the Orkney and Shetland Islands.

29th March 1940

BEF:- Two Hurricanes of 73 Squadron intercepted and damaged a Do17, but one British pilot was shot down and killed by a Bf109E. During two combats, 1 Sqn pilots claimed a Bf109 and three Bf110s shot down without loss.

30th - 31st March 1940

- nil -

"Green To Black"

On the morning of 3rd April 1940, several reconnaissance He111s were ineffectively engaged off Scotland by Skuas of the Royal Navy and by a Gladiator of the Sumburgh Fighter Flight. The returning Heinkels reported a convoy off Peterhead, but more He111s - of II/KG26 - were already airborne, across the North Sea. British radar plotted them at around noon and a lone Spitfire pilot, Flg Off E.N.Ryder of 41 Sqn, was scrambled to investigate. He found *Oberstleutnant* Hafele's 1H+AC off Whitby and attacked. Although he succeeded in shooting the bomber down, return fire hit his Spitfire hard. Thus far no fighter pilot had ever succeeded in ditching a Spitfire successfully, for the weight of the big Merlin immediately pulled the fighter straight down into the depths. Now it was Norman Ryder's turn. As usual, the heavy Merlin engine pulled the nose straight down and the fighter headed for the bottom of the ocean, with Ryder still in the cockpit. He struggled free and swam to the surface to be rescued by a fishing boat. Of his experience he was later to say, "At first the water was a pretty green colour, but as I went down it got darker and darker. When it turned black I knew it was time to get out!" From that moment Norman Ryder would be known as "Green-To-Black Ryder", a nickname that would follow him throughout his Air Force career.

Group Captain Edgar Norman Ryder CBE DFC*

Norman Ryder was serving with 41 Squadron at the outbreak of war, flying Spitfires with this unit until he was rested from operations in January 1941. He later became Commanding Officer of 56 Squadron before taking command of the Kenley Wing. On 31st October 1941, while leading the Wing on a Ramrod operation near Gravelines, he was shot down and captured. He remained with RAF after war, retiring on 28th October 1960.

The Waiting Game

Victory List

3.4.40	He111	destroyed	7.9.40	Do17	damaged
15.8.40	Ju88	prob destroyed	10.9.40	Ju88	damaged
5.9.40	Bf109	prob destroyed	15.9.40	He111	shd destroyed
5.9.40	Bf109	destroyed	25.10.40	Bf109	prob destroyed
6.9.40	Bf109	destroyed	30.10.40	Bf109	destroyed
7.9.40	Bf109	prob destroyed	27.11.40	Bf109	destroyed

Summary - March 1940

Air Combat Claims:
13:1:2

Missing/destroyed aircraft:
Five Hurricanes and two Gladiators. Four pilots killed.

Notes:

72 Sqn,	equipped with Spitfire Is, took on a few Gladiator I/IIs for a matter of weeks.
92 Sqn	replaced Blenheim IFs with Spitfire Is.
145 Sqn	received Hurricane Is, retaining Blenheim IFs until May.
229 Sqn	replaced Blenheim IFs with Hurricane Is.
234 Sqn	replaced Battles and Blenheim IFs with Spitfire Is.
245 Sqn	replaced Battles and Blenheim IFs with Hurricane Is.
607 Sqn	received Hurricane Is, retaining Gladiator Is.

April 1940

1st April 1940
BEF:- 1 Squadron pilots fought Bf110s near Thionville, claiming three shot down. One Hurricane was shot down, pilot safe.

2nd April 1940
UK:- Hurricanes of 504 Squadron engaged reconnaissance He115s off the east coast, claiming three damaged near the South Knock lightship. One Hurricane was lost.

BEF:- 1 Squadron pilots, chasing a Do17 near St Avold, were 'bounced' by Bf109s. One Hurricane was shot down and the pilot baled out unhurt. Two other RAF pilots each claimed a Messerschmitt destroyed.

3rd April 1940
UK:- An He111 was shot down by a 41 Squadron Spitfire pilot while attacking a British convoy off Whitby. The Spitfire was shot down by return fire and ditched, pilot rescued.

4th - 6th April 1940
- nil -

7th April 1940
BEF:- A flight of 73 Squadron Hurricanes, patrolling near Thionville, met sixteen Bf109Es. RAF pilots claimed one shot down and a 'probable' for the loss of one Hurricane. The RAF pilot baled out wounded.

8th April 1940
UK:- At dusk, Hurricanes engaged an incoming Heinkel raid off Scotland. 111 Squadron pilots were awarded a 'probable' while those from 43 Squadron claimed three destroyed. One of these, an aircraft from *6./KG 26*, crash-landed on Wick airfield. The pilot was under the impression that he was force-landing on the sea at a seaplane base. When the bomber had slithered to a halt the door opened, a dinghy was tossed out and two German crewmen leaped out with no boots on!

Chapter Four
Blitzkrieg In The West

While the war between the Western Allies and Germany had proceeded in a fairly quiet fashion since September 1939, a 'shooting war' had broken out elsewhere. In November 1939 hostilities had commenced between Finland and the Soviet Union. By Spring 1940, Britain and France had announced their intention to despatch an international force to Scandinavia, ostensibly to assist the Finns, but in reality with a deeper motive; iron ore. Sweden, a major producer of high grade ore, was a major supplier to Germany. Because of Sweden's geographical location, the Germans had denied such supplies to Britain. A force of Allied troops in Scandinavia would therefore be in a position to deny Germany this vital product. Accordingly the Germans had set their own plans in motion for the occupation of Norway, used to transport the ore during the winter months, and Denmark. This operation, code-named *Weserübung*, was planned for early in April. Diplomatic notes were passed between the Allied governments and the Swedes, who were rightly concerned about possible infringements of their neutrality. In the meantime the Russo-Finnish war had ended.

Aware that the Germans were considering a take-over of Scandinavia, the Allied governments pressed those in the threatened countries to allow their troops as a precautionary measure. The Swedes refused, while the Norwegians stayed silent. As a compromise, the Allies began to sow minefields in Norwegian waters, the British government now having been warned that a German invasion was imminent. In Britain an Expeditionary Force was being readied to be rushed to the area should the Germans attack.

The blow fell before dawn on 9th April, when German Divisions rolled across the Danish frontier, this advance was co-ordinated with a simultaneous seaborne and paratroop

The Fighter Command War Diaries

invasion of Norway. The so called 'Phoney War' appeared to be over. At once Gladiators of 263 Squadron commenced preparation for embarkation to Norway together with the prepared Expeditionary Force.

Note: *From this point theatres of operation will be identified as 'UK', 'BEF France' and 'BEF Norway'.*

April 1940

9th April 1940

- nil -

10th April 1940:

UK:- Several formations of German bombers were engaged by Hurricane pilots off Scotland. An He111 was shot down near Ronaldsay Island by 43 Squadron. Another bomber was destroyed and a second damaged near Kinnaird Head by 605 Squadron, while a third was destroyed near Scapa Flow by 111 Squadron.

BEF France:- An He111 was claimed destroyed off Cap Griz Nez by an 87 Squadron Hurricane pilot.

11th - 19th April 1940

- nil -

20th April 1940

BEF France:- A Do17 was destroyed by a 1 Squadron Hurricane pilot, who crash-landed due to return fire. Further 1 Squadron pilots fought an escorted German bomber, an He111 being claimed as destroyed as were two Bf109s. An 'He113' (misidentified Bf109) was claimed as a 'probable'. In a third engagement by 1 Squadron, four further Bf109Es were claimed as destroyed. No losses were sustained by the RAF unit.

21st April 1940

BEF France:- 73 Squadron pilots fought Bf109s, claiming two destroyed, a 'probable' and a 'damaged'. One Hurricane crash-landed, pilot wounded. A second combat by 73 Squadron resulted in one Bf109 being claimed destroyed, followed by claims of 2:3:2 against Bf110s.

22nd April 1940

- nil -

23rd April 1940

BEF France:- 73 Squadron pilots claimed a Bf110 damaged, but lost two Hurricanes to Bf109s. Both pilots were wounded.

24th April 1940

BEF Norway:- Gladiators of 263 Squadron arrived at Lesjaskog, Norway, to operate from the frozen lake.

25th April 1940

BEF Norway:- An He115 was claimed destroyed by 263 Squadron Gladiator pilots but, before they returned to base, an He111 arrived over Lesjaskog. It bombed the lake where four Gladiators were destroyed and several pilots wounded. Attacks continued throughout the day resulting in seven further Gladiators being burnt on the ground. Two He111s were claimed shot down during later patrols for the loss of two Gladiators, which force-landed and were strafed to destruction by the *Luftwaffe*.

26th April 1940

BEF Norway:- 263 Squadron lost a Gladiator due to engine failure. The pilot baled out unhurt.

27th April 1940

BEF Norway:- The remaining three 263 Squadron Gladiators were destroyed by ground crew before the unit evacuated Norway.

28th - 30th April 1940

- nil -

The Gloster Gladiator I and II
Basic Specification
Dimensions Span: 32 feet 3 inches Length: 27 feet 5 inches Height: 10 feet 4 inches

Armament: Two .303 inch Browning machine guns mounted in fuselage side, two more in faired mounting beneath lower wings.

Power Plant: (Mk I) One Bristol Mercury IX/IXS radial engine (Mk II) One Bristol Mercury VIIIA/VIIIAS.

Performance:
Max Speed: (Mk I) 253 mph, (Mk II) 231 mph
Initial Climb: (Mk I) 2,300 ft/min, (Mk II) 2.430 ft/min
Ceiling: (Mk I) 33,000 feet, (Mk II) 32,900 feet

Service History

The Gladiator, the last biplane fighter to see service with the Royal Air Force, was designed to meet Air Ministry Specification F.7/30. It was to replace the World War One generation of fighters currently in service and was a radical modification of the Gloster Gauntlet. The prototype - the S.S.37 - retained the engine, fuselage and tail assembly of the earlier aircraft, but had an improved wing and undercarriage system, plus heavier armament. Following successful trials, the Air Ministry ordered the new fighter in July 1936, 480 examples eventually serving with the RAF. During the first year of war it saw service in Britain with 247, 263, 603, 605 607 and 615 Squadrons, plus the Sumburgh Fighter Flight. It was not phased out until the winter of 1940/41, when 263 Squadron, which had borne the brunt of the RAF air fighting over Norway in April/May 1940, finally became operational with Whirlwinds.

Summary - April 1940

Air Combat Claims:
30:7:8

Missing/destroyed aircraft:
8 Hurricanes, 14 Gladiators and 1 Spitfire. Four pilots were wounded.

64 Sqn	replaced Blenheim IFs with Spitfire Is.
141 Sqn	replaced Blenheim IFs and Gladiators Is with Defiant Is.
615 Sqn	received Hurricane Is, retaining Gladiator IIs until May.

May 1940

1st - 6th May 1940

- nil -

7th May 1940

UK:- 263 Squadron, with a new complement of Gladiators, prepared to return to Norway together with 46 Squadron, equipped with Hurricanes.

8th May 1940

- nil -

9th May 1940

UK:- 605 Squadron pilots claimed a Do17 destroyed off Wick, while others from 43 Squadron claimed another shot down near Dunnet Head.

BEF France:- 87 Squadron pilots claimed a Bf110 destroyed over the Maginot Line, then attacked and damaged a Do17, one Hurricane force-landing due to return fire.

10th May 1940

The world was rapidly to learn a new word - *Blitzkrieg* - when the German blow fell. Simultaneous attacks were made by airborne forces upon Rotterdam and Fort Eban Emael in Holland, while German armour rolled across the Dutch and French frontiers. The main weight bypassed the Maginot Line and came down through the Ardennes forest, always thought to be impassable, to threaten Sedan. The shooting war in the west had begun. Home-based fighter squadrons flew escorts and ground attack missions to Holland. The Hurricane squadrons of the BEF were involved in heavy fighting near Lille, Rouvres, Verdun and over Belgium as the *Luftwaffe* sought to destroy the Allied airfields.

10th May 1940 "The Balloon Goes Up"

At dawn, the German attack upon France and the Low Countries began. The armoured assault, while not unexpected, stunned the western Allies with its speed, power and particularly the massive air cover and tactical support provided by the *Luftwaffe*. One of the first contacts came in the early hours, when a lone 600 Squadron Blenheim fought Heinkels off the French coast and returned damaged.

To the north, the Germans had landed paratroops on and around Rotterdam airfield and the Hague. At noon Blenheims of 600 Squadron set out to attack these. They strafed a Ju52 on Rotterdam airfield, but as they were climbing away a pack of Bf110s from *I./ZG 1* fell upon them. Flg Off Hayes managed to get away, but the other five aircraft were all shot down by the more agile Bf110s, all flown by German pilots who were, in the course of time, to win the *Ritterkreuz* for valour[1]. 600 Squadron Blenheims flew a further patrol in the early afternoon, when an He111 was claimed probably destroyed off the Belgian coast by two crews.

Defiants were in action for the first time, Flight Lieutenant Cooke of 264 Squadron joined four other (unidentified) fighters in shooting down an He111 off Belgium, while 604 Squadron Blenheim flew an escort sortie to the Hague, strafing the airfield. Four Ju52s were destroyed and three 'probables' but one Blenheim was lost to ground fire. Pilot Officer I.K.S.Joll and his crew returned later.

The main actions were fought over France and Belgium. 73 Squadron scrambled Hurricanes at 0400 hours. These engaged three Do17s near their base at Rouvres and claimed one damaged. One Hurricane was shot down, Flying Officer Orton force-landing unhurt. Ten minutes later, three 85 Squadron Hurricanes, airborne from Seclin, found a trio of Hs126s and claimed all three destroyed. Meanwhile more fighters from this unit found a pair of Ju88s, one being shot down near Mons. Return fire damaged one Hurricane and wounded the pilot, Pilot Officer Mawhood, who was able to put his aircraft down safely.

Within a few minutes a trio of 607 Squadron Hurricanes, scrambled to intercept bombers approaching their base at Vitry-en-Artois, engaged a group of He111s near Conde. Two were attacked and claimed damaged, but one of the fighters was hit by 'friendly AA fire'

---

1. *Oberleutnant* Werner Streib, *Unteroffizier* Paul Gildner, *Leutnant* Reinhold Knacke and *Leutnant* Wolfgang Schenk.

Meanwhile more pilots from 85 Squadron were chasing a lone bomber near Lille, where they attacked and claimed it probably destroyed. At the same time other Hurricanes from 87 Squadron took on Dorniers attacking Senon, one being claimed shot down.

A half-hour later, at 0500 hours, more incoming raids were reported, the 'phoney war' stalwarts of 1 and 73 Squadrons, plus 607 Squadron Hurricanes, rising to engage them. 73 Squadron took on Dorniers approaching their airfield and succeeded in damaging one, but one Hurricane was shot down and a second badly damaged. 1 Squadron pilots claimed an He111 destroyed while patrolling near the Maginot Line and 607 Squadron - which would prove to be the most successful unit of this days fighting - claimed another near St Quentin. Flying Officer L.Fredman of 615 Squadron also engaged a Heinkel and claimed it damaged while flying a Gladiator.

Between 0515 and 0730 hours, 1, 73, 85, 87 and 607 Squadrons were in action again, claiming eight further bombers destroyed, plus two 'probables ' and three damaged. Three Hs126s were also destroyed, one by Squadron Leader J.W.C.More, CO of 73 Squadron, and two by Sergeant G.L.Nowell of 87 Squadron. 1 Squadron lost a Hurricane, abandoned after a forced landing, and two more of 85 Squadron were badly shot-up. All three pilots were unharmed.

There was a pause until 11.30 hours, the RAF pilots taking what little rest they could while their aircraft were patched up, refuelled and rearmed. Then, at 1130 hours, the attacks were renewed. By mid afternoon a further ten bombers had been claimed, with six more reported as 'probably destroyed'. One Hurricane of 87 Squadron force-landed with battle damage.

By early afternoon it had become apparent that the forward airfields were becoming untenable, and the Hurricane squadrons were ordered to withdraw. 'B' Flight of 1 Squadron, evacuating to Berry-au-Bac, ran straight into a group of bombers, the pilots claiming two He111s and a Do17 destroyed. One Hurricane was shot down, the pilot baling out. At the same time (1430 hours) 607 Squadron, accompanied by a couple of Morane Saulnier MS406s, tore into another group of Heinkels. Two were claimed destroyed, three 'probables' and four damaged for the loss of a single Hurricane, this pilot being wounded.

By early evening the BEF fighter pilots had reported the destruction of nine more bombers, with one 'probable' and five damaged. German fighters were reported for the first time when Pilot

Officer J.R.Cock claimed to have damaged one, but this is likely to to have been a Do17, these two types frequently misidentified for each other. Two Hurricanes of 607 Squadron were hit and force-landed.

At 1610 hours, 501 Squadron arrived in France from England as reinforcements and, at 1800 hours, flew its first patrol during which a Do17 was met and claimed shot down.

With dusk approaching there was no let-up from the *Luftwaffe*. The French-based squadrons claimed a further twelve bombers destroyed, three 'probables' and two damaged. 3 Squadron, operating from England, claimed six Heinkels shot down and three damaged in three separate combats. One Hurricane was hit and force-landed. Another, lost in darkness at 2230 hours, was abandoned over the English coast on return.

During the fierce fighting that had taken place not a single Hurricane pilot had been lost, although at least three were wounded. Six Blenheims and eight Hurricanes had been shot down and at least three more of the latter - of 615 Sqn - had been destroyed in airfield attacks. Against these losses, the fighter squadrons had claimed 62 enemy aircraft destroyed, 18 'probables' and 21 damaged. But the worst was yet to come, for the Bf109 units, heavily engaged against the Dutch, French and Belgian air forces - and the RAF light bombers - had not yet shown their mettle against the RAF fighters.....

Note: *Due to the confused nature of the air fighting during May and June 1940, many records of British Expeditionary Force fighter units were either not completed or in some cases lost completely. Thus it is not possible to provide as complete a picture of daily activities as the author would wish for. The following account of the BEF in France had been pieced together from surviving documents such as Operation Record Books, Combat Reports, Log Books and Daily Summaries. For the many errors and omissions the author apologises.*

| Fighter Command Defiants ||||||||
Unit	Dest	P.D.	Dam	MIA	Cat E	KIA	MIA	WIA
264 Sqn	1[1.]	0	0	0	0	0	0	0

| Fighter Command Blenheims ||||||||
Unit	Dest	P.D.	Dam	MIA	Cat E	KIA	MIA	WIA
600 Sqn	1	1	0.	5	0	0	10	0
600 Sqn	1	0	0(G)					

| 604 Sqn | 4 | 3 | 0(G) | 0 | 1 | 0 | 0 | 0 |

BEF Hurricanes

Unit	Dest	P.D.	Dam	MIA	Cat E	KIA	MIA	WIA
1 Sqn	5	0	0	0	3	0	0	0
3 Sqn	6	0	3	0	2	0	0	1
73 Sqn	5	0	2.	0	1	0	0	1
85 Sqn	14	5	0	0	1	0	0	1
87 Sqn	12	6	5	0	0	0	0	0
501 Sqn	1	0	0	0	0	0	0	0
607 Sqn	17	6	10	0	1	0	0	1
615 Sqn	0	0	1[2]	0	3[3]	0	0	

1. Shared with unknown unit.
2. By Gladiator
3. Bombed on ground

11th May 1940

The German forces were now advancing through Holland while in Belgium the spearheads were threatening Maastricht, where two vital bridges spanned the River Meuse. The Belgian Army had failed to destroy these, and thus it fell to the RAF to attempt the task. Airfield attacks continued across France, Belgium and Holland. Fighters operating from England flew

---

Combat Report

11th May 1940
87 Squadron

I was on a patrol with five other aircraft when we spotted a great number of Junkers 87s dive-bombing over Brussels. We attacked them and I hit one which appeared to be put out of action and go down in the forest S of Brussels. At the same time three Dornier 17s escorted by Messerschmitt 109s appeared overhead. The 109s ran away and S/Ldr Dewar and I attacked one of the Dorniers. After chasing it across country on the deck we succeeded in shooting it down approximately 15 miles NE of Brussels.

- P/O H.T.Mitchell, 87 Squadron.

Blitzkrieg in the West

offensive patrols over the North Sea and the Dutch and Belgian coasts.

Fighter Command Hurricanes

Unit	Dest	P.D.	Dam	MIA	Cat E	KIA	MIA	WIA
3 Sqn	1	0	0	0	0	0	0	0
17 Sqn	5	1	0	4	1	0	4[1]	0

Fighter Command Spitfires

Unit	Dest	P.D.	Dam	MIA	Cat E	KIA	MIA	WIA
19 Sqn	1	0	0	0	0	0	0	0
54 Sqn	0	0	0	1	0	0	1	0

BEF Hurricanes

Unit	Dest	P.D.	Dam	MIA	Cat E	KIA	MIA	WIA
1 Sqn	13	1	0	0	1	0	0	0
73 Sqn	6	1	4	0	1	0	0	0
79 Sqn	1	0	0	0	1	0	0	1
85 Sqn	7	4	0	1	1	0	1	0
87 Sqn	9	0	0	0	0	0	0	0
501 Sqn	6	0	0	0	0	0	0	0
607 Sqn	7	2	2	0	0	0	0	1

1. 2 PoW

Luftwaffe Combat Reports

Orders: Freijagd (fighter sweep) and cover in the area west of Sedan. The Staffel flew at 5,000m (16,404 feet) covering a Stuka unit. This was attacked by six Hurricanes. I took the covering Schwarm to engage and shot down a Hurricane, which crashed in flames.

- Oberleutnant Hans-Karl Mayer 1 Staffel, Jagdgeschwader 53

I flew as the third man in Leutnant Zeis' Schwarm. At 16.20 hours enemy aircraft were sighted below us, which were about to attack another Schwarm. I rolled and dived into the combat. Suddenly I saw, right beneath me, a Hurricane right behind another Bf109 of our Staffel (Lt Groten). because I was in a very favourable position, I was able to get behind the Hurricane with a gentle turn and opened fire from 100m to 50m. The Hurricane spun down in flames.

- Uunteroffizier Höhnisch, 1 Staffel, Jagdgeschwader 53

Note: the Hurricanes were probably from 3 Squadron. Flt Lt Stephens managed to force-land while Plt Off Jeffrries baled out of his fighter.

12th May 1940

The BEF squadrons were involved in heavy fighting over Maastricht and Sedan, while the UK units flew offensive patrols to Holland

\multicolumn{8}{c}{Fighter Command Spitfires}
Unit	Dest	P.D.	Dam	MIA	Cat E	KIA	MIA	WIA
66 Sqn	1	0	0	0	0	0	0	0

\multicolumn{8}{c}{Fighter Command Defiants}
Unit	Dest	P.D.	Dam	MIA	Cat E	KIA	MIA	WIA
264 Sqn	2	0	0	0	0	0	0	0

\multicolumn{8}{c}{Fighter Command Blenheims}
Unit	Dest	P.D.	Dam	MIA	Cat E	KIA	MIA	WIA
SD Flt	0	1	0	0	0	0	0	0

\multicolumn{8}{c}{BEF Hurricanes}
Unit	Dest	P.D.	Dam	MIA	Cat E	KIA	MIA	WIA
1 Sqn	6	3	1	0	2	0	0	1
3 Sqn	13	1	0	0	0	0	0	0
73 Sqn	1	0	0	0	0	0	0	0
79 Sqn	5	2	0	0	1	0	0	0
85 Sqn	7	0	0	0	0	0	0	0
87 Sqn	5	0	0	0	2	1	0	1
501 Sqn	11	1	0	0	4	2	0	0
607 Sqn	3	0	0	0	1	0	0	1
615 Sqn	1	0	0	0	1	1	0	0

13th May 1940

The German advance continued in the north, while the master-stroke, an armoured thrust through the Ardenne Forest towards Sedan, took the Allied forces by surprise. By the end of the day the River Meuse had been reached and, if *Panzers* were not stopped, the whole of France would be open. UK-based fighters flew offensive patrols between Breda and Rotterdam.

\multicolumn{8}{c}{Fighter Command Spitfires}
Unit	Dest	P.D.	Dam	MIA	Cat E	KIA	MIA	WIA
66 Sqn	3	0	3	0	1	0	0	0

\multicolumn{8}{c}{Fighter Command Defiants}
Unit	Dest	P.D.	Dam	MIA	Cat E	KIA	MIA	WIA
264 Sqn	7	0	3	1	4	0	2	0

Unit	Dest	P.D.	Dam	MIA	Cat E	KIA	MIA	WIA
1 Sqn	7	0	0	0	1	0	0	1
3 Sqn	5	0	0	1[1]	2[2]	2	1	0
73 Sqn	3	1	0	0	1	0	0	1
85 Sqn	2	10[3]	0.	0	1	0	0	0
87 Sqn	1	0	0	0	0	0	0	0
501 Sqn	5	0	0	0	0	0	0	0
607 Sqn	2	0	0	1	0	0	1[4]	0
615 Sqn	0	0	0	0	1	1	0	0

BEF Hurricanes

1. Pilot died as PoW
2. Aircraft lost in mid-air collision
3. 'possibles'
4. PoW

Above: He111s of III./KG 55 over France during the Blitzkrieg.
(H.Scholl)
Left: The Bf110 proved an effective weapon during the campaign in France, but missions against an effective fighter defence showed its weaknesses
(H.Scholl)

The Boulton Paul Defiant I and II variants.
Basic Specification
Dimensions: Span: 39 ft 4 in Length 35 ft 4 in Height 11 ft 4 in
Power Plant: One Rolls Royce Merlin III rated at 1,030 hp at 16.250 ft
Armament: Four Browning .303 in machine-guns mounted in a Boulton-Paul AIID power-operated turret.

Performance:
Max Speed: 304 mph at 17,000 ft
Initial Climb: 1,900 ft/min
Ceiling: 30,350 ft.

Service History
In 1935, the development of the hydraulic-operated power turret by the Boulton-Paul company caused the Air Ministry to issue a specification (F9/35) calling for a twin-seat interceptor fighter carrying all armament in such a turret. Although the design produced exceeded the performance requirements specified, the aircraft was doomed to failure in its designed rôle. The reason was that the specification was flawed in three major respects. First, no twin-seat fighter of the time could ever hope to match the performance and maneouvreability of a contemporary single-seat aircraft. This was due to the added weight of the second crewman. Secondly, the high inherent drag caused by a four-gun turret, however streamlined. hthe Finally, the concentration of all armament in that turret and with no provision for fixed forward-firing armament proved to be a mistake.

When prototype Defiant flew on 11th August 1937, an order for 87 production models already having been placed, since the Defiant's only competitor, the Hawker Hotspur, had been abandoned. In December 1939 the first Defiants arrived to equip 264 Squadron and, in April 1940, 141 Squadron followed suit. 264 saw heavy action during the Battle of France and over Dunkirk in May, pilots claiming seventy-six confirmed victories and seven 'damaged' for the loss of ten Defiants and fourteen aircrew, with seven more fighters shot-up.

The *Luftwaffe* pilots soon got the measure of the Defiant however. On 19th July 141 Squadron, on an early Channel patrol, was bounced by the veteran Bf109E pilots of *Hauptmann* Hannes Trautloft's *III Gruppe, JG 51*, losing six out of nine with one more badly damaged. It was the beginning of the end for the Defiant as a day fighter. 141 Squadron moved to Scotland six days later. Three more Defiants were shot down on 24th August, including that flown by Squadron leader Hunter, CO of 264 Squadron Another were lost on 26th and again three on 28th. Next day 264 Squadron was withdrawn from the battle.

If the Defiant had been found wanting in daylight, it found its niche as a reasonably successful night fighter, operating in this rôle with nine further units. In the autumn of 1941 it was fitted with AI Mk.4 (Defiant Mk.IA). The final operational version was the Defiant II, powered by a Merlin XX. It had a slightly lengthened fuselage and the improved AI Mk.6. The last operational use of the Defiant was with 515 Squadron, using *Mandrel* radar jamming equipment in support of Bomber Command operations, serving in this way until mid-1943.

14th May 1940

Heavy fighting was now taking place in the areas of Louvain and Sedan as the Allied Air Forces strove to halt the German advance which would open up the whole of central France. Further north the German Army had now reached the Meuse. At 16.00 hours the German spearhead crossed the river and, by nightfall, three Divisions were across. The way was open to the Channel. In Holland the city of Rotterdam was subjected to a raid that would lead to the Dutch surrender before nightfall. RAF fighters engaged the *Luftwaffe* fighter cover over Belgium, as well as escorting the Allied bombers in near-suicidal attacks in the Sedan sector.

BEF Hurricanes								
Unit	Dest	P.D.	Dam	MIA	Cat E	KIA	MIA	WIA
1 Sqn	14	1	0	0	3	2	0	0
3 Sqn	18	2	0	0	4	1	0	1
73 Sqn	6	1	4	0	4	3	0	0
79 Sqn	6	0	1	0	2	1	0	1
85 Sqn	4.5	0	0	0	0	0	0	0
87 Sqn	1.5	2	0	0	4	2	0	2[1]
501 Sqn	6	0	1	0	0	0	0	0
504 Sqn	2	1	1	0	4	3	0	0
607 Sqn	1[2]	0	2	3	0	0	3	0
615 Sqn	1	0	0	0	0	0	0	0

1. Both pilots died of their injuries
2. Plus seven 'possibles'.

15th May 1940

The previous day's air fighting in the Sedan area had been the heaviest yet seen and was a total disaster for the western Allies. The French bomber forces had been all but destroyed, while the RAF had lost two-thirds of the bombers despatched to this area. The Official History stated that, *'No higher rate of loss in an operation of comparable size has ever been experienced by the RAF'*. Under the heaviest air cover possible, the Germans rapidly advanced to the so-called 'Dyle Line' running northwest from Sedan to Ostend. Holland and most of Belgium had already fallen, while France was shrinking by the minute.

An army request for six more RAF fighter squadrons to be sent to France was opposed by the Chief of Air Staff, Air Chief Marshal Sir Cyril Newall. He put forward the argument that no facilities existed in France to support six new units and promised that the necessary support would be given by squadrons operating from the British mainland.

On 14th May the French Premier had urgently requested that ten more Hurricane units be sent to France. Air Chief Marshal Dowding, C-in-C Fighter Command, protested vigorously, putting his case to the Cabinet on the 15th. His letter concluded with the words:

"I believe that, if an adequate fighter force is kept in this country, if the fleet remains in being and if Home Forces are suitably organised to resist invasion, we should be able to carry on the war single-handed for some time, if not indefinitely. But, if the Home Defence Force is drained away in desperate attempts to remedy the situation in France, defeat in France will involve the final, complete and irremediable defeat of this country".

Winston Churchill, determined to see for himself, flew to Paris next day. He saw the total breakdown of both the French Command and the situation generally. He returned, convinced of the rightness of Dowding's case. No further Hurricane units were despatched. Not only had Hugh Dowding's remarkably accurate forecast spared Fighter Command to fight the inevitable battle to come, but undoubtedly saved Britain from quick defeat.

During the day the outnumbered BEF squadrons attempted in vain to stem the massive onslaughts.

BEF Hurricanes								
Unit	Dest	P.D.	Dam	MIA	Cat E	KIA	MIA	WIA
1 Sqn	5	1	0	0	0	0	0	0
3 Sqn	4	1	0	1	5	2	1[1]	0
73 Sqn	4	1	1	0	3	0	0	2
85 Sqn	4	0	1	0	3	0	0	2
87 Sqn	4	1	0	0	1	1	0	0
501 Sqn	3	0	0	0	2	0	0	0
504 Sqn	3	2	4	0	0	0	0	0
607 Sqn	4	0	0	0	2	1	0	1
615 Sqn	4	1	2	1	1	0	1[2]	1

1. PoW
2. PoW

16th May 1940

By dawn the situation had deteriorated almost beyond hope of recovery. The Germans had torn a hole, some sixty miles wide, in the Allied defences west of Sedan, with *General* Heinz Guderian's *Panzers* already some 55 miles west of Sedan. The previous evening the French Prime Minister M Paul Reynaud had spoken to Winston Churchill by telephone: *'We are defeated'*, he said, *'We have lost the battle'*. meanwhile the Allied forces in the north were withdrawing southwards, leaving Belgium to its fate.

While the events were unfolding in France, the aircraft carrier HMS *Furious* sailed, carrying the replacement 263 Squadron Gladiators plus Hurricanes of 46 Squadron to Norway.

| BEF Hurricanes ||||||||
Unit	Dest	P.D.	Dam	MIA	Cat E	KIA	MIA	WIA
3 Sqn	1	0	0	0	0	1	0	0
73 Sqn	0	0	1	0	0	0	0	0
79 Sqn	3	0	0	0	1	0	0	0
85 Sqn	4	0	0	0	6	2	0	3
87 Sqn	4[1]	0	0	0	2	1	0	0
504 Sqn	1	1	2	0	0	0	0	0
607 Sqn	0	0	0[2]	0	0	0	0	0
615 Sqn	1	0	0	1	2	1	1[3]	1

1. Plus 4 'possibles'.
2. 1 'doubtful'.
3. PoW

17th May 1940

Brussels was captured and, further south, German *Panzer* spearheads had crossed the River Oise and were heading for St Quentin. Home-based squadrons were again in action, flying patrols and bomber escorts to France. An indication of the air superiority now enjoyed by the *Luftwaffe* is shown by the experience of 82 Squadron; twelve Blenheim bombers were intercepted by Bf109Es from *I./Jagdgeschwader 3* and eleven were shot down.

| Fighter Command Spitfires ||||||||
Unit	Dest	P.D.	Dam	MIA	Cat E	KIA	MIA	WIA
65 Sqn	1	0	0	0	0	0	0	0

| BEF Hurricanes ||||||||
Unit	Dest	P.D.	Dam	MIA	Cat E	KIA	MIA	WIA
1 Sqn.	5	2	0	0	3	0	0	0
3 Sqn.	1	1	0	0	2	0	0	1
56 Sqn	6	2	1	0	0	0	0	0
73 Sqn	1	2	0	0	0	0	0	0
79 Sqn.	1	0	1	1	0	0	1[1]	0
85 Sqn.	2	1	0	0	0	0	0	0

Blitzkrieg in the West

Unit	Dest	P.D.	Dam	MIA	Cat E	KIA	MIA	WIA
213 Sqn	0	0	0	0	1	0	0	1
242 Sqn	1	0	0	0	1	0	0	0
245 Sqn	1	0	0	0	2	0	0	0
504 Sqn	1	0	0	0	0	0	0	0
601 Sqn	0	0	0	0	1	0	0	0
607 Sqn	5	0	0	0	1	0	0	0
615 Sqn.	4	0	0	0	2	0	0	0

1. PoW

Wing Commander Ian Richard Gleed DFC

'Widge' Gleed was serving with 46 and later 266 Squadrons before transferring to 87 Squadron, with which he fought during the Battle of France and Battle of Britain, rising to command this unit. He led the squadron throughout 1941, mainly operating Hurricanes from the Scilly Isles against German reconnaissance bombers. He was promoted to Wing Commander and successively led the Middle Wallop and Ibsley Wings before being posted abroad to the Middle East, to lead 244 Spitfire Wing in the Tunisian Campaign. He was killed in action on 16th April 1943.

Victory List

13.5.40	Bf109	destroyed	7/8.5.41	Do17	destroyed
19.5.40	He111	destroyed*	24.5.41	Do17	damaged*
19.5.40	Do17	destroyed	28.5.41	Ju88	prob destroyed*
19.5.40	Bf109	destroyed	13.5.42	Ju88	prob destroyed*
19.5.40	Bf109	damaged	23.3.42	Ju88	destroyed
20.5.40	Ju88	destroyed*	17.4.42	Bf109	destroyed
20.5.40	Bf109	destroyed	25.4.42	Bf109	damaged
21.5.40	Do17	destroyed*	5.5.42	FW190	prob destroyed
15.8.40	Bf110	destroyed	7.3.43	MC202	damaged
15.8.40	Bf110	destroyed	17.3.43	Bf109	destroyed
15.8.40	Bf109	prob destroyed	30.9.40	Bf110	destroyed
25.8.40	Bf110	destroyed	30.9.40	Ju88	prob destroyed
25.8.40	Bf110	damaged	30.9.40	Do17	damaged
25.8.40	Bf109	damaged	* Shared claims		

Fighter Command Hurricanes

Unit	Dest	P.D.	Dam	MIA	Cat E	KIA	MIA	WIA
17 Sqn	4	1	1	2	0	0	2	0
151 Sqn	6	0	1	0	0	0	0	1

18th May 1940

In the week that had passed since the German invasion had begun, RAF fighter pilots and aircrew had claimed 356 German aircraft destroyed, with 55 more probably destroyed and 58 damaged, all in air combat. In the same period 117 RAF fighter aircraft had been lost together with 51 pilots and six air gunners. The BEF had suffered very heavily in this respect, with 44 pilots dead, missing or captured and 108 fighters lost. The term 'lost' does not necessarily indicate that the aircraft were all damaged beyond repair. Had the casualties occured in the United Kingdom it is likely that a large number would have been repaired, perhaps very quickly. However, when an aircraft was forced to land in a French field during a fast-moving ground campaign, it would simply be abandoned as the pilot sought to find transport to return to his unit.

Home-based squadrons were now being sent to operate from French airfields but, as these excursions were normally of short duration, their operations will continue to be classed as 'Fighter Command'. The Germans were now being fiercely engaged in the St. Quentin area as they sought to cut France in two, isolating the British forces between the German forces and the sea.

Fighter Command Hurricanes

Unit	Dest	P.D.	Dam	MIA	Cat E	KIA	MIA	WIA
17 Sqn.	1	2	0	0	0	0	0	0
32 Sqn.	0	1	1	0	0	0	0	0
56 Sqn.	10	2	0	0	3	2	0	1
111 Sqn.	10	3	3	0	2	1	0	0
145 Sqn.	3	3	1	0	1	0	0	0
151 Sqn.	3	0	1	0	2	0	0	0
213 Sqn.	1	0	2	0	0	0	0	0
229 Sqn.	2	0	1	1	3	0	1[1.]	1
253 Sqn	8	5	1	0	5	0	0	0
601 Sqn.	3	1	2	0	2	0	0	0

BEF Hurricanes

Unit	Dest	P.D.	Dam	MIA	Cat E	KIA	MIA	WIA
1 Sqn.	3	0	0	1	1	0	1[2.]	0
3 Sqn	1	0	0	0	2	0	0	0
17 Sqn	4	1	1	2	0	0	2	0
79 Sqn	4	0	3	0	1	0	0	1
85 Sqn	1	0	0	2	0	1	2[3.]	0
87 Sqn	3	2	1	0	0	0	0	0
151 Sqn	6	0	1	0	0	0	0	1
242 Sqn	1	1	0	1	2	0	1[4.]	1
504 Sqn	0	0	1	1	1	1	1[5.]	0
607 Sqn	0	1	3	0	3	1	0	0
4 CFF[6.]	1	0	2	0	0	0	0	0

1- 5. PoWs
6. Continental Ferry Flight

18/19th May 1940

An He111 was claimed destroyed off Dunkirk by a 604 Squadron Blenheim flown by Flying Officer A.S.Hunter.

19th May 1940

By nightfall, German armoured columns had reach the line Cambrai-Peronne. They were now more than halfway across France, the tanks rolling steadily across the old Somme battlefields, with the British forces being compressed into a decreasing area.

Fighter Command Hurricanes

Unit	Dest	P.D.	Dam	MIA	Cat E	KIA	MIA	WIA
17 Sqn	4	2	1	1	1	0	1[1.]	0
32 Sqn	3	4	2	1	0	0	1[2.]	0
56 Sqn	0	0	1	0	0	0	0	0
111 Sqn	3	2	1	0	3	2	0	0
145 Sqn	2	1	0	0	1	1	0	0
213 Sqn	4.5	1	1	0	1	0	0	0
242 Sqn	1	0	0	0	0	0	0	0
253 Sqn	1	1	2	0	4	3	0	1
601 Sqn	5	1	0	0	3	0	0	0

			BEF Hurricanes					
Unit	Dest	P.D.	Dam	MIA	Cat E	KIA	MIA	WIA
1 Sqn	5	2	5	0	2	0	0	2
3 Sqn	8.5	0	0	0	0	0	0	0
73 Sqn	7	1	1	0	2	0	0	0
79 Sqn.	1	0	0	0	0	0	0	0
85 Sqn	14	2	1	0	3	1	0	0
87 Sqn	10	2	1	0	3	0	0	2
501 Sqn.	0	1	0	0	0	0	0	0
504 Sqn.	1	1	0	0	3	0	0	0
607 Sqn.	2	0	0	1	0	0	1[3]	0
615 Sqn.	0	2	0	0	1	0	0	0

1. - 3. PoWs

19/20th May 1940

One 604 Sqn Blenheim was reported missing from patrol.

20th May 1940

Heavy ground fighting took place in the area of Arras. Amiens fell, while further south the German armoured spearhead reached the Channel at Abbeville. France was now cut in two, with the British and Belgians almost surrounded in the north.

			Fighter Command Hurricanes					
Unit	Dest	P.D.	Dam	MIA	Cat E	KIA	MIA	WIA
32 Sqn	0	0	1	0	1	0	0	0
213 Sqn.	2.75	1	0	0	0	0	0	0

			BEF Hurricanes					
Unit	Dest	P.D.	Dam	MIA	Cat E	KIA	MIA	WIA
3 Sqn	4	0	2	0	0	0	0	0
79 Sqn	2.25	1	3	0	2	1	0	0
85 Sqn	3[1]	0	0	0	4	3	0	0
87 Sqn	6	0	5	0	0	0	0	0
501 Sqn	0	1	0	0	0	0	0	0
504 Sqn	0	0	0	0	1	0	0	1
607 Sqn	0	0	0	1	0	0	1[2]	0
615 Sqn.	3	0	1	0	1	0	0	0
60 Wg[3]	1	0	0	0	0	0	0	0

1. plus 3 'possibles'
2. PoW
3. Wg Cdr Harry Broadhurst.

21st May 1940

An Allied armoured counteroffensive in the Arras sector confused the Germans - albeit temporarily - into thinking that a far larger Allied force was deployed against them. Thus their advance halted as they consolided to deal with the threat. RAF fighter activity was confined to the home-based squadrons, some operating from forward French bases. The BEF Hurricane units were either moving bases or attempting to evacuate to England. Off Norway, 263 Sqn Gladiators commenced flying out to Bardufoss. Three aircraft crashed in bad weather; one pilot was injured and the other two were killed.

Fighter Command Spitfires

Unit	Dest	P.D.	Dam	MIA	Cat E	KIA	MIA	WIA
74 Sqn	2	4	0	0	1	0	0	0

23rd May 1940 - Rescue at Calais/Marck

In the early morning Spitfires of 74 Sqn flew a patrol, catching an Hs126 near Guines at 06.00 hours. This was shot down by Squadron leader White and Flight Lieutenant Measures, but Laurie White did not return. He was seen to force-landed on Calais Marck aerodrome. Immediately, 54 Squadron laid plans to rescue him. Flight Lieutenant James Leathart was to pilot a Miles Master to land on the battered airfield, with Spitfires flown by Pilot Officers Al Deere and Johnny Allen flying as cover. At 10.30 hours, the trio set off and, as they approached the coast, Deere stayed with Leathart, ordering Allen to climb above the clouds in order to warn of any approaching Germans. He quickly reached 12,000 feet, by which time the Master had landed.

Squadron Leader White scrambled into the Master and Leathart opened the throttle but, as the little aircraft left the ground, two things happened almost simultaneaously. Johnny Allen radioed sighting a *Staffel* of Bf109s approaching and dived to engage them, while a Bf109 came streaking from the clouds firing at the Master. It flew straight in front of Al Deere, who gave him a quick burst of gunfire. The '109 broke hard, with Deere turning inside him as Johnny Allen called, *'I'm surrounded. Can you help me?'* The German now in front of Deere pulled into a vertical climb, giving the Spitfire pilot a no-deflection shot that caused the Messerschmitt to stall and dive into the sea just offshore. Deere immediately climbed at full throttle to help Allen, but almost at once saw two more Bf109s. Turning inside one of them, he gave a long burst that knocked pieces off it and, as it dived away he took on the other one, chasing it down to 'zero feet' and expending all his ammunition at it before breaking upwards into cloud.

Meanwhile Johnny Allen, having originally sighted twelve Messerschmitts 3,000 feet below, had courageously taken them on in an atttempt to divert their attention from the Master below:

"*I attacked closest Me109 and it did a stall turn and dived into cloud. I followed, shooting for five seconds till he was lost in cloud. I dived through cloud and enemy aircraft was still diving, smoke pouring from him. I climbed again hoping to draw attention away from aerodrome and found many enemy aircraft still above clouds. Two Me109s dived on me and I did a head-on attack. First Me109 shot past (the other tried to do a beam attack which was unsuccessful, tracer shooting well behind). One-second burst got in at the leader. This manoeuvre was repeated twice more and each time I found enemy aircraft orbitting above the clouds. I managed to get in two bursts five seconds each at both, diving into cloud smoke pouring from their engines.*"

The Master had, early on, landed again and the two occupants evacuated the aircraft and dived into a nearby ditch. From there they witnessed the battle above them. The composite Combat Report submitted by 54 Squadron says it all:

"*A series of dogfights ensued in which Red Leader attacked a further two enemy aircraft and Red 17 attacked three enemy aircraft. Great credit is due to Red 17, who who attempted successfully to keep as many Me109s as he could above the cloud so that the Master might have the best possible chance of landing. The pilot of the Master, together with the 74 Squadron pilot, witnessed most of the fight and confirm that 3 enemy aircraft crashed - one in the sea and two on land. The first was shot down by Pilot Officer Deere (also witnessed by P/O Allen) and one of the other two was the first one attacked by P/O Allen (this the pilot of the Master saw crash in flames immediately he had landed; it was diving from a great height).*

"*Enemy offensive tactics were to outnumber the Spitfires by 2 to 1 on every attack - adopting line astern - so that evasive measures of the Spitfires could be followed. There was no 'squadron' or 'section'*

Johnny Allen, Bob Stanford-Tuck, Alan Deere, Adolph 'Sailor' Malan and James Leathart at their investiture, cheering HM King George VI.. At this time Bob Tuck and Malan were both Flight Commanders, with 92 and 74 Squadrons respectively.

formation apart from this. The enemy aircraft appeared to hold their fire until they were well placed. Evasive measures were to dive steeply, pulling out suddenly, going vertically upwards and pushing the stick forward. Half rolls from all positions and stall turns (particularly to the left) were used. An Me109 chasing a Spitfire broke away to assist another Me109 being chased by a Spitfire. Cloud was used whenever possible as a means of escape, and because of this the three remaining enemy aircraft attacked cannot be confirmed as losses. The above was obtained partly from the pilots and partly from the pilot of the Master, who was able to watch the battle from the ground.

"Red Leader Pilot Officer A.C.Deere Red 17 Pilot Officer J.L.Allen"
Allen's aircraft had been hit by a few bullets in his epic fight, but like Deere he got back safely, followed by James Leathart and Laurie White in the Master, Leathart later saying, 'We waited about ten minutes after the fight ended and, when it seemed safe, made a hasty take-off and a rather frightened trip back to England and safety'

Leathart received the DSO for his part in the action, while Al Deere and Johnny Allen were each awarded a richly deserved DFC.

"The Debut of 19 Squadron"

19 Squadron, the first to receive Spitfires, had sat largely inactive during the Phoney War and the major part of the Battle of France. Now, with the British Expeditionary Force falling back to the coast at Dunkirk and Calais, came their first real call to action. Air Vice-Marshal (then Pilot Officer) Michael Lyne remembers:

"At 9.30 on 26th May we climbed towards Dunkirk, twelve of us in sections of three - a mistake which the fighter pilots of World War I could have corrected if they had been asked. But the new 'high-tech' air force thought that it had left the past behind.....

"Having reached the end of the patrol line at Dunkirk, we ran back towards Calais, being stubbornly defended by British and French troops. As we approached Calais at about 10,000 feet we saw ahead of us a large formation of dive-bombers heading in the same direction and at our height. Above and in front of them, heading away from us, was the formation of covering fighters. I was in the leading section with the C.O., Squadron Leader Geoffrey Stevenson. He had been a friend of Douglas Bader at Cranwell and was a daring amateur jockey. But he was also a top grade flying instructor 'A1' grade. His flying was smooth and controlled and he was accustomed to following in detail the well proven training system of the Royal Air Force Central Flying School. Alas we had left the only well proven fighter system in the mists of World War I. All we had in its place was a pedantic book laying out four attacks for use against unescorted bombers.

"Geoffrey followed the book to the letter - including trying to reduce the squadron's overtaking speed to the modest 30 mph tha would allow a long and destructive burst from our eight Browning machine guns. But the cads in the Ju87s seemed to be doing only about 130 mph. I remember so clearly Geoffrey's order "No. 19 Squadron, throttling back" as we came up on the unsuspecting bombers.....they obviously looked on us as part of the escort and did not fire. I ought to have been dismayed, for we were down to a lethally low speed and the German fighters could not forever remain out of position. My target was well within my sights, the order to 'Fire!' came and the three rearmost Ju's were hit, then we had to break to avoid running into the middle of the formation. I broke right and Geoffrey and Wattie broke left, and from that moment we were on our own, yet still in the area of conflict. The fighters must have come down on us as we broke. I saw Wattie hit in the cockpit by a cannon bursting round, then seemed to be alone in a peaceful sky. So peaceful that I remember taking a moment to wonder what the little corkscrews of smoke were outside my port wing.

The steady 'Thump, thump' of the Me's cannon quite close behind explained it all. He must have been as much of a beginner as I was and, as I turned, he overshot and was gone."

After a pass at some Ju87s circling near Calais, he returned to Hornchurch with a slightly damaged Spitfire, but Geoffrey Stevenson was shot down and captured, while 'Wattie' was never seen again. But the day was only half over. At 16.00 hours the squadron, now led by the dynamic Brian Lane took off again for another patrol in the same area, but with rather different results, the squadron breaking formation as eight Bf109s dived on them:

"We were then involved in a fierce dogfight in which the superiority of the German pilots became evident. You could be sure if you had a lone Me in your sights there would be another one behind you. In my case the pair stayed together above me and for a moment we circled, watching one another. Then the leader dropped his nose as I pulled mine up and fired.

"I didn't stop to observe the results, for his burst slammed into my knee. The pain was appalling, but a lucky by-product of this tremendous blow was to kick my rudder hard over and put my Spitfire into a right-hand spin, usually taken as a sign that the target has been fatally hit. I had no more problems with the enemy and could concentrate on my own situation....."

Michael Lyne recovered the Spitfire with difficulty and, with the radio out of action and the Merlin engine overheating, found himself in cloud, heading towards Kent. By immense good fortune his fading engine kept him airborne until he reached the coast at Walmer, where he belly-landed, just missing many people walking on the seafront as he glided in. Quickly he found himself on a stretcher in the Royal Marine Hospital at Deal:

"The severely wounded destroyer casualties were pouring in. Compared to them I was lucky and, by the end of 26th May 1940 was in good hands and starting the long trek back to 21st February 1941 and the Spitfire cockpit once more".

The Fighter Command War Diaries

		Fighter Command Hurricanes						
Unit	Dest	P.D.	Dam	MIA	Cat E	KIA	MIA	WIA
17 Sqn	1	0	0	0	0	0	0	0
151 Sqn	1	0	0	0	0	0	0	0
229 Sqn	2	0	0	0	1	1	0	0
253 Sqn.	0	0	0	1	0	0	1[1.]	0
601 Sqn	0	0	0	0	1	0	0	0

1. PoW

22nd May 1940

The German spearheads now reached Boulogne, but were halted by the stubborn resistance of the defenders. Winston Churchill returned to France to re-assess the situation, now clearly a disaster of the first magnitude.

		Fighter Command Hurricanes						
Unit	Dest	P.D.	Dam	MIA	Cat E	KIA	MIA	WIA
32 Sqn	5	1	0	0	1	0	0	0
56 Sqn	1	1	0	0	1	0	0	0
145 Sqn	4	5	1	0	0	0	0	0
151 Sqn	5	2	0	0	0	0	0	0
213 Sqn	0	3	0	0	0	0	0	0
229 Sqn	2	0	0	1	0	0	1	0
242 Sqn	3	0	0	0	0	0	0	0
605 Sqn	0	0	0	4	1	0	4	0

		Fighter Command Spitfires						
Unit	Dest	P.D.	Dam	MIA	Cat E	KIA	MIA	WIA
54 Sqn	0	2	0	0	0	0	0	0
65 Sqn	0	1	0	0	0	0	0	0
74 Sqn	3	0	0	0	1	0	0	0

		Fighter Command Blenheims						
Unit	Dest	P.D.	Dam	MIA	Cat E	KIA	MIA	WIA
604 Sqn	0	0	1	0	0	0	0	0

		BEF Norway Gladiators						
Unit	Dest	P.D.	Dam	MIA	Cat E	KIA	MIA	WIA
263 Sqn	1	0	0	0	1	1	0	0

23rd May 1940

British troops at Calais had now been surrounded, while the larger body of British forces was being steadily pressed towards

Dunkirk. Meanwhile *Feldmarschall* von Runstedt, in response to requests from his field commanders, ordered that the *Panzers* halt for necessary maintenance and to rest the tired crews. Goering, aware of this, immediately telephoned Hitler, requesting that the *Luftwaffe* be allowed 'to finish the job' at Dunkirk. His subordinate, *General* Kesselring, protested that they had not the resources, but was overruled. Hitler agreed to Goering's request and the die was cast.

Fighter Command Hurricanes								
Unit	Dest	P.D.	Dam	MIA	Cat E	KIA	MIA	WIA
32 Sqn	1	0	0	0	1	0	0	1
56 Sqn	0	0	1	0	0	0	0	0
145 Sqn	0	1[1]	0	0	0	0	0	0
242 Sqn	0	0	0	4	0	0	4	0
253 Sqn	4	2	1	1	1	0	1	0

Fighter Command Spitfires								
Unit	Dest	P.D.	Dam	MIA	Cat E	KIA	MIA	WIA
54 Sqn	2	4	0	0	0	0	0	0
74 Sqn.	1	0	0	1	1[2]	0	1	0
92 Sqn	20[3]	3	1	4	0	0	4	0

BEF Hurricanes								
Unit	Dest	P.D.	Dam	MIA	Cat E	KIA	MIA	WIA
1 Sqn	1	0	0	0	0	0	0	0
73 Sqn	1	1	0	0	0	0	0	0

BEF Norway Gladiators								
Unit	Dest	P.D.	Dam	MIA	Cat E	KIA	MIA	WIA
263 Sqn	1	0	0	0	1	0	0	0

1. Shared victory
2. See 'Rescue at Calais/Marck'
3. Includes 9 'unconfirmed destroyed'

24th May 1940

The German advance was now halted on Hitler's orders as he acceded to Goering's request to 'let the Luftwaffe finish off the British Army'. Hitler did have another reason; the armoured forces had suffered a high attrition rate due to mechanical failure and crew fatigue in addition to the combat losses. With the bulk of France still to conquer, the *Führer* wanted his *Panzers* fresh, rested and eager. For the first time came the feeling that the *Luftwaffe* was not quite as effective as had been first thought when von Kleist's Armoured Group, a short distance from Dunkirk, reported, *"Enemy air superiority. Very heavy activity by enemy fighters. Luftwaffe operations against enemy sea transport remain ineffective"*.

Over Norway, an He111 was destroyed and a Bf110 damaged by 263 Sqn Gladiator pilots.

Fighter Command Spitfires								
Unit	Dest	P.D.	Dam	MIA	Cat E	KIA	MIA	WIA
54 Sqn	13	0	3	2	0	0	2	0
65 Sqn	1	0	0	0	0	0	0	0
74 Sqn	6	3	0	1	0	0	1	0
92 Sqn	0	0	0	2	2	0	2	0

Fighter Command Hurricanes.								
Unit	Dest	P.D.	Dam	MIA	Cat E	KIA	MIA	WIA
242 Sqn	0	0	0	2	0	0	2	0

Fighter Command Defiants								
Unit	Dest	P.D.	Dam	MIA	Cat E	KIA	MIA	WIA
264 Sqn	1	0	0	0	0	0	0	0

BEF France Hurricanes								
Unit	Dest	P.D.	Dam	MIA	Cat E	KIA	MIA	WIA
73 Sqn	1	0	0	1	1	0	1	0

BEF Norway Gladiators								
Unit	Dest	P.D.	Dam	MIA	Cat E	KIA	MIA	WIA
263 Sqn	1	0	1	0	0	0	0	0

25th May 1940

The port of Boulogne, having been besieged for several days, was captured after many British serviceman had been evacuated. Calais however, was being bitterly contested, the *Luftwaffe* sending in a mass *Stuka* attack in the morning, opposed by the RAF. So far had the situation deteriorated that the British Secretary of State for War, Anthony Eden, now authorised a complete British withdrawal to the coast. As the BEF ground forces closed in on Dunkirk, most *Luftwaffe* units were operating some distance away against purely French targets and thus the assembling troops were spared the start of Goering's *'finishing off the British army'*.

			Fighter Command Spitfires					
Unit	Dest	P.D.	Dam	MIA	Cat E	KIA	MIA	WIA
54 Sqn	5	0	3	1	2	0	1	0
92 Sqn	1	0	0	0	0	0	0	0
			Fighter Command Hurricanes					
Unit	Dest	P.D.	Dam	MIA	Cat E	KIA	MIA	WIA
17 Sqn	5	0	3	0	0	0	0	0
151 Sqn	0	0	0	0	2	2	0	0
Unit	Dest	P.D.	Dam	MIA	Cat E	KIA	MIA	WIA
242 Sqn	1	0	0	0	0	0	0	0
605 Sqn	6	5	0	0	0	0	0	0
			BEF Hurricanes					
Unit	Dest	P.D.	Dam	MIA	Cat E	KIA	MIA	WIA
1 Sqn	0	0	0	1	0	0	1	0
73 Sqn	1	0	0	0	0	0	0	0
501 Sqn	0	0	1	0	1	0	0	0
			BEF Norway Gladiators					
Unit	Dest	P.D.	Dam	MIA	Cat E	KIA	MIA	WIA
263 Sqn	3	0	0	0	0	0	0	0

26th May 1940

Calais finally fell, following further *Stuka* raids. However the *Luftwaffe*'s main target had not yet become Dunkirk, since the Germans were again busily attacking French positions further afield. The British government, now recognising that defeat was inevitable and believing that around 35,000 troops might be saved, put *'Operation Dynamo'* into effect. At dusk an armada of small ships supporting the Royal Navy setting out to rescue the embattled British from the beaches.

46 Sqn Hurricanes arrived in Norway, landing at Skaanland.

			Fighter Command Spitfires					
Unit	Dest	P.D.	Dam	MIA	Cat E	KIA	MIA	WIA
19 Sqn	11	1	0	3	0	0	3	0
54 Sqn	7	2	0	0	0	0	0	0
65 Sqn	8	0	8	1	1	0	1	0
74 Sqn	0	1	0	0	0	0	0	0
			Fighter Command Hurricanes					
Unit	Dest	P.D.	Dam	MIA	Cat E	KIA	MIA	WIA
17 Sqn	2	0	2	2	0	0	2	0
32 Sqn	1	0	0	0	0	0	0	0
145 Sqn.	0	1	0	0	0	0	0	0
605 Sqn	2	0	0	1	0	0	1	0

BEF Hurricanes

Unit	Dest	P.D.	Dam	MIA	Cat E	KIA	MIA	WIA
73 Sqn	1	0	0	1	0	0	1	0

BEF Norway Gladiators

Unit	Dest	P.D.	Dam	MIA	Cat E	KIA	MIA	WIA
263 Sqn	7	1	0	0	0	0	0	0

27th May 1940

This day proved to be the first major encounter between the RAF Fighter Command home-based squadrons and the *Luftwaffe*. The Germans at last unleashed their full might against the vast fleet commencing the mass rescue of the British Army at Dunkirk. The RAF proved equal to the task by claiming 53 confirmed victories, the Germans losing at least 33 aircraft and suffering severe damage to at least a dozen more. *Fliegerkorps II reported 'A bad day: With sixty-four aircrew missing, seven wounded and twenty-three aircraft gone, todays losses exceed the combined total of the last ten days'.* On the ground, Hitler allowed the tanks to advance, but no closer than 15 miles from Dunkirk. To the north, the Belgian government surrendered. By the end of the first day of the naval operations, 7,669 soldiers had been rescued from the beaches.

In Norway, Gladiators were again in action and a 46 Squadron Hurricane was lost in a crash at Skaanland. The squadron later transferred to Bardufoss due to the unpreparedness of Skaanland as an operational base.

Fighter Command Hurricanes

Unit	Dest	P.D.	Dam	MIA	Cat E	KIA	MIA	WIA
17 Sqn	1	0	1	0	0	0	0	0
56 Sqn	4	4	0	0	3	0	0	1
79 Sqn	4	2	0	0	0	0	0	0
145 Sqn	3	2	0	3	3	0	3	0
213 Sqn	4	0	0	0	0	0	0	0
601 Sqn	5	2	1	1	1	0	1	0
605 Sqn.	0	0	0	3	0	0	3	0

Fighter Command Defiants

Unit	Dest	P.D.	Dam	MIA	Cat E	KIA	MIA	WIA
264 Sqn	10	0	0	0	0	0	0	0

Fighter Command Spitfires

Unit	Dest	P.D.	Dam	MIA	Cat E	KIA	MIA	WIA
19 Sqn	2	2	0	0	0	0	0	0
54 Sqn	2	0	0	1	0	0	1	0
65 Sqn	6	3	0	0	1	0	0	1
74 Sqn	9	1	0	0	2[1.]	0	0	0
610 Sqn	5	2	0	3	0	0	3	0

BEF France Hurricanes

Unit	Dest	P.D.	Dam	MIA	Cat E	KIA	MIA	WIA
73 Sqn	1	0	0	0	0	0	0	0
501 Sqn	11	3	2	0	0	0	0	0

BEF Norway Hurricanes

Unit	Dest	P.D.	Dam	MIA	Cat E	KIA	MIA	WIA
46 Sqn	0	0	0	0	1	0	0	0

BEF Norway Gladiators

Unit	Dest	P.D.	Dam	MIA	Cat E	KIA	MIA	WIA
263 Sqn	2	0	0	0	2	0	0	1

1. One pilot was captured, but escaped, evaded and returned.

28th May 1940

Fortune, having dealt the British Army many bitter blows in recent days, now smiled. The weather turned bad, bringing the cloudbase down to some 300 feet over the Dunkirk beachhead and salient, thus preventing further mass assaults from the *Luftwaffe*. The attacks were infrequent and sporadic and, by the end of the day, a further 17,804 soldiers had been plucked from the beaches.

Both Hurricanes and Gladiators were in action over Norway. In addition to aerial victories being claimed by both types, two Do26s were discovered on the water and were strafed and set on fire by Hurricane pilots.

Fighter Command Spitfires

Unit	Dest	P.D.	Dam	MIA	Cat E	KIA	MIA	WIA
19 Sqn	2	0	0	0	0	0	0	0
54 Sqn	0	0	1	0	1	0	0	0
65 Sqn	2	0	0	0	1	0	0	0
616 Sqn	2	1	0	0	0	0	0	0

Fighter Command Hurricanes

Unit	Dest	P.D.	Dam	MIA	Cat E	KIA	MIA	WIA
213 Sqn	8	0	2	2	3	0	2	1
242 Sqn	2	1	0	2	0	0	2	0

The Fighter Command War Diaries

Fighter Command Defiants

Unit	Dest	P.D.	Dam	MIA	Cat E	KIA	MIA	WIA
264 Sqn	6	0	0	0	0	0	0	0

BEF Norway Hurricanes

Unit	Dest	P.D.	Dam	MIA	Cat E	KIA	MIA	WIA
46 Sqn	1	0	0(A)	0	0	0	0	0
46 Sqn	2	0	0(G)	0	0	0	0	0

BEF Norway Gladiators

Unit	Dest	P.D.	Dam	MIA	Cat E	KIA	MIA	WIA
263 Sqn	1	0	0	0	0	0	0	0

29th May 1940

The bad weather continued throughout the morning, but a clearing of the skies in the early afternoon brought another series of mass *Luftwaffe* attacks against the fleet of ships off Dunkirk. Despite this, the RAF fighters were able to provide sufficient daylight cover for another 47,310 troops to be rescued.

Fighter Command Spitfires

Unit	Dest	P.D.	Dam	MIA	Cat E	KIA	MIA	WIA
64 Sqn	1	0	1	3	1	0	3	0
610 Sqn	4	0	0	2	0	0	2	0

Fighter Command Hurricanes

Unit	Dest	P.D.	Dam	MIA	Cat E	KIA	MIA	WIA
17 Sqn	2	0	2	0	0	0	0	0
56 Sqn	3	0	3	1	1	0	1	0
151 Sqn	3	0	0	0	2	0	0	1
213 Sqn	4	3	3	0	0	0	0	0
229 Sqn	0	0	0	1	0	0	1	0
242 Sqn	11	0	0	0	0	0	0	0

Fighter Command Defiants

Unit	Dest	P.D.	Dam	MIA	Cat E	KIA	MIA	WIA
264 Sqn	39[1]	0	2	0	0	0	1	0

BEF Norway Hurricanes

Unit	Dest	P.D.	Dam	MIA	Cat E	KIA	MIA	WIA
46 Sqn	6	0	0	0	3	2	0	0

BEF Norway Gladiators

Unit	Dest	P.D.	Dam	MIA	Cat E	KIA	MIA	WIA
263 Sqn	0	1	0	0	0	0	0	0

1. See inset

The Two-Seaters in Action

At 14.30 hours on 29th May, Squadron Leader Philip Hunter led twelve Defiants of 264 Squadron off to provide cover for the Dunkirk evacuation. A large number of Bf109s and '110s were met, escorting Stukas, and a massive dogfight began. The squadron claimed seven Bf109s, ten Bf110s and two *Stukas* shot down, with another '109 damaged. Pilot Officer Kay's Defiant (L6957) was badly shot up and his gunner, Leading Aircraftman Jones, baled out into the sea and was never seen again.

The second cover sortie commenced at 18.55 hours and, on this occasion, eighteen Ju87 *Stukas*, one Ju88 and a Bf110 were claimed destroyed, with another Stuka claimed as damaged. Two Defiants were hit, but all returned safely. Honours went to Flight Lieutenant N.G.Cooke, with five *Stukas*, two Bf109s and a Bf110 credited. Pilot Officer T.D.Welsh claimed four destroyed as did Sgt R.Thorne, while Pilot Officer R.W.Stokes, Pilot Officer E.G.Barwell and Pilot Officer D.Whitley claimed three apiece.

The press hailed this as a great victory, but the truth is rather different. The *Luftwaffe* actually lost around twenty aircraft that day, of which only one was a *Stuka*. The real success of the two operations was that none of the RAF were lost, since the Defiant, hampered in speed and manouevreability by the bulky turret, was a hopeless aircraft in daylight. The crews fought courageously - indeed, by the end of the battle, Hunter was dead, as was Cooke and Whitley - and their claims were made in good faith. However it would be some time before the authorities recognised it as a failure in daylight and relegated it to nightfighting, in which rôle it served very well indeed.

Sqn Ldr Philip Hunter of 264 Sqn (left) briefs his crews. After 264's initial successes, the Bf109 pilots soon got the measure of the Defiant, but the gallant crews fought bravely on into August.
(D.Brocklehurst)

Flight Lieutenant John Terrance Webster DFC

Served pre-war with 46, 17 and 80 Squadrons before being posted to 41 as a Flight Commander and remained with this unit from the outbreak of war. He fought over Dunkirk and through the Battle of Britain and had the distinction of engaging and wounding the celebrated German *Experte Major* Werner Mölders on 28th July. He was killed at North Benfleet on 5th September when he was shot down, together with his CO, Squadron Leader H.R.L.Hood, who also died.

Victory List

31.5.40	Bf109	destroyed	29.7.40	Ju87	damaged
31.5.40	He111	destroyed*	5.8.40	He111	damaged
1.6.40	Ju88	destroyed	8.8.40	Bf109	destroyed
1.6.40	Ju88	destroyed	8.8.40	Bf109	destroyed*
19/20.6.40	He111	prob destroyed	8.8.40	Bf109	prob destroyed
27.7.40	Bf109	destroyed	8.8.40	Bf109	prob destroyed
28.7.40	Bf109	damaged	5.9.40	Bf109	destroyed
28.7.40	Bf109	damaged	5.9.40	Bf109	destroyed
29.7.40	Bf109	destroyed	5.9.40	Bf109	damaged

* indicates shared claims

30th May 1940

Bad weather again prevented the *Luftwaffe* from operating in force over Dunkirk, only two engagements being reported by covering RAF fighters. The daily total of rescued soldiers rose to 53,823, bringing the overall figure to well over 100,000 - three times the original estimate.

Fighter Command Hurricanes

Unit	Dest	P.D.	Dam	MIA	Cat E	KIA	MIA	WIA
213 Sqn	1	0	0	0	0	0	0	0
245 Sqn	1	2	0	0	0	0	0	0

31st May 1940

Luftwaffe bombers returned to Dunkirk at dawn, but the *Stukas*, so deadly against shipping, were notably absent. Again the RAF fought bravely and well, allowing 68,014 soldiers to be lifted from the beaches, the highest daily figure of *'Operation Dynamo'*.

			Fighter Command Spitfires					
Unit	Dest	P.D.	Dam	MIA	Cat E	KIA	MIA	WIA
41 Sqn	2	0	0	0	0	0	0	0
64 Sqn	4	0	0(A)	1	0	0	1	0
64 Sqn	2	0	0(G)	0	0	0	0	0
222 Sqn	0	0	1	0	1	0	0	0
609 Sqn	7	3	0	3	0	0	3	0
610 Sqn	2	0	0	1	1	0	1	0

Where Was The RAF at Dunkirk?

On 26th May 1940, orders for the commencement of Operation Dynamo were put into effect. Fighter Command was ordered to *'Ensure the protection of the Dunkirk beaches (three miles on either side) from first light to darkness by continuous fighter patrols in strength.'* Between 26th May and 4th June, when the evacuation was completed, RAF fighter pilots defending Dunkirk had claimed 276 enemy aircraft destroyed, 85 'probables' and 53 damaged. They lost 96 fighters, with another 54 badly damaged (Cat 2). A further two bombers were claimed destroyed in ground strafes. In addition, eleven more German aircraft were claimed as confirmed, with three 'probables' and two damaged by BEF pilots, but these were almost certainly to the southwest, far from the Dunkirk area.

The Army survivors, huddled on the Dunkirk beaches, have often put forward the bitter question *'Where was the RAF?'* and, from their own point of view, this may seem justified. Amid the smoke of battle few aircraft except for *Luftwaffe* bombers were seen. However the troops on the beaches were not to know that the bulk of the air fighting was occurring many miles behind them, as the RAF sought to stop the *Luftwaffe* from reaching Dunkirk. Besides causing great damage to the German air attackers they caused very many bombers to jettison their loads to evade attack, rendering them ineffective. Over 338,000 soldiers were eventually rescued but, if it had not been for the sacrifices made by Fighter Command, far fewer men would have returned to fight again.

Wing Commander Michael Nicholson Crossley DSO, DFC

The 'Red Knight' was a Flight Commander with 32 Squadron at the outbreak of war and fought throughout the Battle of France and the Battle of Britain, as Flight Commander of 'Red Flight', rising to command the unit. He remained with the squadron until April 1941 and was then posted to the USA to fly as a test pilot with the British Air Commission. He returned to the United Kingdom in 1943 to lead the Detling Wing, but contracted tuberculosis, which prevented him from flying. He left the RAF in 1946 and died in South Africa in 1987.

Victory List

19.5.40	Bf109	destroyed	15.8.40	Bf110	destroyed*
22.5.40	Bf109	destroyed	15.8.40	Ju88	prob destroyed
26.5.40	Ju88	destroyed	16.8.40	Bf109	destroyed
8.6.40	He111	destroyed	16.8.40	Ju88	destroyed
8.6.40	He111	destroyed	16.8.40	Bf110	prob destroyed
20.7.40	Bf109	destroyed*	18.8.40	Ju88	destroyed
20.7.40	Bf109	prob destroyed	18.8.40	Bf110	prob destroyed
25.7.40	Bf109	prob destroyed	18.8.40	Do17	damaged
12.8.40	Bf109	destroyed	18.8.40	Bf109	destroyed
12.8.40	Bf109	prob destroyed	25.8.40	Bf109	destroyed
15.8.40	Ju88	destroyed	25.8.40	Do17	destroyed
15.8.40	Ju88	destroyed	* indicates shared claim		

Fighter Command Hurricanes

Unit	Dest	P.D.	Dam	MIA	Cat E	KIA	MIA	WIA
17 Sqn	1	0	1	0	0	0	0	0
111 Sqn	8	0	0	0	0	0	0	0
145 Sqn	2	0	0	0	0	0	0	0
213 Sqn	6	1	0	3	2	0	3	0
242 Sqn	6	0	0	1	0	0	1	0
245 Sqn	0	0	0	0	1	0	0	0

Fighter Command Defiants

Unit	Dest	P.D.	Dam	MIA	Cat E	KIA	MIA	WIA
264 Sqn	10	0	2	2	3[1]	0	4	0

1. Two Defiants lost to collision.

Summary May 1940

Air Combat Claims:
876:183:154
plus 9:3:0 Ground

Missing/destroyed aircraft:
255 Hurricanes, 46 Spitfires, 10 Defiants and 7 Blenheims lost.
160 pilots and 10 gunners killed or missing, 42 pilots wounded

Notes:

46 Sqn	Embarked for the Scandinavian campaign on 9th May with Hurricane Is.
79 Sqn	Temporarily detached to France (10th - 21st May)
85 Sqn	Returned from France to Debden, dets Martlesham Heath and Castle Camps.
87 Sqn	Returned from France to Debden.
238 Sqn	Formed at Tangmere with Spitfire Is on 16th.
249 Sqn	Formed at Church Fenton with Hurricane Is on 16th, immediately moved to Leconfield to re-equip with Spitfire Is, but next month reverted to Hurricane Is.
257 Sqn	Formed at Hendon with Spitfire Is on 16th, but immediately replaced these with Hurricane Is.
604 Sqn	received Gladiator Is for a few weeks only, retaining Blenheim Is.

Peter 'Prossor' Hanks was a flight commander with No.1 Squadron at the outbreak of war and fought throughout the 'Phoney War' and the Battle of France, claiming seven confirmed kills. He later fought in the Middle East, rising to the rank of Group Captain with at least 13 victories and winning the DSO, DFC and AFC for his leadership. (D.Sarkar)

June 1940

1st June 1940

Savage air combats over Dunkirk took place throughout the day and, due to the increasing losses to naval units, Admiral Ramsay decreed that *'Operation Dynamo'* should proceed henceforth only under cover of darkness. Even with the high level of *Luftwaffe* activity, however, another 64,429 men were rescued.

Fighter Command Spitfires								
Unit	Dest	P.D.	Dam	MIA	Cat E	KIA	MIA	WIA
19 Sqn	10	5	3	0	1	0	0	0
41 Sqn.	4	2	0	2	0	0	2	0
64 Sqn	1	4	0	1	0	0	1	0
222 Sqn	5	2	0	2	2	0	2	1
609 Sqn	1	1	2	1	0	0	1	0
616 Sqn	3	2	5	0	1	0	0	0

Fighter Command Hurricanes								
Unit	Dest	P.D.	Dam	MIA	Cat E	KIA	MIA	WIA
17 Sqn	0	0	1	0	2	0	0	0
43 Sqn	11	5	1	1	1	0	1	1
111 Sqn	0	0	1	0	0	0	0	0
145 Sqn	8	0	1	1	0	0	1	0
151 Sqn	0	1	0	0	0	0	0	0
229 Sqn	1	2	0	0	0	0	0	0
242 Sqn	6	3	0	0	0	0	0	0
245 Sqn	4	2	0	2	0	0	0	0

BEF France Hurricanes								
Unit	Dest	P.D.	Dam	MIA	Cat E	KIA	MIA	WIA
73 Sqn	2	0	0	2	0	0	2	0

2nd June 1940

With no shipping targets, the Luftwaffe concentrated its attacks on the beaches themselves, RAF fighters flying cover to the troops. The air fighting was less intense however.

Fighter Command Spitfires								
Unit	Dest	P.D.	Dam	MIA	Cat E	KIA	MIA	WIA
66 Sqn.	4	1	0	1	2	0	1	0
72 Sqn	3	4	0	0	0	0	0	0

Unit	Dest	P.D.	Dam	MIA	Cat E	KIA	MIA	WIA
92 Sqn	12	7	6	0	0	0	0	0
266 Sqn	1	6	0	2	0	0	2	0
611 Sqn	1	4	3	2	0	0	2	0

Fighter Command Hurricanes

Unit	Dest	P.D.	Dam	MIA	Cat E	KIA	MIA	WIA
32 Sqn	1	1	0	1	0	0	1	0
111 Sqn	2	4	4	0	1	0	0	0
151 Sqn	1	2	0	0	0	0	0	0

BEF Norway Hurricanes

Unit	Dest	P.D.	Dam	MIA	Cat E	KIA	MIA	WIA
46 Sqn	2	0	1	0	0	0	0	0

BEF Norway Gladiators

Unit	Dest	P.D.	Dam	MIA	Cat E	KIA	MIA	WIA
263 Sqn	9	3	0	1	0	0	1	0

3rd June 1940

The previous night had seen 26,256 men rescued from Dunkirk. By day, only one fighter engagement was reported by home-based fighters:

Fighter Command Hurricanes

Unit	Dest	P.D.	Dam	MIA	Cat E	KIA	MIA	WIA
17 Sqn	1	0	0	1	0	0	1	1

BEF France Hurricanes

Unit	Dest	P.D.	Dam	MIA	Cat E	KIA	MIA	WIA
73 Sqn	2	0	0	2	0	0	2	0
501 Sqn	0	0	0	1	1	0	1	0

4th June 1940

On this date General Weygand, the French Commander, requested that a further twenty RAF fighter squadrons be sent to France but this was refused. Winston Churchill summed up the situation in his usual style: '.... *We shall fight on the beaches, we shall fight on the landing-grounds, we shall fight in the fields and in the streets, we shall fight in the hills; we shall never surrender...*'

With another 26,746 soldiers rescued, 'Operation Dynamo' was drawing to a close. Daylight activity was slight over the area:

			Fighter Command Spitfires					
Unit	Dest	P.D.	Dam	MIA	Cat E	KIA	MIA	WIA
616 Sqn	0	0	0	1	0	0	1	0

			BEF France Hurricanes					
Unit	Dest	P.D.	Dam	MIA	Cat E	KIA	MIA	WIA
1 Sqn	7	1	4	0	0	0	0	0
501 Sqn	0	0	2	0	0	0	0	0

1. Aircraft lost in an accident.

5th June 1940

The previous night brought the great evacuation to a close with the rescue of 26,175 men, bringing the overall total to a staggering 338,226 - nearly ten times as many as had been first envisaged. Now, with the British Army neutralised, the *Luftwaffe* operations moved south. *Operation Paula* began as the airfields around Paris were attacked. For the home-based fighter squadrons of the RAF the defensive coastal fighting was over.

			BEF France Hurricanes					
Unit	Dest	P.D.	Dam	MIA	Cat E	KIA	MIA	WIA
1 Sqn	2	4	0	1	1	0	1	0
73 Sqn	1	0	0	0	0	0	0	0
501 Sqn	5	1	0	0	0	0	0	0

6th June 1940

Fighter Command assumed a different rôle when bombers were escorted to bomb Abbeville.

			Fighter Command Hurricanes					
Unit	Dest	P.D.	Dam	MIA	Cat E	KIA	MIA	WIA
17 Sqn	1	2	0	1	0	0	1	0
111 Sqn	4	1	0	0	1	0	0	1

			BEF France Hurricanes					
Unit	Dest	P.D.	Dam	MIA	Cat E	KIA	MIA	WIA
73 Sqn	0	0	0	0	1	1[1.]	0	0
501 Sqn	1	0	2	0	0	0	0	0

1. Flg. Off. E.J.Kain killed in flying accident.

The First Of The Many

While the British, for no clear reason, have always considered the Battle of Britain to have begun on either 1st or 10th July 1940, the Germans view is that it really began on the night of 18th June 1940. This was when the first major attacks on the British mainland were carried out by the Heinkels of *Stab* and *II Gruppe Kampfgeschwader 4 'General Wever'*. Targets in Cambridgeshire, Essex, Yorkshire, Durham, East Anglia and Surrey were attacked, most damage occurring in Cambridge, Southend and Canvey Island. Many Blenheims from the fledgling nightfighter force were scrambled, as were several single-seaters. The first contacts were made by Pilot Officer L.H.G.Kells of 29 Squadron, who endeavoured to engage three bombers off Felixstowe. While the unit ORB states that he was unsuccessful, it appeared that he was credited with a 'probable' by Fighter Command. An unknown Hurricane pilot was credited with an He111 'probable' at 23.10 hours, while Pilot Officer J.D.Humphreys of 29 Squadron claimed one shot down at around midnight. The first claim that can be confirmed from the German loss tables occurred at 00.30 hours. Flight Lieutenant A.G.Malan of 74 Squadron hunted down another Heinkel over Chelmsford. The Spitfire pilot shot down '5J+GA' of *Stab./KG 4* into a garden at Springfield Road, after *Oberleutnant* Corpus and his crew had baled out. Twenty minutes later Flight Lieutenant R.M.B.D.Duke-Woolley of 23 Squadron found '5J+DM' of Stab *II Gruppe*, commanded by the *Kommandeur Major* Dieter *Freiherr* von Massenbach. Following several attacks by the Blenheim - which was itself hit by return fire - the bomber was ditched offshore at Cley-next-the-Sea, Norfolk and this crew too were captured.

There were no further interceptions until 01.15 hours, when several fights took place. Malan found another He111, this one from *4 Staffel*, which he blasted into the sea just off Felixstowe. From this only the body of of *Hauptmann* Prochnow, the *Staffelkapitän*, was recovered. Meanwhile a pitched battle was raging over Cambridgeshire, where *Oberleutnant* Joachim von Arnim's *4 Staffel* aircraft was simultaneously engaged by a 23 Squadron Blenheim and a 19 Squadron Spitfire. Their combined gunfire proved devastating, but so was that thrown back by the rear gunner, who shot down both Flying Officer G.W.Petre's Spitfire and Squadron Leader J.S.O'Brien's Blenheim. Petre baled out unhurt as did O'Brien, but Pilot Officer King-Clark and Corporal Little were both killed. The bomber crashed at Six Mile Bottom, Cambs, one of the crew being killed. (Claims were assessed separately. Petre was awarded credit for a 'confirmed' and O'Brien a 'probable').

A similar action took place over East Anglia, again involving 29 Squadron. Pilot Officer J.S.Barnwell and his navigator Sergeant K.L.Long took off from Martlesham Heath at 00.25 hours and, about an hour later, his Blenheim was seen chasing an enemy aircraft across the airfield and out to sea. Flames were seen coming from both the front guns of the Blenheim and the Heinkel rear gun position. The starboard engine of the bomber was seen to catch fire and it went down out of control. Barnwell and Long failed to return and are believed to have engaged two further bombers before their loss. No such German loss actually occurred and it seems more likely that it was Barnwell's aircraft that had been seen falling away. He was, however, awarded posthumous credit for a victory.

Other Spitfire pilots claimed success this night. Pilot Officer J.A.P.Studd of 66 Squadron attacked a Heinkel, claiming a 'probable'. Flying Officer G.E.Ball of 19 Squadron avenged the treatment received by Petre by intercepting and destroying '5J+EP' from *6 Staffel KG 4*. This crashed into the sea off Margate at 02.15 hours and *Leutnant* Bachaus was captured together with two of his crew.

One further RAF fighter was lost when Sgt Close's 23 Squadron Blenheim was shot down by a bomber. He was killed, but Leading Aircraftman Karasek baled out unhurt.

The night had proved expensive for the fighter crews. Seven bombers had been claimed destroyed with three 'probables', five being actually lost, but four fighters had been shot down with the loss of five aircrew.

The Bristol Blenheim IF
Basic Specifications

Dimensions: Span: 56 ft 4 in. Length: 42 ft 9 in. Height: 12 ft 0 in.

Armament: One fixed .303in Vickers machine-gun in nose, four .303 in Browning machine-guns in ventral belly pack and one .303in Vickers 'K' machine-gun in dorsal turret.

Power Plant: Two Bristol Mercury XV radial engines rated at 840 hp.

Performance

Max Speed: 285 mph.
Initial Climb: 1,500 ft/min.
Ceiling: 31,500 ft.

Service History

The Blenheim began life as the Bristol Type 142, a venture funded by Lord Rothermere as a fast executive aircraft capable of carrying a pilot and six passengers at 240 mph. The result was a low-wing all-metal monoplane, which first flew on 12th April 1935. Tests soon showed that it was considerably faster than any RAF fighter in service, reaching a speed of 307 mph, which caused the Air Ministry to issue a specification for a light bomber to be developed from the 142, now known as 'Britain First'. The fuselage and wing inner sections were re-designed to provide a bomb-bay, a dorsal turret and the necessary nose-glazing. With performance reduced, but still acceptable, the new aircraft went into production as the Blenheim I.

The Blenheim was to give sterling bomber service as the Mark I and, with a lengthened nose and Bristol Mercury XV engines, the Mark IV. However, the Air Ministry soon perceived the need for gun-pack, became the Mark If. At the outbreak of war it partially equipped seven squadrons, this figure doubling by January 1940.

The first operations were daylight ground strafing missions during the 'Phoney War' and the first day of the campaign in France. Its debut as a night fighter came in June and, while it was adequate in that rôle, it was was soon realised that its speed was insufficient to provide the necessary defence, while the armament was simply not heavy enough. A night fighter needed sufficient firepower to destroy its target in one devastating attack, since an opponent, jinking away into the darkness, rarely gave the crew a second chance.

By late 1940 the Blenheim was already being being supplanted by the Bristol Beaufighter. However the first AI (Airborne Interception) experiments had taken place with the Blenheim. The first success to an AI-equipped Blenheim occurred on the night of 22nd July 1940, when Flight Lieutenant G.Ashfield of the Fighter Interception Unit claimed a Do17 destroyed off the south coast. As Beaufighters became available the Blenheim squadrons dwindled until, by the end of the Blitz in May 1941, only the newly-formed No 68 Sqn retained this aircraft, but was already phasing them out. Thus the Blenheim If passed into history, having begun a proud history of nightfighting with the RAF in the Second World War that would be carried on by its successors the Beaufighter and the superlative Mosquito.

7th June 1940

Fighter Command flew another bomber escort, again to Abbeville, and fighter squadrons also flew fighter sweeps over northern France:

The aircraft carrier HMS *Glorious* was engaged and sunk off Norway by the German battle cruisers *Scharnhorst* and *Gneisenau* while evacuating the pilots, ground crews and surviving aircraft of 46 and 263 Sqns. Of the 1,519 casualties from *Glorious* and the destroyers *Acasta* and *Ardent* - both also sunk whilst attempting to defend *Glorious* - 41 were ground staff and a further 18 were pilots.

\	\	\	Fighter Command Hurricanes					
Unit	Dest	P.D.	Dam	MIA	Cat E	KIA	MIA	WIA
17 Sqn	1	1	0	2	0	0	2	0
32 Sqn	3	0	0	0	0	0	0	0
43 Sqn	7	0	0	2	5	0	2	2

Unit	Dest	P.D.	Dam	MIA	Cat E	KIA	MIA	WIA
56 Sqn	1	0	0	0	0	0	0	0
79 Sqn	4	4	0	0	0	0	0	0
111 Sqn	4	0	0	0	0	0	0	0
151 Sqn	0	0	0	2	0	0	2	0
601 Sqn	2	0	0	1	1	0	1	0

Fighter Command Spitfires

Unit	Dest	P.D.	Dam	MIA	Cat E	KIA	MIA	WIA
610 Sqn	1	0	0	0	0	0	0	0

BEF Norway Hurricanes

Unit	Dest	P.D.	Dam	MIA	Cat E	KIA	MIA	WIA
46 Sqn	5	0	2	0	0	0	0	0

8th June 1940

Offensive patrols were flown over northern France:

Fighter Command Hurricanes

Unit	Dest	P.D.	Dam	MIA	Cat E	KIA	MIA	WIA
32 Sqn	7	1	0	2	1	0	2	0
79 Sqn	3	0	0	0	0	0	0	0
151 Sqn	2	0	0	0	1	0	0	0

BEF France Hurricanes

Unit	Dest	P.D.	Dam	MIA	Cat E	KIA	MIA	WIA
501 Sqn	1	2	0	4	0	0	4	0

9th June 1940

The German thrust across France had now reached the Seine. The second phase of this began with German armour driving southeast, past Rheims, to engage and destroy the major part of the French army now in the area between Paris amd Metz. Fighter Hurricanes flew a patrol to Rouen.

Fighter Command Hurricanes

Unit	Dest	P.D.	Dam	MIA	Cat E	KIA	MIA	WIA
17 Sqn	0	0	0	0	1	0	0	0
242 Sqn	2	1	0	1	0	0	1	0

10th June 1940

The Germans crossed the River Seine and the French government, having declared Paris an open city, now fled to Tours. It would now be just a matter of time before France was overrun. The BEF units were now either evacuating to England or fighting their way towards Marseilles.

Fighter Command Spitfires

Unit	Dest	P.D.	Dam	MIA	Cat E	KIA	MIA	WIA
74 Sqn	0	0	2	0	0	0	0	0

Fighter Command Hurricanes

Unit	Dest	P.D.	Dam	MIA	Cat E	KIA	MIA	WIA
111 Sqn	2	0	5	0	0	0	0	0

11th June 1940

Even with the evacuation of Dunkirk, British troops were not only still in France but still fighting. The 51st Highland Division, trapped at St Valery-en-Caux with no hope of rescue, finally surrendered. Fighter Command units operated over this area during the day:

Fighter Command Hurricanes

Unit	Dest	P.D.	Dam	MIA	Cat E	KIA	MIA	WIA
32 Sqn	2	1	0	1	0	0	1	0
111 Sqn	6	2	2	0	0	0	0	0
145 Sqn	1	0	0	0	0	0	0	0
615 Sqn	1	0	1	0	0	0	0	0

BEF France Hurricanes

Unit	Dest	P.D.	Dam	MIA	Cat E	KIA	MIA	WIA
73 Sqn	1	0	0	0	0	0	0	0

12th June 1940

There were a few engagements against the lone German reconnaissance aircraft. Additionally, Fighter Command flew offensive patrols to Le Havre.

Fighter Command Spitfires

Unit	Dest	P.D.	Dam	MIA	Cat E	KIA	MIA	WIA
64 Sqn	1	0	0	0	0	0	0	0
610 Sqn	1	0	0	0	0	0	0	0

Fighter Command Hurricanes

Unit	Dest	P.D.	Dam	MIA	Cat E	KIA	MIA	WIA
17 Sqn	5	0	0	0	0	0	0	0
242 Sqn	3	0	0	0	0	0	0	0
17 Sqn	5	0	0	0	0	0	0	0

13th June 1940

In France, the French government moved on to Bordeaux on the Atlantic coast. There were still a few BEF Hurricane units in

France, 73 Squadron pilots claiming an He111 shot down and a second damaged near Le Mans, possibly an aircraft from *2 Staffel Kampfgruppe 126.*

			BEF France Hurricanes					
Unit	Dest	P.D.	Dam	MIA	Cat E	KIA	MIA	WIA
73 Sqn	1	0	2	0	0	0	0	0

14th June 1940

Fighter Command Hurricanes flew patrols to the Seine area and escorted bombers. Two Hurricanes were shot down by Bf109s from *8./JG26.*

			Fighter Command Hurricanes					
87 Sqn	0	0	3	0	0	0	0	0
111 Sqn	0	0	0	0	1	0	0	0
242 Sqn	2	0	0	0	0	0	0	0
245 Sqn	0	0	0	0	1	0	1	0
			BEF France Hurricanes					
Unit	Dest	P.D.	Dam	MIA	Cat E	KIA	MIA	WIA
1 Sqn	1	0	0	1	1	0	1	0

What General Weygand called the Battle of France is over. I expect that the Battle of Britain is about to begin. The whole might and fury of the enemy must very soon be turned on us.

Hitler knows that he will have to break us in this island or lose the war. If we can stand up to him, all Europe will be free and the life of the world may move forward into broad, sunlit uplands. But if we fail, then the whole world, including the United States, including all that we have known and cared for, will sink into the abyss of a new dark age, made more sinister, and perhaps more protracted, by the lights of perverted science.

Let us therefore brace ourselves to our duties and so bear ourselves, that if the British Empire and its Commonwealth last for a thousand years, men will still say: 'This was their finest hour'.'

- Winston S Churchill 18th June 1940

15th June 1940

After two days of negotiations, Paris surrendered.

			BEF France Hurricanes					
Unit	Dest	P.D.	Dam	MIA	Cat E	KIA	MIA	WIA
73 Sqn	0	0	0	1	0	0	1	0

16th June 1940

- nil -

17th June 1940

Fighter Command Spitfires flew a patrol over Abbeville:

			Fighter Command Spitfires					
Unit	Dest	P.D.	Dam	MIA	Cat E	KIA	MIA	WIA
54 Sqn	1	2	0	0	0	0	0	0

			BEF France Hurricanes					
Unit	Dest	P.D.	Dam	MIA	Cat E	KIA	MIA	WIA
1 Sqn	1	0	0	0	0	0	0	0

17/18th June 1940

An He115 was shot down off Ostend by a 604 Squadron Blenheim crew.

			Fighter Command Blenheims					
Unit	Dest	P.D.	Dam	MIA	Cat E	KIA	MIA	WIA
604 Sqn	1	0	0	0	0	0	0	0

18th June 1940

Hurricanes escorted bombers to Cherbourg, where Hurricane pilots from 151 Squadron found an He111 of *5./KG 1*. This was attacked and claimed probably destroyed by Wing Commander F.V.Beamish and was actually a total loss.

			Fighter Command Hurricanes					
Unit	Dest	P.D.	Dam	MIA	Cat E	KIA	MIA	WIA
151 Sqn	0	1	0	2	0	0	2	0

18/19th June 1940

The first major attacks on Britain took place when He111s of *KG 4* bombed Cambridge, Southend and Canvey Island in addition to other minor raids. Many fighters were scrambled to intercept. (See pages 87-88)

| Fighter Command Spitfires ||||||||
Unit	Dest	P.D.	Dam	MIA	Cat E	KIA	MIA	WIA
19 Sqn	2	0	0	0	1	0	0	0
66 Sqn	0	1	0	0	0	0	0	0
74 Sqn	2	0	0	0	0	0	0	0

| Fighter Command Blenheims ||||||||
Unit	Dest	P.D.	Dam	MIA	Cat E	KIA	MIA	WIA
23 Sqn	1	1	0	0	1	2	0	0
29 Sqn	2	1	0	1	0	0	2	0

| Fighter Command Hurricanes ||||||||
Unit	Dest	P.D.	Dam	MIA	Cat E	KIA	MIA	WIA
605 Sqn	0	1	0	0	0	0	0	0

19th June 1940

Escort to Amiens and defensive patrols:-

| Fighter Command Hurricaness ||||||||
Unit	Dest	P.D.	Dam	MIA	Cat E	KIA	MIA	WIA
3 Sqn	2	0	0	0	0	0	0	0
66 Sqn	0	1	0	0	0	0	0	0
79 Sqn	1	0	1	0	0	0	0	0

19/20th June 1940

Several raiders crossed the British coast, mainly in the Tyne/Tees area, where fighters made several interceptions:

| Fighter Command Spitfires ||||||||
Unit	Dest	P.D.	Dam	MIA	Cat E	KIA	MIA	WIA
41 Sqn	0	1	0	0	0	0	0	0
222 Sqn	1	0	1	0	0	0	0	0
616 Sqn	0	1	0	0	0	0	0	0

20th June 1940

Day: 245 Sqn Hurricanes flew a patrol to Boos airfield, France. Four Ju52s were strafed and reported destroyed while a further twenty were damaged.

21st June 1940

- nil -

22nd June 1940

The French government accepted the terms for an armistice, which would not come into force for another two days. In the air, Squadron Leader J R Kayll led nine Hurricanes of 615 Squadron to Rouen, where He111s escorted by Bf110s were found and attacked

| Fighter Command Hurricanes |||||||||
Unit	Dest	P.D.	Dam	MIA	Cat E	KIA	MIA	WIA
615 Sqn	2	5	3	1	0	0	1	0

23rd June 1940

A Bf109 was claimed probably destroyed off Calais by 245 Sqn.

| Fighter Command Hurricanes |||||||||
Unit	Dest	P.D.	Dam	MIA	Cat E	KIA	MIA	WIA
245 Sqn	0	1	0	0	0	0	0	0

24th June 1940

The French government formally signed an armistice with the Germans. Britain was finally alone.

While the Germans sifted through the wreckage of countless RAF aircraft on the continent Fighter Command braced itself for the coming onslaught.

(Defiant at Breda - G.J.Zwanenberg)

Chapter Five
The Battle of the Channel

With the Battle of France over, Britain now stood alone. For more than six weeks the *Luftwaffe* was to make small-scale forays over Britain and would seek to close the Channel to British shipping. Very often the question has been asked: *'Why did the Luftwaffe not attack in force at once?'* The truth is that, for that period, the Germans were incapable of launching any such assault. The campaign in France had cost them dear, both in aircraft and crews. Most of the combat units required re-equipping or major repairs. The crews needed a rest. Therefore the brunt of the air fighting during late June and most of July would be borne by *Jagdgeschwader 3, 27,* and *51*. Other units were placed 'on line' as they returned from Germany, until, by the second week of August, the Germans were as strong, if not stronger, than they had been on the first day of the *Blitzkrieg*. The British forces, equally exhausted, could take no such respite, for the Germans could strike at any moment. While the German High Command was confident about the result of the coming battle, this confidence was not entirely shared by the *Luftwaffe* aircrews. Firstly, the concept of the campaign was to regard the Channel as a 'wide river', which was definitely not the case. Secondly, some of the German pilots had faced the RAF before, in the First World War, and held their courage and skill in high regard, a view reinforced by the tenacious defence of Dunkirk. They knew that the battle would be harder than their superiors realised.

Most of the fighting was to take place over the sea and here the RAF fighter pilots were placed at a marked disadvantage. Not only was the British Air-Sea Rescue organisation practically non-existent, but the personal survival equipment issued to British pilots was primitive - a 'Mae West' life jacket. On the 'other side' the Germans had a well organised ASR system, while their pilots were issued with dinghies and sea marker dye, rendering their chances of survival and rescue from the sea far higher than their British counterparts.

Naturally, the movement of *Luftwaffe* units back to Germany had been noted by British intelligence. Thus while vigilance could not be relaxed, the Air Ministry decided that offensive actions against France could continue. The opening weeks of the Battle of Britain would see several such missions being flown. These actions, while small-scale, often led to vicious engagements. However, they were as nothing compared to the storm that everyone knew must surely come.....

Note: *During the period of the Battle of Britain, any description of the air fighting must necessarily be highly curtailed. Space alone precludes any attempt other than to divide the day into separate 'raids', with the merest mention of particular targets. Since the objectives of individual attacks are well documented elsewhere, the author believes that the achievements and sacrifices of Fighter Command aircrew are of more importance in this volume than descriptions of raids. British losses will be classified as either 'MIA' (missing) or 'Cat E' (destroyed). Occasionally a figure will appear in squared brackets. This indicates a Cat E loss reported by Fighter Command in AIR16 960, but which has not been found from ORB/Movement Card records. It should be noted that this does not indicate that the loss did not happen. ORBs, understandably, are at times incomplete. Movement Cards also contain many errors, usually of date. Staff were more concerned with keeping aircraft flying than dealing with paperwork. Hence aircraft could be 'written off' strength many days and sometimes weeks after the event, a true date being guessed at by the person responsible for the records. Indeed, fairly recently a 213 Squadron Hurricane wreck was excavated which appears in no record of the battle. The Movement Card records its loss as being in mid-August, yet the fighter was actually shot down in September, nearly a month later.*

25th June 1940

65 Squadron Spitfires flew a fighter sweep over Abbeville, where they were engaged by fifteen Bf109s.

Unit	Dest	P.D.	Dam	MIA	Cat E	KIA	MIA	WIA
				Spitfires				
65 Sqn	3	3	0	0	0	0	0	0

The Battle of the Channel

25/26th June 1940

There were many small formations of German aircraft plotted over the British Isles. Many fighters were scrambled and interceptions took place over Scotland, along the northeast coast and near Brighton. Two Spitfires were lost, both after successful interceptions

\multicolumn{8}{c}{Spitfires}							
Unit	Dest	P.D.	Dam	MIA	Cat E	KIA	MIA	WIA
72 Sqn	1	0	0	0	0	0	0	0
222 Sqn	1	0	0	0	1	0	0	1
602 Sqn	0.5	0	0	0	0	0	0	0
603 Sqn	1.5	0	0	0	1	0	0	0
616 Sqn	1	1	0	0	0	0	0	0

\multicolumn{8}{c}{Hurricanes}							
Unit	Dest	P.D.	Dam	MIA	Cat E	KIA	MIA	WIA
601 Sqn	1	0	0	0	0	0	0	0

26th June 1940

- nil -

27th June 1940

Hurricanes flew escort to a bomber reconnaissance of St Valéry. 79 Squadron was attacked by Bf109s and two Hurricanes were shot down by Bf109Es from *II./JG 51*, pilots killed.

\multicolumn{8}{c}{Hurricanes}							
Unit	Dest	P.D.	Dam	MIA	Cat E	KIA	MIA	WIA
79 Sqn	0	0	0	0	2	2	0	0

28th June 1940

Hurricanes escorted another bomber reconnaissance to Calais and Boulogne and again Bf109s were engaged. One 151 Squadron Hurricane was shot down. The pilot baled out and was rescued.

\multicolumn{8}{c}{Hurricanes}							
Unit	Dest	P.D.	Dam	MIA	Cat E	KIA	MIA	WIA
79 Sqn	0	0	0	0	2	2	0	0
151 Sqn	0	0	0	0	1	0	0	0

Air Vice-Marshal Alexander Vallence Riddell Johnstone CB, DFC, AE

'Sandy' Johnstone flew with 602 Squadron during 1940 and by August took command of the squadron, leading it throughout the Battle of Britain. He later led a Spitfire Wing on Malta and later still, led another Wing in Burma. He remained with the RAF postwar, retiring on 14th December 1968 with the rank of AVM.

Victory List

Date	Aircraft	Result	Date	Aircraft	Result
25/26.6.40	He111	destroyed	7.9.40	Ju88	damaged
19.8.40	Ju88	destroyed	7.9.40	He111	damaged
25.8.40	Bf109	destroyed	9.9.40	Do17	destroyed*
25.8.40	Bf110	destroyed	30.9.40	Ju88	destroyed
4.9.40	Bf110	destroyed	6.11.40	Ju88	damaged*
7.9.40	Bf109	prob destroyed			

* indicates shared claims

28/29th June 1940

There were a few isolated raiders over Britain. An He111 was claimed probably destroyed by a 23 Squadron Blenheim crew near Norwich and another was reported destroyed by a 616 Squadron Spitfire pilot off Hornsea.

			Blenheims					
Unit	Dest	P.D.	Dam	MIA	Cat E	KIA	MIA	WIA
23 Sqn	0	1	0	0	0	0	0	0

			Spitfires					
Unit	Dest	P.D.	Dam	MIA	Cat E	KIA	MIA	WIA
616 Sqn	1	0	0	0	0	0	0	0

29th June 1940

There was one interception, a Do215 being destroyed by 72 Squadron Spitfires 100 miles east of May Island.

			Spitfires					
Unit	Dest	P.D.	Dam	MIA	Cat E	KIA	MIA	WIA
72 Sqn	1	0	0	0	0	0	0	0

The Battle of the Channel

30th June 1940: Gestures of Defiance

In the late morning an escorted bomber mission was flown to Merville, twelve Blenheims of 107 Squadron being escorted by Hurricanes of 111 and 615 Squadrons. Bf109s of *I./JG 20* and almost certainly *I.(J)/LG 2* were scrambled to intercept, and found the British formation in the target area. The Hurricane pilots allowed themselves to be drawn away from their charges. 111 Squadron reported a bloodless encounter, while three 'probables' were claimed by Flight Lieutenant Sanders, Flying Officer Giddings and Pilot Officer Young of 615 Squadron. Meanwhile the bombers came under attack. Three were shot down by Bf109 pilots, a fourth bomber receiving battle damage. In addition, Hurricanes were claimed by *Leutnant* Kolbow, *Unteroffizier* Kroll and *Feldwebel* Klotz of *I./JG 20* and by *Hauptmann* Herbert Ihlefeld of *I.(J)/LG 2*.

In the mid-afternoon a second escort mission was flown, when 21 Hurricanes from 56 and 151 Squadrons escorted twelve 110 Squadron Blenheims to Vignacourt. On this occasion Bf109s from *III./JG 3* were airborne, engaging as the force departed. Six Messerschmitts attacked 151 Squadron, and Wing Commander F.V.Beamish claimed two shot down in flames while Flight Lieutenant Smith and Flying Officer Allen each claimed a 'probable' before Squadron Leader E.M.Donaldson was shot down. He baled out into the Channel from where he was rescued unhurt.

Meanwhile Sergeants Smythe and Hillwood of 56 Squadron had become separated, meeting five Bf109s near Le Treport. Each claimed a Bf109 destroyed with Hillwood adding a 'probable'. It is likely that one of these pilots brought down *Oberleutnant* Kupka of *9./JG 3*, who was killed when his fighter crashed at Mon Robert. During this engagement Hurricanes were claimed by *Oberfeldwebel* Heitmann, *Unteroffizier* von Boremski and *Gefreiters* Wessling and Pfeiffer. One further Bf109 was lost when *Unteroffizier* Rauhaut of *I.(J)/LG 2* was shot down and killed near St Omer, reportedly by a Blenheim gunner, but more likely to have fallen to 615 Squadron pilots. A further victory, claimed as a Spitfire, was reported by *Leutnant* Hans Kolbow of *I./JG 20*.

30th June 1940

A bomber escort was flown to Merville during which 615 Squadron was engaged. A second bomber escort to Vignacourt involved 56 and 151 Squadrons. One bomber was intercepted by Spitfires off Peterhead.

Spitfires								
Unit	Dest	P.D.	Dam	MIA	Cat E	KIA	MIA	WIA
603 Sqn	0	0	1	0	0	0	0	0

Hurricanes								
Unit	Dest	P.D.	Dam	MIA	Cat E	KIA	MIA	WIA
56 Sqn	2	1	0	0	0	0	0	0
151 Sqn	2	2	0	0	1	0	0	0
615 Sqn	0	3	0	0	0	0	0	0

Summary - June 1940

Air Combat Claims:
    216:109:58

Missing/destroyed aircraft:
    58 Hurricanes, 17 Spitfires, 2 Blenheims and 1 Gladiator missing/Cat E
    50 pilots and 2 gunners killed/missing
    7 pilots wounded.

Notes:

1 Sqn	(Hurricanes Is) returned from France to Northolt, det Hawkinge.
17 Sqn	(Hurricanes I) was temporarily detached to France (8th - 19th)
19 Sqn	commenced re-equipment with Spitfire IBs
46 Sqn	(Hurricane I) returning from Norway. Sunk aboard HMS *Glorious* on 8th June. Squadron reformed at Digby on 19th.
73 Sqn	(Hurricanes I) returned from France to Church Fenton, det Sherburn-in-Elmet.
74 Sqn	replaced Spitfire Is with Spitfire IIAs.
98 Sqn	formed at Kaldadarnes Iceland with Hurricane Is, but downgraded to Flight status (1423 Flt) on 15th July.
238 Sqn	replaced Spitfire Is with Hurricane Is.
263 Sqn	replaced Gladiator I/IIs with Hurricane Is.
600 Sqn	relinquished Blenheim IVFs, retaining Blenheim IFs.
607 Sqn	having lost all Gladiators in France, became operational on Hurricane Is.

1st July 1940: The Red Cross No Protection

Shortly after dawn, Blue Section of 72 Squadron patrolled off Sunderland and sighted an He59 heading south-east at 500 feet. Although the aircraft was clearly marked with Red Cross insignia, Blue 1 (Flight Lieutenant Graham) ordered Flying Officer Wilcox and Flight Sergeant Steere to attack. The Heinkel, engaged upon a search for an He115 reported missing during the night, stood no chance of escape. At 06.12 hours *Unteroffizier* Lelsen ditched the crippled D-ASAH and the crew took to their dinghy, from where they were subsequently rescued by a Royal Naval cruiser.

This was the first occasion that an unarmed ambulance aircraft had been shot down. The machine was later beached and examined. No armament was found. It had always been suspected that such aircraft were employed on 'spying' missions near the British coast and were armed. Despite any evidence to support these suspicions the British government was to issue a warning to the Germans that ambulance aircraft found in the area of operations would be attacked without warning. While it would be foolish to suppose that returning German air-sea rescue crew would not report on events they had witnessed, it is clear that their prime purpose was indeed to rescue shot-down airmen. They would go to extraordinary length to pick up not only their pilots and aircrew, but also British pilots, who would otherwise almost certainly have drowned.

The Fighter Command War Diaries

July 1940

1st July 1940

German aircraft were plotted mainly off the northeast coast and Scotland. Intercepting fighter units claimed three destroyed and two damaged

Spitfires

Unit	Dest	P.D.	Dam	MIA	Cat E	KIA	MIA	WIA
64 Sqn	0.5	0	0	0	0	0	0	0
72 Sqn	1	0	0	0	0	0	0	0
602 Sqn	0	0	1	0	0	0	0	0
616 Sqn	1	0	1	0	0	0	0	0

Hurricanes

Unit	Dest	P.D.	Dam	MIA	Cat E	KIA	MIA	WIA
145 Sqn	0.5	0	0	0	0	0	0	0

2nd July 1940

There was only one interception, this occurring when Flight Lieutenant W.J.Leather led a section of 611 Squadron Spitfires to destroy a Do17 off Withernsea.

Spitfires

Unit	Dest	P.D.	Dam	MIA	Cat E	KIA	MIA	WIA
611 Sqn	1	0	0	0	0	0	0	0

3rd July 1940

Isolated *Luftwaffe* bombers and reconnaissance aircraft were plotted from Scotland, down the east coast and the Channel. There were several interceptions and combats. Although six Spitfires and one Hurricane suffered damage, all returned safely

Spitfires

Unit	Dest	P.D.	Dam	MIA	Cat E	KIA	MIA	WIA
54 Sqn	0	0	1	0	0	0	0	0
603 Sqn	3	0	0	0	0	0	0	0
610 Sqn	0	1	1	0	0	0	0	0
616 Sqn	1	0	0	0	0	0	0	0

Hurricanes

Unit	Dest	P.D.	Dam	MIA	Cat E	KIA	MIA	WIA
32 Sqn	1	0	0	0	0	0	0	0
43 Sqn	0	0	1	0	0	0	0	0
56 Sqn	1	0	0	0	0	0	0	0
145 Sqn	0	1	0	0	0	0	0	0

4th July 1940

The Germans raided the Portland naval base in the morning. Later a convoy was attacked off the east Kent coast, attacks continuing into the early evening as it passed Dover and proceeded westwards. Defending fighters from 32 and 79 Squadrons engaged the attackers claiming two destroyed for the loss of a Hurricane. Later in the afternoon a few He111s attacked the Bristol works at Filton. 92 Squadron engaged and claimed one and a 'probable'. The shot-down Heinkel (of *4./KG 54*) was chased from Weston-Super-Mare to Dorset, where it crash-landed. Pilot Officer C.H.Saunders and Sergeant R.H.Fokes landed beside the crashed Heinkel and helped the German crew escape from their burning bomber. During the engagements a further five British fighters were damaged, three seriously.

				Spitfires				
Unit	Dest	P.D.	Dam	MIA	Cat E	KIA	MIA	WIA
92 Sqn	1	1	0	0	0	0	0	0

				Hurricanes				
Unit	Dest	P.D.	Dam	MIA	Cat E	KIA	MIA	WIA
32 Sqn	2	0	0	0	0	0	0	0
79 Sqn	0	0	0	1	0	0	1	0

5th July 1940

There was one successful interception. An He111 was destroyed near Folkestone in the early morning by 65 Squadron Spitfires. Spitfires of 64 Squadron flew a patrol over France, meeting Bf109s of *II./JG 51* near Le Touquet and losing one pilot. One Messerschmitt was claimed shot down over the Channel as the Spitfires returned.

				Spitfires				
Unit	Dest	P.D.	Dam	MIA	Cat E	KIA	MIA	WIA
64 Sqn	1	0	0	1	0	0	1	0
65 Sqn	1	0	0	0	0	0	0	0

6th July 1940

Few raiders were reported. An He111 was claimed destroyed and another damaged by 74 Squadron Spitfire pilots over the

Dover Straits, while a Do17 was reported shot down by 603 Squadron Spitfire pilots near Aberdeen.

			Spitfires					
Unit	Dest	P.D.	Dam	MIA	Cat E	KIA	MIA	WIA
74 Sqn	1	1	0	0	0	0	0	0
603 Sqn	1	0	0	0	0	0	0	0

7th July 1940

The Germans began a series of 'hit and run' raids along the south coast from Plymouth to Dover, losing several aircraft to RAF fighters. An interception off Scotland caught a Ju88, which was claimed destroyed by 602 Squadron pilots.

			Spitfires					
Unit	Dest	P.D.	Dam	MIA	Cat E	KIA	MIA	WIA
54 Sqn	0	0	0	0	2	0	0	2
64 Sqn	2	0	0	0	0	0	0	0
65 Sqn	3	0	0	3	0	0	3	0
234 Sqn	0	0	1	0	0	0	0	0
602 Sqn	1	0	0	0	0	0	0	0

			Hurricanes					
Unit	Dest	P.D.	Dam	MIA	Cat E	KIA	MIA	WIA
43 Sqn	0	0	1	0	1	0	0	0
79 Sqn	0	0	0	0	1	0	0	0
145 Sqn	1	0	0	0	0	0	0	0
601 Sqn.	1	0	0	0	0	0	0	0

8th July 1940

Lone German bombers and reconnaissance aircraft were mainly engaged upon airfield harrassment during the day. British fighter units made several interceptions around the coastline, ranging from Scotland in the north, to Land's End in the south

			Spitfires					
Unit	Dest	P.D.	Dam	MIA	Cat E	KIA	MIA	WIA
41 Sqn	0.5	0	0	0	0	0	0	0
66 Sqn	1	0	0	0	1	0	0	0
74 Sqn	1	0	0	0	0	0	0	0
92 Sqn	1	0	0	0	0	0	0	0
234 Sqn	1	0	0	0	0	0	0	0
602 Sqn	0	0	1	0	0	0	0	0

The Battle of the Channel

		Hurricanes						
Unit	Dest	P.D.	Dam	MIA	Cat E	KIA	MIA	WIA
85 Sqn	1	0	0	0	0	0	0	0
249 Sqn	0.5	0	0	0	0	0	0	0

A convoy attack off Dover brought several vicious combats and, although a Dornier was claimed damaged by 610 Squadron, the majority of the engagements were against Bf109s

		Spitfires						
Unit	Dest	P.D.	Dam	MIA	Cat E	KIA	MIA	WIA
54 Sqn	2	0	0	0	0	0	0	0
65 Sqn	1	1	0	1	0	0	1	0
74 Sqn	2	0	0	0	0	0	0	0
610 Sqn	1	0	0	1	0	0	1	0

8th July 1940: Spitfire I versus Bf109E

In the mid afternoon came a short fighter clash, a Luftwaffe pilot recalling the event vividly:

"Our radar had reported a flight of enemy fighters in the middle of the Dover Straits, so I led my Schwarm in that direction. Suddenly I saw a single Spitfire coming out of the clouds in a gentle dive. I quickly got behind him and opened fire with my cannon and machine guns, hitting him with the first burst. At once the cockpit hood came off and the wheels came down. I stopped firing and moved quite close towards him. I could see quite plainly the pilot getting out. He was wearing a yellow flying helmet and gloves. He fell over the side and his parachute opened. I circled around it and was about to radio his position to our rescue service when a whole flight of Spitfires appeared from the clouds and I was forced to break away and take cover. Unfortunately Leutnant Johann Böhm decided to remain and fight them. He did not return.'

- Major Josef Fözö, *Gruppenkommandeur II. / JG 51*

Combat Report

I was Red Leader of 'A' Flight No 74 Squadron, with No 2 of Blue Section also in company. The four of us were on interception patrol over Dover when I sighted four Me109s flying in line astern on my starboard beam. I gave the order 'Line Astern' and turned to starboard, climbing up under the tail of the rear Me109. I gave him a short 30° deflection shot and he immediately half-rolled and dived to ground level followed by Red 2. In trying to follow him I blacked myself out and lost sight of him, but I saw another Me109 also flying at low level so I dived on him from about 3,000 feet. He immediately dived to ground level and used evasive tactics by flying along the valleys behind Dover and Folkestone, which only allowed me to fire short deflection bursts at him. After two of these bursts smoke or vapour came from the radiator beneath his port wing and other bursts appeared to enter the fuselage. He eventually landed with his wheels up as I fired my last burst at him in a field near Eltham. The pilot was apparently uninjured and I circled round him till he was taken prisoner.

- Sergeant E.A.Mould No 74 Squadron

There is little doubt that the lone Spitfire engaged by Major Fözö was that flown by Squadron Leader Desmond Cooke of 65 Squadron, who disappeared while leading his unit in a battle climb through thick cloud near Dover. It had always been believed that his loss was due to engine failure, which may well have been the indirect cause of his loss. The Austrian Leutnant Böhm was engaged by 74 Squadron aircraft and was chased inland at low level, finally crash-landing at Elham, Kent, after an accurate burst of fire from Sergeant E.A.Mould. Both he and his aircraft were captured. (The unit badge displayed on the side of the grey-dappled Messerschmitt, often referred to as the 'Weeping Pelican', was in fact a cartoon representation of the former Prime Minister, Neville Chamberlain and was supposed to be a Secretary bird).

The Battle of the Channel

Left: The 'Secretary Bird' emblem of II./JG51 on Hans Illner's fighter. (H.Illner) Right: Leutnant Böhm is taken into captivity. (D.Brocklehurst)

			Hurricanes				
Unit	Dest	P.D.	Dam	MIA	Cat E	KIA	MIA	WIA
79 Sqn	0	0	0	1	1	0	1	1[1.]
32 Sqn	0	1	0	0	1	0	0	0

1. Died of wounds

9th July 1940

There were a few interceptions of lone bombers, 610 Squadron pilots claiming a Do215 shot down over the Channel. 17 Squadron claimed a Do17 destroyed off Orfordness and 602 Squadron a Ju88 destroyed near May Island. The major engagements, however, came following a radar warning of an enemy build-up over the Pas de Calais. Fighter units were scrambled to intercept the raid, which was targetted against a convoy in the Thames estuary, the engaging pilots sighting 100-plus enemy aircraft approaching their target. However, the heavy German escort succeeded in holding the meagre British forces away from the bombers, all claims being made against the German escort fighters.

			Spitfires				
Unit	Dest	P.D.	Dam	MIA	Cat E	KIA	MIA	WIA
65 Sqn	3	1	1	0	0	0	0	0

			Hurricanes					
Unit	Dest	P.D.	Dam	MIA	Cat E	KIA	MIA	WIA
79 Sqn	1	1	1	0	0	0	0	0
151 Sqn	2	0	1	0	1	0	0	0

To the west, Bf110s had flown a sweep over the Southampton area, possibly as a diversion for the above attack. 43 Squadron engaged, pilots claiming three Bf110s destroyed. The CO, Squadron Leader George Lott, was shot down by a pilot from *II./JG 2* and baled out, badly wounded.

			Hurricanes					
Unit	Dest	P.D.	Dam	MIA	Cat E	KIA	MIA	WIA
43 Sqn	3	0	0	0	1	0	0	1

A short while after the main raid in the east, *Luftwaffe* aircraft were again plotted off Ramsgate. These were Bf109s of *JG 51* escorting an He59 rescue aircraft. 54 Squadron engaged, Pilot Officer J.A.Allen bringing down the Heinkel, while 2:2:0 was claimed against the escorts. Two Spitfires were reported missing and Flying Officer A.C.Deere crash-landed after a head-on collision with *Feldwebel* Hans Illner, who also got back.

			Spitfires					
Unit	Dest	P.D.	Dam	MIA	Cat E	KIA	MIA	WIA
54 Sqn	3	2	0	2	0	0	2	0

The final attack came in the early evening, when Ju87s escorted by Bf109s raided Portland and were met by 609 Squadron.

			Spitfires					
Unit	Dest	P.D.	Dam	MIA	Cat E	KIA	MIA	WIA
609 Sqn	2	1	0	1	0	0	1	0

Three more fighters were badly damaged in the above actions.

10th July 1940

There were several interceptions of lone bombers in the early morning.

			Spitfires					
Unit	Dest	P.D.	Dam	MIA	Cat E	KIA	MIA	WIA
66 Sqn	1	0	0	0	0	0	0	0
92 Sqn	0	1	1	0	0	0	0	0

			Hurricanes					
Unit	Dest	P.D.	Dam	MIA	Cat E	KIA	MIA	WIA
145 Sqn	1	0	0	0	0	0	0	0
242 Sqn	1	0	0	0	0	0	0	0

The Battle of the Channel

A German fighter sweep in the Dover Straits was engaged by Spitfires.

				Spitfires				
Unit	Dest	P.D.	Dam	MIA	Cat E	KIA	MIA	WIA
74 Sqn	2	1	3	0	0	0	0	0
610 Sqn	0	1	0	0	0	0	0	0

The main attack came early in the afternoon, when heavily escorted Do17s of *KG 2* struck a convoy off Folkestone

				Spitfires				
Unit	Dest	P.D.	Dam	MIA	Cat E	KIA	MIA	WIA
64 Sqn	4	2	2	0	0	0	0	0
74 Sqn	1	0	7	0	0	0	0	0

				Hurricanes				
Unit	Dest	P.D.	Dam	MIA	Cat E	KIA	MIA	WIA
32 Sqn	1	0	0	0	0	0	0	0
56 Sqn	3	0	2	0	1	0	0	0
111 Sqn	4	0	1	1	0	0	1	0

11th July 1940

During the day there were three separate attacks on a convoy near the Isle of Wight. The first attack resulted in:-

				Hurricanes				
Unit	Dest	P.D.	Dam	MIA	Cat E	KIA	MIA	WIA
501 Sqn	0	0	0	1	0	0	1	0

'Head-On'

At this time Squadron Leader J.M.Thompson's 111 Squadron pilots were trying out a new tactic; the head-on charge. On 10th July 1940 Thompson led his nine fighters in line abreast formation in a head-on attack on the KG2 Dorniers, all pilots blazing away and knocking down two of the bombers in the first pass. One was an 'accident' however, for the wing of Flying Officer T.P.Higgs' Hurricane slammed into one bomber. Both aircraft spun into the sea and Higgs was killed. Flying Officer H.M.Ferris claimed a third Dornier damaged before disposing of a Bf109 and returned, badly shot-up by other German escorts. The head-on attack was later to be copied by other units, notably 92 Squadron, and was almost invariably to prove as devastating as 111 Squadron's debut had been.

13th July 1940: Convoy attack

In the convoy attack off Portland, the Germans had again made the mistake of assuming that their twin-engined fighters, if deployed in sufficient numbers, would overwhelm the smaller British single-seaters. They had paid the price, but when they sent a force to attack another convoy approaching the Dover Straits an hour later, the *Stuka* escorts were Bf109s, and the story was rather different.

The bombers were a dozen Ju87Bs from *IV./LG 1*, escorted by 30 Messerschmitts from *II./JG 51*. 56 Squadron had already been despatched on a Channel patrol, and these blundered straight into the German force. *Hauptmann* Josef Fözö was leading II/JG51 and recalled:

"In the middle of the damned Channel our radar warned us to look out for many enemy aircraft. The Stukas were attacked by 16-20 Hurricanes. Unfortunately for them when sliding into firing position, they came between the Stukas and our close-escort formation. We opened fire immediately, and three Hurricanes separated from the formation, two dropping and one gliding down to the water heavily smoking. At that instant I saw a Stuka diving for the water to try to head back to the French coast. It was being chased by a single Hurricane. One Messerschmitt followed, but this Messerschmitt was also chased by a Hurricane. I saw the deadly dangerous situation and dived down. There were now five aircraft nosing down to the water. The Stuka received heavy damage, and crashed on the beach near Wissant with the crew badly wounded. Feldwebel John hit the Hurricane, which disappeared into the Channel, the right wing cutting the water surface like the fin of a shark, and my Hurricane dropped like a stone close to the one that John had shot down."

Both Sergeants Cowsill and Whitfield failed to return. Cowsill was credited with a Ju87 destroyed and actually this dive-bomber returned damaged. Despite claims for a *Stuka* by Flying Officer Brooker, and dive-bombers 'unconfirmed' by Sergeants Smythe, Hillwood and Baker, Flight Lieutenant Coghlan, and Squadron Leader Manton, not another *Stuka* was even hit. Pilot Officer Page and Coghlan then engaged the escorts, claiming one destroyed and an 'unconfirmed' respectively but with similar results. Further Hurricanes were claimed by *Hauptmann* Tietzen, *Unteroffizier* Büder and *Feldwebel* Tornow, the latter reporting that the pilot of one baled out into the sea, and that claimed by Büder was chased inland. Apart from the losses of Whitfield and Cowsill (who were both killed) Baker's Hurricane was badly shot-up, and Coghlan was wounded.

Spitfires

Unit	Dest	P.D.	Dam	MIA	Cat E	KIA	MIA	WIA
609 Sqn	1	1	0	1	1	0	1	1[1]

1. *Pilot died of injuries*

The second raid was larger:

Hurricanes

Unit	Dest	P.D.	Dam	MIA	Cat E	KIA	MIA	WIA
87 Sqn	4	1	0	0	0	0	0	0
238 Sqn	1?	0	0	0	0	0	0	0
501 Sqn	1	0	0	0	0	0	0	0
601 Sqn	2?	4	1	0	0	0	0	0

The third:-

Hurricanes

Unit	Dest	P.D.	Dam	MIA	Cat E	KIA	MIA	WIA
145 Sqn	3	1	0	0	1	0	0	0
601 Sqn	1	6	0	0	1	0	0	1

Additionally, fighter patrols engaged several reconnaissance aircraft, claiming two destroyed

Hurricanes

Unit	Dest	P.D.	Dam	MIA	Cat E	KIA	MIA	WIA
242 Sqn	1	0	0	0	0	0	0	0
601 Sqn	1	0	0	0	0	0	0	0

12th July 1940

One major raid took place when Dorniers and Heinkels attacked convoys off Essex and in the Thames estuary:

Hurricanes

Unit	Dest	P.D.	Dam	MIA	Cat E	KIA	MIA	WIA
17 Sqn	3.5	1	0	0	0	0	0	0
85 Sqn	0	0	1	1	0	0	1	0
151 Sqn	0.5	0	0	1	0	0	1	0

There was also skirmishing off Portland:

Hurricanes

Unit	Dest	P.D.	Dam	MIA	Cat E	KIA	MIA	WIA
145 Sqn	0	1	3	0	0	0	0	0
501 Sqn	0	1	0	1	0	0	1	0

The Fighter Command War Diaries

Additionally, lone reconnaissance aircraft were successfully engaged throughout the day:

Hurricanes							
Unit	Dest	P.D.	Dam	MIA	Cat E	KIA	MIA	WIA
43 Sqn	1	0	0	0	0	0	0	0

Spitfires							
Unit	Dest	P.D.	Dam	MIA	Cat E	KIA	MIA	WIA
74 Sqn	1	0	0	0	0	0	0	0
234 Sqn	0	1	0	0	0	0	0	0
603 Sqn	1	0	0	0	0	0	0	0
609 Sqn	1	0	0	0	0	0	0	0

13th July 1940

Two convoys came under attack, the first, near Portland, in the mid-afternoon:

Spitfires							
Unit	Dest	P.D.	Dam	MIA	Cat E	KIA	MIA	WIA
609 Sqn	1	1	0	0	0	0	0	0

Hurricanes							
Unit	Dest	P.D.	Dam	MIA	Cat E	KIA	MIA	WIA
238 Sqn	2	2	0	0	1	0	0	0

A short while later a convoy was attacked by *Stukas* near Dover:

Spitfires							
Unit	Dest	P.D.	Dam	MIA	Cat E	KIA	MIA	WIA
54 Sqn	1	0	0	0	0	0	0	0
64 Sqn	1	0	0	0	0	0	0	0

Hurricanes							
Unit	Dest	P.D.	Dam	MIA	Cat E	KIA	MIA	WIA
56 Sqn	3	6	0	2	0	0	2	0

Lone bombers were also engaged earlier in the day:

Hurricanes							
Unit	Dest	P.D.	Dam	MIA	Cat E	KIA	MIA	WIA
501 Sqn	1	0	0	0	0	0	0	0

Spitfires							
Unit	Dest	P.D.	Dam	MIA	Cat E	KIA	MIA	WIA
152 Sqn	0	0	1	0	0	0	0	0

14th July 1940

In the mid-afternoon, a convoy off Eastbourne was attacked by *Stukas*:

The Battle of the Channel

			Spitfires				
Unit	Dest	P.D.	Dam	MIA	Cat E	KIA	MIA	WIA
610 Sqn	1	1	0	0	0	0	0	0

			Hurricanes				
Unit	Dest	P.D.	Dam	MIA	Cat E	KIA	MIA	WIA
151 Sqn	2	1[1.]	0	0	0	0	0	0
615 Sqn	2	1	0	0	1	0	0	1[2.]

1. One of the 151 Squadron pilots, Flt Lt R.L.Smith, was flying an experimental two-cannon Hurricane. He was credited with a Bf109 probably destroyed in this engagement.
2. Pilot died of wounds.

15th July 1940

Bad weather prevented any major air actions. 56 Squadron pilots found and attacked a group of Dorniers attacking shipping near the Thames estuary. A few more were engaged near Selsey, 145 Squadron pilots claiming two damaged but 213 Squadron lost a pilot and Hurricane. Other interceptions against lone bombers resulted in two claimed destroyed by 92 and 603 Squadrons.

			Spitfires				
Unit	Dest	P.D.	Dam	MIA	Cat E	KIA	MIA	WIA
92 Sqn	1	0	0	0	0	0	0	0
603 Sqn	1	0	0	0	0	0	0	0

			Hurricanes				
Unit	Dest	P.D.	Dam	MIA	Cat E	KIA	MIA	WIA
56 Sqn	0	1	1	0	0	0	0	0
145 Sqn	0	0	2	0	0	0	0	0
213 Sqn	0	0	0	1	0	0	1	0

16th July 1940

The bad weather continued and only two interceptions were reported:

			Spitfires				
Unit	Dest	P.D.	Dam	MIA	Cat E	KIA	MIA	WIA
603 Sqn	1	0	0	0	0	0	0	0

			Hurricanes				
Unit	Dest	P.D.	Dam	MIA	Cat E	KIA	MIA	WIA
601 Sqn	2	1	0	0	0	0	0	0

17th July 1940

There were a few interceptions against the isolated German aircraft using the bad weather for reconnaissance and 'hit and run' raids. In the north, 603 Squadron reported a pilot missing, cause not known.

				Spitfires				
Unit	Dest	P.D.	Dam	MIA	Cat E	KIA	MIA	WIA
92 Sqn	0	1	0	0	0	0	0	0
603 Sqn	0	0	0	1	0	0	1	0

				Hurricanes				
Unit	Dest	P.D.	Dam	MIA	Cat E	KIA	MIA	WIA
145 Sqn	0	0	1	0	0	0	0	0
615 Sqn	0	0	1	0	0	0	0	0

18th July 1940

Continuing bad weather brought a few interceptions of lone *Luftwaffe* bombers around the coastline:

				Spitfires				
Unit	Dest	P.D.	Dam	MIA	Cat E	KIA	MIA	WIA
609 Sqn	0	1	1	0	1	0	0	0

				Hurricanes				
Unit	Dest	P.D.	Dam	MIA	Cat E	KIA	MIA	WIA
145 Sqn	1	0	0	0	0	0	0	0

The Germans made a feint attack upon a convoy off Dover, where 610 Squadron, ordered to intercept, found only Bf109s and lost one pilot. 111 Squadron escorted Coastal Command Blenheims to attack Le Havre, found an Hs126, and claimed it damaged.

				Spitfires				
Unit	Dest	P.D.	Dam	MIA	Cat E	KIA	MIA	WIA
610 Sqn	0	0	0	1	0	0	1	0

				Hurricanes				
Unit	Dest	P.D.	Dam	MIA	Cat E	KIA	MIA	WIA
111 Sqn	0	0	1	0	0	0	0	0

19th July 1940

The weather improved and the Germans sent Ju87s to attack Portland. These werer engaged by 87 Squadron pilots, who claimed a 'damaged'. Interceptions against lone bombers resulted in:

			Hurricanes					
Unit	Dest	P.D.	Dam	MIA	Cat E	KIA	MIA	WIA
1 Sqn	0	0	1	0	1	0	0	0
145 Sqn	1.5	0	0	0	0	0	0	0
257 Sqn	0.5	0	0	0	0	0	0	0

64 Squadron found some He115 minelayers, escorted by Bf109s, in the Dover Straits, claiming four shot down. 32 Squadron pilots engaged escorted Ju87s near Dover, claiming two shot down and several badly damaged

			Spitfires					
Unit	Dest	P.D.	Dam	MIA	Cat E	KIA	MIA	WIA
64 Sqn	4	0	0	0	0	0	0	0

			Hurricanes					
Unit	Dest	P.D.	Dam	MIA	Cat E	KIA	MIA	WIA
32 Sqn	2	3	1	0	0	0	0	0

Other engagements however were against Bf109 patrols:

			Spitfires					
Unit	Dest	P.D.	Dam	MIA	Cat E	KIA	MIA	WIA
74 Sqn	0	2	0	0	0	0	0	0

			Hurricanes					
Unit	Dest	P.D.	Dam	MIA	Cat E	KIA	MIA	WIA
43 Sqn	2	1	0	1	1	0	1	0
111 Sqn	2	1	0	0	0	0	0	0

The Defiants of 141 Squadron suffered a major disaster off Folkestone when they were bounced by Bf109s from *Hauptmann* Hannes Trautloft's *III./JG 51*. They lost six aircraft for claims of three shot down and one 'probable'. Had it not been for the intervention of 111 Squadron Hurricanes (above) it seems likely that none would returned. As it was, the loss of four pilots and six gunners, with three further pilots wounded, was sufficient to take the squadron 'out of the line'.

			Defiants					
Unit	Dest	P.D.	Dam	MIA	Cat E	KIA	MIA	WIA
141 Sqn	3	1	0	2	4	3	7	3

19/20th July 1940

An He115 minelayer was engaged and probably destroyed and another damaged off Walton, both by 25 Squadron Blenheim

Air Commodore Peter Malam Brothers CBE DSO, DFC*

Peter Brothers was a serving officer with 32 Squadron at the outbreak of war and fought 'cross-Channel' during the Battle of France. He flew throughout the Battle of Britain, moving to 257 Squadron as a Flight Commander in September. In January 1941 he was rested, then joined 457 Squadron on its formation in June, as Commanding Officer. A year later he took command of 602 Squadron and in the autumn, now Wing Commander, became Wing Leader at Tangmere. He later led the Milfield, Culmhead and Exeter Wings, surviving the war and remaining with the RAF until his retirement on 4th April 1973.

Victory List

19.5.40	Bf109	destroyed	22.10.40	Bf109	prob destroyed
23.5.40	Bf110	destroyed	26.3.42	Bf109	destroyed
19.7.40	Bf109	destroyed	29.4.42	FW190	prob destroyed
20.7.40	Bf109	prob destroyed	26.6.42	FW190	damaged
16.8.40	Bf110	destroyed	26.6.42	FW190	damaged
18.8.40	Do17	destroyed	18.8.42	FW190	damaged
18.8.40	Bf109	destroyed	19.8.42	FW190	damaged
24.8.40	Bf109	destroyed	26.1.43	FW190	destroyed
15.9.40	Do17	destroyed	7.8.44	FW190	destroyed
15.9.40	Do17	destroyed			

crews. A Ju88 was claimed probably destroyed off Aberdeen by a 603 Squadron Spitfire pilot.

				Blenheims				
Unit	Dest	P.D.	Dam	MIA	Cat E	KIA	MIA	WIA
25 Sqn	0	1	1	0	0	0	0	0

				Spitfires				
Unit	Dest	P.D.	Dam	MIA	Cat E	KIA	MIA	WIA
603 Sqn	0	1	0	0	0	0	0	0

20th July 1940

There were a number of engagements and interceptions of lone German aircraft and several claims were made, including another He59 ambulance aircraft destroyed by 601 Squadron:

Spitfires								
Unit	Dest	P.D.	Dam	MIA	Cat E	KIA	MIA	WIA
54 Sqn	0	1	0	0	0	0	0	0
603 Sqn	1	0	0	0	0	0	0	0

Hurricanes								
Unit	Dest	P.D.	Dam	MIA	Cat E	KIA	MIA	WIA
56 Sqn	1	0	0	0	0	0	0	0
238 Sqn	0	0	1	0	0	0	0	0
601 Sqn	1	0	1	0	0	0	0	0

In the early and mid-afternoon sweeps by Bf109 units were encountered between Swanage and Dover. 501 Squadron patrolled out as far as the Channel Islands to protect a convoy:

Spitfires								
Unit	Dest	P.D.	Dam	MIA	Cat E	KIA	MIA	WIA
152 Sqn	0	0	0	1	0	0	1	0

Hurricanes								
Unit	Dest	P.D.	Dam	MIA	Cat E	KIA	MIA	WIA
32 Sqn	1	0	0	0	0	0	0	0
43 Sqn	0	1	0	1	0	0	1	0
238 Sqn	2	1	0	0	1	0	0	1[1.]
501 Sqn	3	0	1	1	0	0	1	0

1. Pilot died of wounds.

At 18.00 hours the *Luftwaffe* struck at convoy 'Bosom' off the Kent coast and a minor battle developed, the British fighters attacking from the sun:

Spitfires								
Unit	Dest	P.D.	Dam	MIA	Cat E	KIA	MIA	WIA
65 Sqn	1	0	0	0	0	0	0	0
610 Sqn	0	1	0	0	1	0	0	1

Hurricanes								
Unit	Dest	P.D.	Dam	MIA	Cat E	KIA	MIA	WIA
32 Sqn	1	5	4	1	1	0	1	0
615 Sqn	2	2	1	0	0	0	0	0

21st July 1940

There was little activity. 238 Squadron pilots caught two lone aircraft, a Bf110 and a Do17, shooting both down. The Bf110, a reconnaissance aircraft, had earlier shot down a Fairey Battle near Stockbridge and a Hawker Hart at Old Sarum. A convoy was attacked off the Sussex coast, the attackers being engaged firstly by 43 Squadron. Pilots claimed a Bf109 destroyed and another damaged but lost Pilot Officer De Mancha, who collided with *Leutnant* Kriker of *III./JG 27*. Both pilots were lost. 238 Squadron then arrived, Blue Section engaging Bf110s and claiming one shot down and a 'probable' without loss.

			Hurricanes					
Unit	Dest	P.D.	Dam	MIA	Cat E	KIA	MIA	WIA
43 Sqn	1	0	1	1	0	0	1	0
238 Sqn	3	1	0	0	0	0	0	0

22nd July 1940

There were three interceptions and two claims, 46 Squadron pilots damaging a Do17 near Skegness shortly after dawn. A section of 145 Squadron Hurricanes destroyed another Do17 off Tangmere a little later.

			Hurricanes					
Unit	Dest	P.D.	Dam	MIA	Cat E	KIA	MIA	WIA
46 Sqn	0	0	1	0	0	0	0	0
145 Sqn	1	0	0	0	0	0	0	0

22/23rd July 1940

There were a few isolated raiders over Britain, mainly over Scotland and Wales. A Do17 was intercepted by a Blenheim crew from the FIU, Flying Officer G.Ashfield claiming it shot down off Brighton.

			Blenheims					
Unit	Dest	P.D.	Dam	MIA	Cat E	KIA	MIA	WIA
FIU	1	0	0	0	0	0	0	0

23rd July 1940

The quiet phase continued, with only two successful interceptions reported; a Ju88 was claimed destroyed off Yarmouth by

The Battle of the Channel

242 Squadron Hurricanes. A Do17 met a similar fate off Scotland at the hands of 603 Squadron Spitfire pilots.

Hurricanes							
Unit	Dest	P.D.	Dam	MIA	Cat E	KIA	MIA	WIA
242 Sqn	1	0	0	0	0	0	0	0

Spitfires							
Unit	Dest	P.D.	Dam	MIA	Cat E	KIA	MIA	WIA
603 Sqn	1	0	0	0	0	0	0	0

23/24th July 1940

There was another successful night interception when Sergeant A.McDowall of 602 Squadron claimed an He111 east of Linton.

Spitfires							
Unit	Dest	P.D.	Dam	MIA	Cat E	KIA	MIA	WIA
602 Sqn	1	0	0	0	0	0	0	0

24th July 1940

Following an earlier unsuccessful convoy attack by Do17s off Dover, the main attack of the day centred around a convoy leaving the Thames estuary. This was attacked off Margate by Do17s escorted by Bf109s of *III./JG 26*, which succeeded in keeping most of the intercepting Spitfires away from the bombers:

Spitfires							
Unit	Dest	P.D.	Dam	MIA	Cat E	KIA	MIA	WIA
54 Sqn	2	12	1	0	2	1	0	0
65 Sqn	0	0	7	0	0	0	0	0
610 Sqn	3	0	0	0	0	0	0	0

Several lone bombers were engaged around the British Isles:

Spitfires							
Unit	Dest	P.D.	Dam	MIA	Cat E	KIA	MIA	WIA
64 Sqn	1	0	0	0	0	0	0	0
74 Sqn	0	1	0	0	0	0	0	0
92 Sqn	1	0	0	0	0	0	0	0
603 Sqn	0	0	1	0	0	0	0	0

25th July 1940

Shortly after noon, several diversionary *Luftwaffe* fighter sweeps were flown in the Dover Straits, with the clear intention of exhausting the defending RAF pilots by numerous scrambles:

The Vickers Supermarine Spitfire I Series.
Basic Specification

Dimensions: Span 36 feet 10 inches. Length 29 feet 11 inches. Height 11 feet 5 inches.

Power Plant: One Rolls-Royce Merlin II or III inline liquid cooled engine.

Armament: Eight .303 inch Browning machine-guns mounted in wings.

Performance

Max speed: 362 mph at 18,500 feet.
Max Climb: 2,500 ft/min
Ceiling 31,900 feet.

The Spitfire I, developed from the successful Schneider Trophy racing seaplanes, was designed by R.J.Mitchell to meet Air Ministry Specification F.5/34. It was originally a private venture design based on the somewhat inferior Goshawk engine but, when the Rolls-Royce company assured Supermarine's that their new PV-12 engine would deliver 1,000 hp, Mitchell modified his design to accept the private venture engine, the new aircraft easily exceeding the AM Spec. The PV-12 engine became the Merlin, the Supermarine Type 300 became the Spitfire, the AM Spec. was rewritten as F.37/34 for production of the new fighter and thus was one of the most successful 'marriages' in aviation history consummated.

The prototype was ready early in 1936 and was first flown on 5th March by Captain J "Mutt" Summers, Vickers Chief Test Pilot. It was soon apparent that the new fighter was an outstanding aircraft and, on 3rd June, the Air Ministry contracted for an initial production of 310 aircraft, followed by and order for 600 more in 1937. The first Spitfires arrived at No.19 squadron in June 1938 and, by the time war was declared, nine squadrons had been fully equipped and more than 2,000 aircraft were on order.

The AOC-in-C Fighter Command, Air Chief Marshal Dowding, clearly realised the importance of the Spitfire, since none were allowed to join the BEF in France. This was almost certainly due to his foresight in realising that, should the BEF be defeated, a strong fighter defence would be required in Britain. It was also clear that the narrow track undercarriage of the aircraft would be unsuitable for the rough field operations. Thus, when the Battle of Britain began, nineteen squadrons of Spitfires were operational, despite heavy losses incurred during the Dunkirk evacuation.

The Spitfire I won immortality in the skies over Britain during the summer and autumn of 1940. Its aesthetic beauty won the admiration of the British public, eclipsing, somewhat unfairly, its stable-mate the Hurricane. The Hurricane was actually more stable and destroyed more enemy aircraft. It also had a rather better 'kill' rate in terms of ammunition expended due to its stability and concentrated gunfire pattern. The thin wings of the Spitfire were prone to flexing under high-G conditions, spreading the cone of fire. Therefore a burst of fire from the widely staggered Brownings of the Spitfire, while more likely to achieve hits, was less likely to cause significant damage. A variation of the Mark I was the Mark IB, equipped with twin 20mm Hispano cannon, but these proved unreliable in action, tending to jam due to the ammunition-feed system. No 19 squadron, equipped for a short time with Spitfire IBs, protested and was allowed to return to eight-gun Mark IAs. Despite these early problems, the Spitfire was to prove the most successful RAF fighter ever built.

				Spitfires				
Unit	Dest	P.D.	Dam	MIA	Cat E	KIA	MIA	WIA
65 Sqn	1	0	0	0	0	0	0	0

				Hurricanes				
Unit	Dest	P.D.	Dam	MIA	Cat E	KIA	MIA	WIA
32 Sqn	0	1	0	0	0	0	0	0
615 Sqn	1	1	0	0	0	0	0	0

The main thrust in the east came a few hours later when a convoy off Dover was attacked by Ju88s. The battle developed into a series of raids that were to last for several hours, with some squadrons landing to refuel and rearm before taking off again:

				Spitfires				
Unit	Dest	P.D.	Dam	MIA	Cat E	KIA	MIA	WIA
54 Sqn	1	0	0	1	2	1	1	0
64 Sqn	3	0	1	2	0	0	2[1.]	0
74 Sqn	0	0	1	0	0	0	0	0
610 Sqn	7	4	1	0	1	0	0	0

1. Pilot captured, but died of wounds

				Hurricanes				
Unit	Dest	P.D.	Dam	MIA	Cat E	KIA	MIA	WIA
56 Sqn	2	1	1	0	0	0	0	0
111 Sqn	1	0	4	0	0	0	0	0

Meanwhile the second thrust of the *Luftwaffe* attack hit Portland, where two squadrons engaged:

				Spitfires				
Unit	Dest	P.D.	Dam	MIA	Cat E	KIA	MIA	WIA
152 Sqn	4	0	4	0	1	0	0	1

				Hurricanes				
Unit	Dest	P.D.	Dam	MIA	Cat E	KIA	MIA	WIA
87 Sqn	0	1	0	0	0	0	0	0

A few hours later, Blue Section of 1 Squadron found a Bf109 patrol off the Isle of Wight and claimed one destroyed and a 'probable'. During the day lone bombers were engaged off Scotland, the east coast and over the Irish Sea:

				Hurricanes				
Unit	Dest	P.D.	Dam	MIA	Cat E	KIA	MIA	WIA
1 Sqn	1	1	0	0	0	0	0	0
3 Sqn	1	0	0	0	0	0	0	0

				Spitfires				
Unit	Dest	P.D.	Dam	MIA	Cat E	KIA	MIA	WIA
92 Sqn	0	1	0	0	0	0	0	0
222 Sqn	0	1	0	0	0	0	0	0

26th July 1940

Bad weather brought a halt in the German effort against British Channel convoys. Instead, Bf109s flew *Freijagds* in the area of the Isle of Wight, where 601 Squadron pilots claimed two 'probables' and a 'damaged' for the loss of one Hurricane pilot to *Oberleutnant* Max Dobislav of *III./JG 27*. Later in the day Flight Lieutenant S.C.Walch of 238 Squadron claimed a Bf109 destroyed south of Swanage. Another *Freijagd* to the east resulted in a Bf109 being claimed shot down off Folkestone by Flight Sergeant W.H.Franklin of 65 Squadron. One of the few reported solo bombers, a Ju88, was attacked and claimed probably destroyed off Pembroke by 92 Squadron Spitfire pilots.

| Spitfires ||||||||
Unit	Dest	P.D.	Dam	MIA	Cat E	KIA	MIA	WIA
65 Sqn	1	0	0	0	0	0	0	0
92 Sqn	0	1	0	0	0	0	0	0

| Hurricanes ||||||||
Unit	Dest	P.D.	Dam	MIA	Cat E	KIA	MIA	WIA
238 Sqn	1	0	0	0	0	0	0	0
601 Sqn	0	2	1	1	0	0	1	0

26/27th July 1940

Yet another successful interception was effected when Pilot Officer John Cock of 87 Squadron caught an He111 near Portishead and shot it down.

| Hurricanes ||||||||
Unit	Dest	P.D.	Dam	MIA	Cat E	KIA	MIA	WIA
87 Sqn	1	0	0	0	0	0	0	0

27th July 1940

With slightly better weather, *Stukas* and Bf109s set out to attack the convoy *'Bacon'* sighted off Portland by reconnaissance aircraft. Three squadrons engaged, 238 Squadron claiming a Ju87 and 145 Squadron a Bf109 both destroyed. 609 Squadron lost one pilot shot down and killed off Weymouth. Bf109s flew flew *Freijagds* to the east in the early evening, 41 Squadron claiming one destroyed off Folkestone. 501 Squadron reported another Bf109 'probably destroyed' off Dover, but lost one of its pilots shot down and killed by *Leutnant* Framm of *III./JG 27*. Three solo aircraft were also engaged. 234 Squadron claimed a Ju88 damaged off Land's End and 504 Squadron shot an He111 down into the Irish Sea. Squadron Leader J.R.Kayll led five of

The Fighter Command War Diaries

his 615 Squadron pilots to massacre an He59 off the North Foreland.

				Spitfires				
Unit	Dest	P.D.	Dam	MIA	Cat E	KIA	MIA	WIA
234 Sqn	0	0	1	0	0	0	0	0
609 Sqn	0	0	0	1	0	0	1	0

				Hurricanes				
Unit	Dest	P.D.	Dam	MIA	Cat E	KIA	MIA	WIA
145 Sqn	1	0	0	0	0	0	0	0
238 Sqn	1	0	0	0	0	0	0	0
504 Sqn	1	0	0	0	0	0	0	0
615 Sqn	1	0	0	0	0	0	0	0

28th July 1940

The first engagement was against a single Ju88, intercepted and destroyed by 234 Squadron Spitfires shortly after dawn. No further action took place until the early afternoon, when a large force of *Luftwaffe* aircraft was plotted moving out across the Dover Straits. Several RAF units were scrambled and the squadrons claimed eight enemy aircraft destroyed, five probables and a damaged for the loss of three aircraft and one pilot. A later patrol by 111 Squadron Hurricanes found two He59s in the Channel area and destroyed them both.

				Spitfires				
Unit	Dest	P.D.	Dam	MIA	Cat E	KIA	MIA	WIA
41 Sqn	0	0	3	0	0	0	0	0
74 Sqn	5	5	0	1	1	0	1	1
234 Sqn	1	0	0	0	0	0	0	0

				Hurricanes				
Unit	Dest	P.D.	Dam	MIA	Cat E	KIA	MIA	WIA
111 Sqn	2	0	0	0	0	0	0	0
257 Sqn	0	0	0	0	1	0	0	0

29th July 1940

The day began with a large scale *Stuka* raid on port installations at Dover:

				Spitfires				
Unit	Dest	P.D.	Dam	MIA	Cat E	KIA	MIA	WIA
41 Sqn	2	3	1	1	2	0	1	0
64 Sqn	5	0	2	0	0	0	0	0

126

The Battle of the Channel

28th July 1940: Fighter Clash Over Dover

A heavy raid developed shortly before 14.00 hours when Bf109s of *III./JG 26* escorted *Stukas* towards Dover, with *Stab* and *I./JG 51* covering. The first RAF units in the area were 74 and 257 Squadrons, which were engaged by the Bf109s while the *Stukas*, unaccountably, turned away. 257 Squadron, airborne from Hawkinge, were apparently the first in action, making no claims but sustaining damage to Sgt Forward's Hurricane, which was classified as a 'write-off' after his return. It was almost certainly claimed by *Gefreiter* Brügelmann of *III./JG 26*. The 74 Squadron pilots then engaged the Messerschmitts with more vigour than accuracy, making the following claims:

   F/L A.G.Malan Bf109 destroyed & 1 damaged
   F/L D.P.D.G.Kelly Bf109 destroyed
   P/O J.C.Freeborn Bf109 destroyed
   P/O P.C.F.Stevenson Bf109 destroyed & 2 damaged
   P/O H.R.Gunn Bf109 destroyed
   P/O H.M.Stephen Bf109 damaged
   P/O P.C.B.St.John Bf109 damaged

Not a single *Luftwaffe* fighter was actually hit however, but Sergeant E.A.Mould was shot down, almost certainly by *Major* Adolf Galland who claimed a Hurricane. Mould baled out wounded, while *Oberleutnant* Joachim Müncheberg shot down and killed Pilot Officer J.H.R.Young over the Goodwin Sands. Most of 74 Squadron then retired as *JG 51* came in to find eleven Spitfires of 41 Squadron below them. The *Geschwaderkommodore*, *Major* Mölders, recalled:

"I flew together with my wingman, Oberleutnant Kirchheiss, north of Dover. Suddenly I saw three British fighters, far behind them a lot of Spitfires in the mist. The three Spitfires were somewhat below us. I attacked this section. When I approached, both the outer Spitfires turned, but the Spit' in the middle flew straight on. I got behind it and opened fire from 60m. At once the right wing caught fire, thick smoke and flame, and the Spit' went down. I pulled up and saw 8-10 Spitfires behind me. I was frightened for a moment. There was only one chance - to go straight through the formation. I swept through the crowd. The first Spitfires were surprised, but one of the rearmost was watchful. He fired with all guns and hit me! It rattled in my aircraft, I had hits in the cooling system, wing and fuel tank. I broke away, and dived with everything I had: 700 kph towards the Channel. The engine was working well thank God! The Spitfires chased me and my flag of smoke, but then Oberleutnant Leppla, who

had seen the incident, rushed to my assistance. He snapped the Spitfire sitting directly behind me, and after a few seconds it went down wrapped in a large cloud of smoke. When I reached the coast the engine began to stutter and, during the landing, the undercarriage collapsed and I made a perfect belly-landing. When I tried to get out of the cockpit my legs were strangely weak, and I saw bloodstains. In hospital I discovered the reason: three splinters in the thigh, one in the knee and one in the left foot. I had felt nothing in the heat of combat"

Mölders had attacked Flying Officer A.D.J.Lovell, who was wounded and crashed when landing at Manston. Flight Lieutenant J.T.Webster, steep-turning, caught Mölders' aircraft in his gunsight and opened fire. He badly damaged the *Kommodore's* aircraft, then attacked another. This is believed to have been that which returned damaged but with the pilot unhurt. Pilot Officer G.H.Bennions fired on a third, claiming it damaged. He is thought to have been responsible for the loss of *Gefreiter* Gebhardt of *2./JG 51*, who was subsequently reported missing. Pilot Officer P.C.F.Stevenson of 74 Squadron was far out over the Channel when he sighted Werner Mölders' crippled fighter heading for home, trailing smoke. Stevenson was then bounced by Richard Leppla and his aircraft damaged. Further towards England, Pilot Officer J.C.Freeborn was bounced by *Oberfeldwebel* Schmid of *I./JG 51* and his fighter was badly damaged.

Other accounts have made 'Sailor' Malan of 74 Squadron victor over Werner Mölders, but this is 'wishful thinking' and was definitely not the case. Malan and most of his pilots, having fought Adolf Galland's *III./JG 26*, had already left the scene.

				Hurricanes				
Unit	Dest	P.D.	Dam	MIA	Cat E	KIA	MIA	WIA
56 Sqn	1	0	0	1	0	0	1	0
501 Sqn	4	2	6	0	0	0	0	0

In the early afternoon, a small group of low-flying bombers attacked a convoy in the same area, 610 Squadron pilots claiming a Do17 damaged. A little later a second convoy, sailing near Harwich, was attacked. A single Ju88 had been engaged and destroyed by 145 Squadron Hurricanes off Worthing.

The Battle of the Channel

Generalleutnant Adolf Galland

Adolf Galland was one of the most charismatic personalities of the *Luftwaffe* fighter forces. He fought in Spain with the *Condor Legion* in 1937-38 and on return was trained as a close support pilot. He transferred to *III./JG 27* and gained his first victories during the French campaign. Then he led *III./JG 26* into the Battle of Britain, becoming *Geschwaderkommodore* on 22nd August. Promoted to Inspector of Fighters in December 1941, he had 94 kills to his credit and had won the Oak Leaves, Swords and Diamonds to his *Ritterkreuz*. Finally he led the Me262-equipped *JV 44* from February 1945, bringing his score to 103. He died in 1996.

Oberst Werner Mölders

Werner Mölders was probably the best fighter tactician of the *Luftwaffe*. Like Galland, he fought in Spain, where he developed the most effective fighter tactics by using basic elements of two aircraft instead of the 'vic' of three employed by the RAF. He led *III./JG 53* throught the 'Phoney War' and was shot down and captured during the Battle of France. On repatriation, he was given command of *III./JG 51* and became *Kommodore* on 20th July 1940. He led his unit to Russia and brought his victory tally to 101 (plus 14 in Spain) before being grounded and promoted to Inspector of Fighters on 7th August 1941. He was killed in a flying accident on 22nd November 1941.

Major Joachim Müncheberg

Müncheberg fought with *III./JG 26* from the outbreak of war. He served under Galland during the Battle of Britain, where he proved himself to be a brilliant fighter pilot and leader. Early in 1941, his 7 *Staffel* operated against Malta, where he quickly built up a large score of Hurricanes. He fought in Russia and the Western Desert, finally commanding *JG 77* and bringing his victory tally to 135. He was killed in action on 23rd March 1943, when he collided with an American Spitfire that he was attacking.

Hurricanes

Unit	Dest	P.D.	Dam	MIA	Cat E	KIA	MIA	WIA
17 Sqn	0.5	0	0	0	0	0	0	0
32 Sqn	1	0	0	0	0	0	0	0
85 Sqn	0	0	1	0	0	0	0	0
151 Sqn	0	1	2	0	0	0	0	0

Spitfires

Unit	Dest	P.D.	Dam	MIA	Cat E	KIA	MIA	WIA
66 Sqn	1.5	0	0	0	1	0	0	1
610 Sqn	0	0	1	0	0	0	0	0

30th July 1940

Bad weather again gave the RAF a breathing space, only two interceptions taking place. An He111 was caught off Montrose by three 603 Squadron Spitfires and was shot down. To the south a Bf110 attempting to attack shipping off Southwold was found by a section from 85 Squadron, meeting the same fate.

Group Captain Adolphus Gysbert Malan DSO DFC*

A former Merchant Navy officer, 'Sailor' Malan was a flight commander with 74 Squadron in 1939, rising to command the unit in August 1940. In 1941 his powers of leadership, his tactical skills and his ability as a fighter pilot were fully recognised and he became one of the first Wing Leaders, commanding the Biggin Hill Spitfire Wing. By late July 1941, he was listed as the top-scoring pilot in Fighter Command, having been credited with 27 confirmed victories and seven more 'shared'. He was then taken off operations and served in Staff positions, returning to Biggin Hill as Station Commander in 1943. He subsequently led 145 (Free French) Wing until after the Normany invasion, and then went to the Advanced Gunnery School at Catfoss. He left the RAF in 1946 and returned to his native South Africa, where he was active for several years in the civil rights movement. He was then diagnosed as having Parkinson's Disease and this illness led to his death on 17th September 1963.

The Battle of the Channel

Victory List

21.5.40	Ju88	destroyed	2.12.40	Bf109	destroyed
21.5.40	He111	prob destroyed	2.2.41	Bf109	destroyed
22.5.40	Ju88	destroyed	5.2.41	Do215	prob destroyed
24.5.40	Do17	destroyed	17.5.41	Bf109	prob destroyed
24.5.40	Do17	destroyed*	17.5.41	Bf109	damaged
27.5.40	Bf109	destroyed	21.5.41	Bf109	damaged
18/19.6.40	He111	destroyed	17.6.41	Bf109	destroyed
18/19.6.40	He111	destroyed	21.6.41	Bf109	destroyed
12.7.40	He111	destroyed*	22.6.41	Bf109	destroyed
19.7.40	Bf109	prob destroyed	23.6.41	Bf109	destroyed
25.7.40	Bf109	damaged	23.6.41	Bf109	destroyed
28.7.40	Bf109	destroyed	24.6.41	Bf109	destroyed
28.7.40	Bf109	damaged	25.6.41	Bf109	destroyed
11.8.40	Bf109	destroyed	26.6.41	Bf109	destroyed
11.8.40	Bf109	damaged	28.6.41	Bf109	destroyed
11.8.40	Bf109	damaged	30.6.41	Bf109	destroyed
11.8.40	Bf109	damaged	2.7.41	Bf109	destroyed*
11.8.40	Bf109	destroyed	3.7.41	Bf109	damaged
13.8.40	Do17	destroyed	4.7.41	Bf109	destroyed
13.8.40	Do17	prob destroyed	4.7.41	Bf109	destroyed*
17.10.40	Bf109	prob destroyed	4.7.41	Bf109	damaged
22.10.40	Bf109	destroyed	5.7.41	Bf10	damaged
23.11.40	Bf109	destroyed	6.7.41	Bf109	destroyed
27.11.40	Bf109	destroyed	23.7.41	Bf109	damaged
27.11.40	Bf109	prob destroyed	*indicates shared claim		

Spitfires
Unit	Dest	P.D.	Dam	MIA	Cat E	KIA	MIA	WIA
603 Sqn	1	0	0	0	0	0	0	0

Hurricanes
Unit	Dest	P.D.	Dam	MIA	Cat E	KIA	MIA	WIA
85 Sqn	1	0	0	0	0	0	0	0

31st July 1940

Haze hampered fighter interceptions during the morning, three combats occurring against the few enemy aircraft reported in the south:

Hurricanes

Unit	Dest	P.D.	Dam	MIA	Cat E	KIA	MIA	WIA
1 Sqn	0	0	1	0	0	0	0	0
111 Sqn	1	0	0	0	0	0	0	0
145 Sqn	0	1	0	0	0	0	0	0

The weather cleared a little in the afternoon, when 74 Squadron scrambled to engage Bf109s near Folkestone:

Spitfires

Unit	Dest	P.D.	Dam	MIA	Cat E	KIA	MIA	WIA
74 Sqn	0	1	0	2	0	0	2	0

The last fight came at 18.20 hours, when a patrol from 501 Squadron attacked and damaged a Do17 near Saltwood.

Hurricanes

Unit	Dest	P.D.	Dam	MIA	Cat E	KIA	MIA	WIA
501 Sqn	0	0	1	0	0	0	0	0

Summary - July 1940

Air Combat Claims:

210:111:94

Missing/destroyed aircraft:

37 Spitfires, 33 Hurricanes and 6 Defiants missing/Cat E.

44 pilots and 4 gunners killed/missing.

Notes:

232 Sqn	formed at Sumburgh with Hurricane Is on 17th.
263 Sqn	received Whirlwind Is, retaining Hurricane Is.
302 Sqn	formed at Leconfield with Hurricane Is on 13th.
303 Sqn	formed at Northolt on 22nd to equip with Hurricane Is
310 Sqn	formed at Duxford with Hurricane Is.

August 1940

1st August 1940

Bad weather again hampered German operations and British interceptions. Five contacts were reported by British fighter patrols, but only two resulted in claims, one by 145 Squadron. A small convoy attack off Great Yarmouth was intercepted by 242 Squadron, a Ju88 being claimed shot down without loss.

			Hurricanes				
Unit	Dest	P.D.	Dam	MIA	Cat E	KIA	MIA	WIA
145 Sqn	0	1	1	1	0	0	1	0
242 Sqn	1	0	0	0	0	0	0	0

2nd August 1940

Continuing bad weather resulted in only two interceptions, one unsuccessful. The other fight saw an He111 claimed damaged by Flight Lieutenant W.G.Clouston of 19 Squadron. Clouston was flying an eight-gun Spitfire rather than the unreliable Spitfire IIB with cannons.

			Spitfires				
Unit	Dest	P.D.	Dam	MIA	Cat E	KIA	MIA	WIA
19 Sqn	0	0	1	0	0	0	0	0

3rd August 1940

The bad weather continued. One combat was recorded, Plt Off C.A.Woods-Scawen of 43 Squadron reporting a Bf109 - claimed as an He113 - destroyed off Hove at noon.

			Hurricanes				
Unit	Dest	P.D.	Dam	MIA	Cat E	KIA	MIA	WIA
43 Sqn	1	0	0	0	0	0	0	0

4th August 1940

- nil -

5th August 1940

A morning *Luftwaffe* sortie (Bf109s covering an Hs126) into the Dover Straits was met by Spitfire squadrons covering a convoy in that area:

				Spitfires				
Unit	Dest	P.D.	Dam	MIA	Cat E	KIA	MIA	WIA
64 Sqn	2	2	0	1	0	0	1	0
65 Sqn	1	2	0	0	0	0	0	0

Later in the day, a few escorted Ju88s attacked a convoy in the same area:

				Spitfires				
Unit	Dest	P.D.	Dam	MIA	Cat E	KIA	MIA	WIA
41 Sqn	0	0	1	0	0	0	0	0
65 Sqn	1	0	1	0	0	0	0	0

				Hurricanes				
Unit	Dest	P.D.	Dam	MIA	Cat E	KIA	MIA	WIA
151 Sqn	1	1	0	0	0	0	0	0

6th August 1940

With the lack of activity still being shown by the Germans, more convoys were despatched. No attacks developed, but a few lone reconnaissance aircraft were sighted. One, a Do17 from *III./KG 3*, approached a convoy off Lowestoft and was shot down by patrolling Hurricanes from 85 Squadron. A Ju88 was claimed probably destroyed off Flamborough Head by 616 Squadron.

				Spitfires				
Unit	Dest	P.D.	Dam	MIA	Cat E	KIA	MIA	WIA
616 Sqn	0	1	0	0	0	0	0	0

				Hurricanes				
Unit	Dest	P.D.	Dam	MIA	Cat E	KIA	MIA	WIA
85 Sqn	1	0	0	0	0	0	0	0

7th August 1940

One engagement was reported, Hurricanes of 249 Squadron fighting Bf109s and Do17s near Gravesend and claiming one shot down and another damaged.

				Hurricanes				
Unit	Dest	P.D.	Dam	MIA	Cat E	KIA	MIA	WIA
249 Sqn	1	0	1	0	0	0	0	0

8th August 1940

In contrast to the relative inactivity of the past day, the 8th was to produce the heaviest fighting yet seen as the Germans sought to attack convoy CW9 (code-named *Peewit*) off the Isle of Wight.

The engagements may be regarded as three separate phases. The first came at around 09.00 hours, when *Stukas*, Bf109s and Bf110s were engaged by RAF fighters:

			Hurricanes				
Unit	Dest	P.D.	Dam	MIA	Cat E	KIA	MIA	WIA
145 Sqn	2	9	5	2	0	0	2	0

The Germans returned shortly after noon, the bombers being again *Stukas* with heavy fighter escort:

			Spitfires				
Unit	Dest	P.D.	Dam	MIA	Cat E	KIA	MIA	WIA
609 Sqn	5	0	2	0	0	0	0	0

			Hurricanes				
Unit	Dest	P.D.	Dam	MIA	Cat E	KIA	MIA	WIA
145 Sqn	2	2	0	0	0	0	0	0
238 Sqn	4	5	0	2	0	0	2	0
257 Sqn	2	0	0	3	0	0	3	0
601 Sqn	1	2	0	0	0	0	0	0

This was followed by Hurricanes of 238 Squadron catching an He59 on an ASR operation and shooting it down. One Hurricane ditched, Squadron Leader H.A.Fenton being rescued by HMS *Basset*.

			Hurricanes				
Unit	Dest	P.D.	Dam	MIA	Cat E	KIA	MIA	WIA
238 Sqn	1	0	0	0	1	0	0	0

The final attack on *Peewit* came some two hours later, more escorted *Stukas* being engaged.

			Spitfires				
Unit	Dest	P.D.	Dam	MIA	Cat E	KIA	MIA	WIA
152 Sqn	3	0	2	0	1	0	0	0
43 Sqn	6	9	4	2	0	0	2	0

			Hurricanes				
Unit	Dest	P.D.	Dam	MIA	Cat E	KIA	MIA	WIA
145 Sqn	6	2	4	3	0	0	3	0
213 Sqn	1	0	0	0	0	0	0	0

To the east, RAF squadrons were kept busy throughout the morning fighting off Bf109 sweeps:

			Spitfires				
Unit	Dest	P.D.	Dam	MIA	Cat E	KIA	MIA	WIA
41 Sqn	3	3	0	0	0	0	0	0

Unit	Dest	P.D.	Dam	MIA	Cat E	KIA	MIA	WIA
64 Sqn	0	5	1	0	2	0	0	2
65 Sqn	0	0	0	0	2	0	0	0

1. One pilot died of wounds

Blenheims

Unit	Dest	P.D.	Dam	MIA	Cat E	KIA	MIA	WIA
600 Sqn	0	0	0	1	0	0	1	0

A Do17, probably checking for results, was claimed damaged by 234 Squadron pilots, following the second major convoy battle. The convoy had been practically annihilated, with seven vessels sunk and thirteen badly damaged. It would not be long before shipping movements were halted completely.

Spitfires

Unit	Dest	P.D.	Dam	MIA	Cat E	KIA	MIA	WIA
234 Sqn	0	0	1	0	0	0	0	0

9th August 1940

Following the heavy fighting over the convoy on the previous day, the only *Luftwaffe* operations proved to be reconnaissances and lone bombers. Two were engaged, an He111 being claimed destroyed by 79 Squadron near Newcastle and a Do17 reported shot down by 605 Squadron off Scotland for the loss of a Hurricane and pilot.

Hurricanes

Unit	Dest	P.D.	Dam	MIA	Cat E	KIA	MIA	WIA
79 Sqn	1	0	0	0	0	0	0	0
605 Sqn	1	0	0	1	0	0	1	0

9/10th August 1940

A 600 Squadron Blenheim was lost, shot down by AA gunfire near Westgate. The crew baled out safely.

Blenheims

Unit	Dest	P.D.	Dam	MIA	Cat E	KIA	MIA	WIA
600 Sqn	0	0	0	0	1	0	0	0

10th August 1940

There was just one inconclusive interception during the day, but it was merely the calm before the storm.....

11th August 1940

During the morning, the Germans sent Bf109s across the Dover Straits in an attempt to attract British fighter units to this area while heavy attacks took place elsewhere. These *Freijagds* resulted in:

			Spitfires					
Unit	Dest	P.D.	Dam	MIA	Cat E	KIA	MIA	WIA
64 Sqn	2	1	0	0	0	0	0	0
74 Sqn	7	4	7	0	1	0	0	0

			Hurricanes					
Unit	Dest	P.D.	Dam	MIA	Cat E	KIA	MIA	WIA
32 Sqn	1	0	1	0	0	0	0	0

A short while later A 610 Squadron Spitfire patrol caught and damaged an He59 off Calais.

			Spitfires					
Unit	Dest	P.D.	Dam	MIA	Cat E	KIA	MIA	WIA
610 Sqn	0	0	1	0	0	0	0	0

While the 11 Group fighters were battling Bf109s south of Dover, the main raid of escorted Ju88s and He111s totalling 100+ aircraft, came thundering in towards Portland. This was met by many squadrons:

			Spitfires					
Unit	Dest	P.D.	Dam	MIA	Cat E	KIA	MIA	WIA
152 Sqn.	1	1	0	1	0	0	1	0
609 Sqn	5	1	0	0	0	0	0	0

			Hurricanes					
Unit	Dest	P.D.	Dam	MIA	Cat E	KIA	MIA	WIA
1 Sqn	2	0	0	0	2	1	0	0
87 Sqn	6	0	3	1	1	0	1	0
145 Sqn	0	5	3	2	0	0	2	0
213 Sqn	10	1	2	2	0	0	2	0
238 Sqn	4	1	0	4	0	0	4	0
601 Sqn	10	3	5	4	0	0	4	0

An hour later two escorted 604 Squadron Blenheim crews found an He59 on the water, being towed by E-Boats. They attacked and sank it. At around the same time (noon), Bf110s from *EGr.210* struck at a convoy off Harwich, several squadrons of fighters being vectored to intercept:-

Spitfires

Unit	Dest	P.D.	Dam	MIA	Cat E	KIA	MIA	WIA
74 Sqn	6	3	5	2	0	0	2	0

Hurricanes

Unit	Dest	P.D.	Dam	MIA	Cat E	KIA	MIA	WIA
17 Sqn	1	2	2	1	0	0	1	0
85 Sqn	2	1	0	0	0	0	0	0

Blenheims

Unit	Dest	P.D.	Dam	MIA	Cat E	KIA	MIA	WIA
604 Sqn	1	0	0(W)[1]	0	0	0	0	0

1. (W) indicates 'on water'

As the Bf110s withdrew yet another formation of German bombers was approaching, Do17s briefed to hit a convoy in the Thames estuary. However the covering Bf109s held the British fighters off, just one bomber being claimed damaged. 74 Squadron, having landed, refuelled and rearmed in record time, were back to catch tail-enders of this fight:

Spitfires

Unit	Dest	P.D.	Dam	MIA	Cat E	KIA	MIA	WIA
64 Sqn	1	2	2	0	0	0	0	0
74 Sqn	3	1	1	0	0	0	0	0

Hurricanes

Unit	Dest	P.D.	Dam	MIA	Cat E	KIA	MIA	WIA
56 Sqn	0	0	0	1	0	0	1[1]	0
111 Sqn	1	0	1	4	1	0	1	0

1. Believed shot down by Spitfire).

The final engagements came in the north-east, when a Ju88 was engaged by 41 Squadron Spitfire pilots, who claimed it destroyed near Thirsk.

Spitfires

Unit	Dest	P.D.	Dam	MIA	Cat E	KIA	MIA	WIA
41 Sqn	1	0	0	0	0	0	0	0

The days fighting had cost the RAF 26 fighters and 20 pilots. Few could now doubt that the long-awaited aerial assault had begun.

Chapter Six
The Battle of the Airfields

12th August 1940

The day opened with a *Luftwaffe* fighter sweep across the Dover Straits, met by Spitfires:

		Spitfires						
Unit	Dest	P.D.	Dam	MIA	Cat.E	KIA	MIA	WIA
610 Sqn	5	6	1	1	0	0	1	0

This sweep had been designed to draw fighters up and exhaust their fuel before Bf110s and 109s from *E.Gr.210* swept in to hit the radar stations around Dover:

		Spitfires						
Unit	Dest	P.D.	Dam	MIA	Cat.E	KIA	MIA	WIA
54 Sqn	1	3	0	0	0	0	0	0

		Hurricanes						
Unit	Dest	P.D.	Dam	MIA	Cat.E	KIA	MIA	WIA
151 Sqn	0	0	0	0	2	0	0	2[1.]

1. *One pilot died of wounds*

E.Gr.210 retired and were immediately followed by a *Stuka* attack upon a convoy off Margate, while Dorniers struck at Lympne and Hawkinge airfields:

		Spitfires						
Unit	Dest	P.D.	Dam	MIA	Cat.E	KIA	MIA	WIA
65 Sqn	1	5	0	0	0	0	0	0

		Hurricanes						
Unit	Dest	P.D.	Dam	MIA	Cat.E	KIA	MIA	WIA
501 Sqn	7	3	4	1	0	0	1	0

Meanwhile a massive raid of 200+ Ju88s, He111s and their escorts was approaching the Isle of Wight, targeted to the radar stations in that area,:

		Spitfires						
Unit	Dest	P.D.	Dam	MIA	Cat.E	KIA	MIA	WIA
152 Sqn	4	1	4	2	0	0	2	0
266 Sqn	4	4	9	1	1	0	1	0
609 Sqn	12	3	2	0	0	0	0	0

Combat Report

12.8.1940

Sighted Squadron of enemy aircraft at 20,000 feet over Dover, dived down from 27,000 feet and engaged. Fired 3 second burst at one Me109 which smoked, caught fire, and then commenced to spin in flames. Fired short burst at second Me109 from 50 yards and observed Glycol streaming from port radiator. I chased the enemy aircraft back to French coast in a dive, firing all the time until ammunition ran out. I pursued the enemy aircraft over Cap Griz Nez and observed him force-land on the beach with his wheels up. Enemy aircraft written off. Two Me109 unconfirmed.

P/O C.F.Gray 'B' Flight, 54 Squadron.

Hurricanes

Unit	Dest	P.D.	Dam	MIA	Cat.E	KIA	MIA	WIA
43 Sqn	0	1	9	0	0	0	0	0
145 Sqn	1	4	0	3	1	0	3	0
213 Sqn	12	0	0	2	0	0	2	0
253 Sqn	0	3	1	1	0	0	1	0
615 Sqn	2	2	1	0	0	0	0	0

In the meantime, further bombers were coming in over Manston, catching 65 Sqn on take-off:

Spitfires

Unit	Dest	P.D.	Dam	MIA	Cat.E	KIA	MIA	WIA
65 Sqn	0	2	1	0	0	0	0	0

Hurricanes

Unit	Dest	P.D.	Dam	MIA	Cat.E	KIA	MIA	WIA
501 Sqn	0	1	2	0	0	0	0	0

In the early evening further raids were mounted in the east, engagements taking place from the Channel to Lympne:

Spitfires

Unit	Dest	P.D.	Dam	MIA	Cat.E	KIA	MIA	WIA
54 Sqn	0	4	0	0	0	0	0	0
64 Sqn	1	2	2	0	1	0	0	0

The Battle of the Airfields

		Hurricanes						
Unit	Dest	P.D.	Dam	MIA	Cat.E	KIA	MIA	WIA
32 Sqn	2	7	2	0	1	0	0	0
56 Sqn	2	0	1	0	1	0	0	1
501 Sqn	1	0	0	0	0	0	0	0

13th August 1940

Eagle Day. (see inset) Total claims and casualties:

		Spitfires						
Unit	Dest	P.D.	Dam	MIA	Cat.E	KIA	MIA	WIA
64 Sqn	1	0	5	0	0	0	0	0
65 Sqn	3	3	0	0	0	0	0	0
74 Sqn	7	3	3	0	1	0	0	0
92 Sqn	1	0	0	0	0	0	0	0
152 Sqn	6	0	3	0	1	0	0	1
609 Sqn	13	3	6	0	1	0	0	0

		Hurricanes						
Unit	Dest	P.D.	Dam	MIA	Cat.E	KIA	MIA	WIA
43 Sqn	2	7	6	0	2	0	0	0
56 Sqn	2	1	5	0	4	0	0	2
87 Sqn	2	0	0	1	0	0	1	0
111 Sqn	6	0	4	0	0	0	0	0
151 Sqn	3	1	0	0	0	0	0	0
213 Sqn	7	1	0	1	0	0	1	0
238 Sqn	10	3	4	1	2	0	1	1
257 Sqn	1	0	1	0	0	0	0	0
601 Sqn	8	22	13	0	1	0	0	1

41 Squadon 1940. Front row 2nd from L Norman Ryder; 4th from L Don Finlay, the CO; 2nd from R 'Hawkeye' Wells.

(D.Sarkar)

13th August 1940 "Adler Tag"

Indications of enemy activity began early when, between 0530 and 0540 hours, two formations of 30+ 'bandits' were plotted in the Amiens area. Thirty minutes later these were moving out towards the eastern Channel, while a third formation, reckoned as 100+ was detected near Dieppe. At once Park made his dispositions, scrambling 151 Squadron to patrol over a convoy in the Thames estuary, 74 Squadron to protect Manston and 111 Squadron to head south and stand guard over Hawkinge, while sections from 43, 85 and 238 Squadrons were sent up to cover their bases. During the next ten minutes the first two formations crossed the French coast at Griz Nez and a fourth 'plot' of 12+ was noticed near Guernsey. Further British units were then ordered up; the rest of 43 Squadron to patrol between Petworth and Arundel, 257 Squadron to patrol the Canterbury line and a section from 17 Squadron to cover Martlesham Heath.

By 0630 hours, the German advance had resolved into two discrete parts, two formations nearing the North Foreland, while the other two were further west, one approaching Littlehampton, the other near Spithead, with a new formation detected in the central Channel. The fighter forces in the west were further strengthened by 601 Squadron, and by the remainder of 238 Squadron, scrambled on base patrol to join the section already patrolling.

The Early Morning Attack in the East

The first formation of bombers, Do17s from *KG 2*, droned up the Thames estuary above cloud, emerging to find 74 Squadron waiting. The Spitfire pilots saw four sections each of ten Do17s in line astern and, with no escorts in sight, charged in to attack the rear section under heavy and accurate return fire. Dorniers were claimed shot down by Pilot Officer Hastings, Squadron Leader Malan, Flight Lieutenant Freeborn, Pilot Officer Szczesny, Sergeant Skinner, and Flight Lieutenant Brzezina, with Malan, Flight Lieutenant Mungo-Park and Pilot Officer Stephen adding 'probables'. Strikes on others were claimed by Hastings, Brzezina and Flying Officer Nelson. Brzezina was then shot down and baled out safely. Two more Spitfires were badly damaged, Szczesny belly-landing unhurt at West Malling. Despite taking casualties, the Dorniers doggedly continued, striking at Eastchurch, which was heavily damaged, and Leysdown satellite airfield on the Isle of Sheppy. *KG 2* crews claimed ten Spitfires destroyed at the former base, actually damaging one 266 Squadron machine, but three Blenheims of 53 Squadron were destroyed. Meanwhile to the east, the second formation, forty *KG 2* Do17s flying in the same formation as the first, were seen by 151 Squadron off the North Foreland. The Hurricanes attacked, but despite claims for Dorniers destroyed by Flight Lieutenant Smith, Flying Officer Milne (2) and Sergeant Saville, they were unable to break up the formation. The bombers continued west and, when between Herne Bay and Whitchurch, 111 Squadron came in to attack. One flight went in head-on while the other flight broke away, then came in for a flank attack. Sergeants Dymond and Craig, Squadron Leader Thompson, Pilot Officer Walker, Flying Officer Ferriss and Pilot Officer McIntyre each claimed a 'Do215', further Dorniers being claimed damaged by Dymond, Thompson and Pilot Officer McIntyre. The Hurricanes flown by Dymond, Craig and McIntyre were all damaged - the former seriously -but no pilot was hurt. The result of this fighter attack was satisfactory, for many Dorniers jettisoned bombs in this area and broke for home.

Three sections of 64 Squadron had been scrambled at 0635 hours and were sent towards the Thames estuary. When it became apparent that they would not intercept, they were ordered southwest towards the coast, catching some of the retreating Dorniers near Dungeness. The Spitfire pilots claimed one destroyed by Flying Officer Woodward, while Pilot Officers Simpson, Roberts, Jones and Flight Sergeants Laws and Gilbert each claimed a Do215 damaged. Simpson's aircraft was hit and he forcelanded safely at base.

The Early Morning attack in the West

While the engagements were taking place over Kent, the formation from Dieppe was approaching Tangmere at 0635 hours, heading towards Arundel. The others from the Guernsey area crossed near Portsmouth at 0640, also heading for Arundel. 213 Squadron and one Flight of 87 Squadron were scrambled to intercept.

The first contact was made by 257 Squadron south of Tangmere, an 'honours even' encounter during which Flying Officer Mitchell claimed a Ju88 damaged while Sergeant D.J.Hulbert's Hurricane was slightly damaged. Then 43 Squadron attacked between Littlehampton and Worthing at 0645 hours followed, five minutes later, by 601 Squadron storming in over the South Downs west of Arundel. Claims for the two units are listed overleaf:

43 Sqn

F/O Woods-Scawen	He111	unconfirmed
F/O Woods-Scawen	He111	unconfirmed
F/L Dalton-Morgan	He111	destroyed
P/O Lane	He111	damaged
Sgt Mills	Bf109	unconfirmed
Sgt Deller	Ju88	unconfirmed
P/O Carey	Ju88	probably destroyed
Sgt Hallowes	Ju88	probably destroyed
P/O Carey	Ju88	damaged
S/L Badger	Ju88	damaged
S/L Badger	Ju88	damaged
P/O Upton	Do17	probably destroyed
F/O Gray	Do17	damaged
Sgt Crisp	Bf110	damaged

601 Sqn

P/O Mayers	Ju88	destroyed
Sgt Hawkings	Ju88	shared destroyed
P/O Grier	Ju88	shared destroyed
S/L Hope	Ju88	shared probably destroyed
F/O Doulton	Ju88	shared probably destroyed
P/O Mayers	Ju88	probably destroyed
F/O McGrath	Ju88	unconfirmed
F/O McGrath	Ju88	probably destroyed
F/O Clyde	Ju88	probably destroyed
F/O Grier	Ju88	probably destroyed
F/L Davis	Ju88	destroyed
F/L Davis	Ju88	shared probably destroyed
P/O Fiske	Ju88	destroyed
S/L Hope	Ju88	damaged
F/O Riddle	Ju88	damaged
P/O Fiske	Ju88	damaged
P/O Mayers	Bf110	damaged

NOTE: 20 Ju88s of I./KG 54 targeted to Farnborough, 18 Ju88s of II./KG 54 targeted to Odiham.

Two 43 Sqn Hurricanes were lost. Flight Lieutenant Dalton-Morgan, shot down over Petworth, baled out slightly wounded while Flying Officer Woods-Scawen baled out unhurt, his Hurricane crashing at Midhurst. Sergeant Noble of this unit force-landed at Tangmere with slight damage and Flying Officer Clyde of 601, his fighter badly shot-up, returned wounded.

238 Squadron, hunting near the Isle of Wight, claimed one success by Sergeant Batt, who claimed an 'He111' destroyed before he was attacked by Bf109s and shot down, crash-landing at Eartham. Sergeant Seabourne was shot down into the sea and later rescued, badly burnt. A single victory was also reported by 87 Squadron, when Wing Commander Dewar, Flying Officer Glyde and Pilot Officer Jay jointly claimed a Ju88 destroyed off Bognor Regis, but Glyde, hit by return fire, was shot down into the sea and lost.

By 0730 hours, there were no German aircraft remaining in the disputed area, but just over four hours later, at 1140 hours, came the next indications, when a force of 20+ was plotted near Cherbourg, heading north-west.

The Mid-day Raids

Ten minutes after the first report, 238 Squadron was scrambled to patrol Portland and within minutes the original enemy force, now 45 miles south-west of St Catherines Point, was joined by a second formation of 12+, flying on a parallel course, heading towards Portland. At once 601 Squadron was scrambled to patrol Swanage and 213 to patrol Portland.

The enemy forces (Do17s and Ju88s at 15,000 ft with escorts, plus more escorts at 20,000 ft) reached Portland at noon, but no bombs were dropped. Combat was joined ten minutes later when 601 and 238 Squadrons, coming in above the German formation, engaged the fighter escorts over Weymouth and Portland, allowing 'B' Flight of 213 Squadron to engage the bombers as they retired. The following claims were made:

601 Squadron

F/O Clyde	Bf110	destroyed
F/O Davis	Bf110	destroyed
P/O Grier	Bf110	unconfirmed
F/O Davis	Bf110	unconfirmed
F/O Davis	Bf110	unconfirmed
P/O Mayers	Bf110	damaged
F/L Hope	Bf110	damaged
P/O Fiske	Bf110	damaged
F/L Hope	Bf110	damaged
P/O Fiske	Bf110	damaged
P/O Fiske	Bf110	damaged
P/O Doulton	Bf110	damaged
F/O Clyde	Bf110	damaged
F/S Pond	Bf110	damaged

238 Squadron

P/O Simmonds	Bf110	destroyed
Sgt Marsh	Bf110	destroyed
P/O Wigglesworth	Bf110	unconfirmed
F/L Hughes	Do17	destroyed

213 Squadron

P/O Larichliere	Ju88	destroyed
Sgt Llewellyn	Ju88	destroyed
P/O Larichliere	Bf109	destroyed

Casualties were again minimal; 601 Squadron lost one Hurricane when Pilot Officer H.C. Mayers baled out slightly wounded off Whitnose, Weymouth and Pilot Officers W.L.M.Fiske and M.D.Doulton returned with slightly damaged Hurricanes.

The Afternoon Raid in the West

The third incursion came in the mid-afternoon. 152 Squadron with ten Spitfires airborne, were on standing patrol over the Portland area when, between 1525 and 1540 hours, the first enemy formations were plotted, three each of 30+ heading towards the British coastline between St Albans Head and St Catherine's Point. With the first reports, 213 and 238 Squadrons were scrambled to patrol over Portland at 5,000 and 20,000 feet respectively. During the next ten minutes, 609 were off to patrol their base at Warmwell and 601 to cover the Bembridge area, with sections from 92 and 43 Squadrons scrambled a little later.

They had not long to wait, for at 1600 hours the first formation - Ju88s of LG 1 covered by a heavy fighter escort - crossed in over the Isle of Wight. 238 Squadron engaged first, but were held off by the fighters, and made the following claims:

238 Squadron

F/L Hughes	Bf110	destroyed
F/L Hughes	Bf110	destroyed
Sgt Davis	Bf110	destroyed
P/O Davis	Bf110	unconfirmed
P/O Simmonds	Bf110	damaged
P/O Simmonds	Bf110	damaged
P/O Simmonds	Bf110	damaged
P/O Simmonds	Bf110	damaged
P/O Urwin-Mann	Bf109	destroyed
Sgt Seabourne	Bf109	destroyed
Sgt Seabourne	Bf109	destroyed
F/L Hughes	Bf109	damaged

Two Hurricanes were shot down. Sergeant H.J.Marsh failed to return, while Sergeant R.A.Little was brought down unhurt at Burton Bradstock.

With 238 Squadron otherwise engaged, the Junkers proceeded towards their main objective of Southampton, which was heavily bombed at 1625 hours. This was not the only target however. While the main battles were taking place over and around the Solent, groups of bombers split from the main formation and headed north, striking at Wroughton, Andover (where a 53 Squadron Blenheim was blown up), Stockbridge, Bishops Waltham, Middle Wallop and Benson in addition to an attack upon Thorney Island.

Meanwhile the second formation, consisting of 50+ Bf109s and Bf110s were engaged by 152 and 213 Squadrons over Portland. Ten minutes later the third formation reached the Solent, where 609 engaged, finding their opponents to be Ju87s with a stepped-up escort of fighters too far behind to intervene:

609 Squadron

P/O Appleby	Bf109	destroyed
F/O Nowierski	Bf109	destroyed
P/O Crook	Bf109	destroyed
F/L McArthur	Bf109	damaged
F/O Nowierski	Bf109	damaged
Sgt Feary	Bf110	damaged
P/O Overton	Ju87	destroyed
P/O Overton	Ju87	destroyed
P/O Miller	Ju87	destroyed
P/O Staples	Ju87	destroyed
F/L Howell	Ju87	destroyed
F/L Howell	Ju87	destroyed
F/O Goodwin	Ju87	destroyed
F/O Goodwin	Ju87	destroyed
Sgt Feary	Ju87	destroyed
F/O Dundas	Ju87	destroyed
P/O Miller	Ju87	probably destroyed
F/O Ostaczewski	Ju87	probably destroyed
F/O Ostaczewski	Ju87	probably destroyed
P/O Appleby	Ju87	damaged
P/O Dundas	Ju87	damaged
P/O Staples	Ju87	damaged

213 Squadron

P/O Larichliere	Bf110	destroyed
P/O Atkinson	Bf109	destroyed
P/O Osmond	Bf109	destroyed

152 Squadron

P/O Marrs	Bf110	destroyed
F/L Boitel-Gill	Bf110	destroyed
F/L Boitel-Gill	Bf110	destroyed
Sgt Baker	Bf110	Probably destroyed
F/L Boitel-Gill	Ju87	destroyed
Sgt Robinson	Bf109	destroyed

The skilful positioning of the squadrons helped keep casualties to a minimum, for just one aircraft and pilot was lost, when Sergeant P.P.Morris of 213 Squadron failed to return. Pilot Officer R.F.Inness of 152 Squadron was wounded, but he brought his Spitfire home to be classified as a 'write-off' after landing. The Spitfire flown by Flying Officer J.C.Dundas of 609 also took a few bullets during the fight.

As the bombers turned for home, they were engaged between Portland Bill and Selsey by 601 Squadron in the area Southampton-Winchester-Botleigh. Elements from 257 Squadron engaged the enemy over Bembridge, 43 Squadron (Isle of Wight), 213 Squadron (15 miles south-west of Selsey Bill), 92 Squadron (over Selsey Bill) and 87 Squadron (over Portland):

601 Squadron

P/O Grier	Bf110	unconfirmed
P/O Clyde	Bf110	unconfirmed
F/O Clyde	Bf110	unconfirmed
Sgt Guy	Bf110	destroyed
F/O Riddle	Bf110	probably destroyed
Sgt MacDonald	Bf110	probably destroyed
P/O McGrath	Bf110	destroyed
F/O Cleaver	Bf110	shared unconfirmed
F/O Cleaver	Bf110	unconfirmed
S/L Hope	Bf110	probably destroyed
F/O ?	Bf110	probably destroyed
F/O Davis	Bf110	probably destroyed
F/O Davis	Bf110	damaged
F/O Cleaver	Bf110	damaged
P/O McGrath	He113	damaged
F/S Pond	Ju88	damaged

	213 Squadron	
F/L Sing	Bf109	destroyed
Sgt Bushell	Bf109	probably destroyed
	87 Squadron	
P/O David	Ju87	destroyed
	257 Squadron	
Squadron	Ju88	destroyed
	43 Squadron	
Sgt Hallowes	Do17	destroyed
	92 Squadron	
F/L Tuck	Ju88	shared destroyed
P/O Watling	Ju88	shared destroyed
F/S Havercroft	Ju88	shared destroyed

No fighters were lost, but Pilot Officer C.A.Capon's 257 Squadron Hurricane was badly shot-up.

The Afternoon Raids Over Kent

While the above raids were being tracked on their inbound flight, more plots were noted in the eastern Channel. A section of 17 Squadron Hurricanes was already patrolling over a convoy off Clacton, two fighters from 1 Squadron were over another convoy near Harwich and 'A' Flight of 65 Squadron were covering Dover. At 1539 hours a plot of 30+ was noted to the north of Cap Griz Nez. At once 'B' Flight of 65 Squadron was ordered away to join their comrades and, within a minute, a second enemy force materialised in the Channel. The forces did not seem large, thus during the next fifteen minutes minimal forces were disposed to deal with them; seven aircraft of 64 Squadron scrambled and sent towards the Dover Straits, 56 Squadron to patrol over Manston and five fighters from 19 Squadron to cover the coastline near Martlesham Heath.

Then the controllers watched the plots anxiously as the first enemy formation - Bf110s and 109s of *E.Gr.210* escorted by more Bf110s from *ZG 26* - tracked steadily north until 50 miles east of Sheerness. They then turned west, heading towards the Thames estuary. Meanwhile the second formation, Ju87s with Bf109 escorts, crossed the coast between Deal and Sandwich and a new formation of Bf109s was plotted to the south of Dover. The RAF paid the price for not treating the raids more seriously, for the thinly spread defences were unable to intercept the *Stukas* as they headed for Detling, which was heavily bombed, another 53 Squadron Blenheim being destroyed and two damaged. The formation of Bf110s, targeted to Rochford, had turned north meanwhile, reached Southend at 1600 hours and then turned south again, having missed their target in cloud. As they crossed the Thames, 56 Squadron was waiting. The vulnerable Bf110s emerged from the clouds to find Hurricanes above. Flying Officer Weaver claimed a Bf110 destroyed and a 'damaged', Pilot Officer Sutton and Flying Officer Mounsden a Bf110 destroyed apiece and Flight Lieutenant Gracie two more 'damaged'. The cost was high however. Four of the twelve Hurricanes were lost. Pilot Officer Joubert and Flying Officer Davies both baled out wounded over Sheppey, Sergeant Hillwood baled out off Sheerness and swam ashore while Flying Officer Brooker crashed attempting to force-land his battered Hurricane at Hawkinge.

One flight of 65 Squadron found the third formation off Manston, Bf109s acting as withdrawal cover, and fought them off the coast. Flight Lieutenant Smart claimed one destroyed and a 'probable', Flight Lieutenant Olive two and a 'probable' and Sergeant Kilner also claimed one probably destroyed for no loss to the unit.

14th August 1940

The first raid built up in the late morning and proved to be Bf109s and Ju87s, which headed towards Dover, where they were hotly engaged shortly after midday:

\\	\\	Spitfires	\\	\\	\\	\\	\\	\\
Unit	Dest	P.D.	Dam	MIA	Cat E	KIA	MIA	WIA
65 Sqn	2	2	0	0	0	0	0	0
610 Sqn	6	1	5	0	0	0	0	0
\\	\\	Hurricanes	\\	\\	\\	\\	\\	\\
Unit	Dest	P.D.	Dam	MIA	Cat E	KIA	MIA	WIA
32 Sqn	1	0	0	0	1	0	0	0
151 Sqn	2	0	1	0	0	0	0	0
615 Sqn	4	0	1	2	0	0	2	0

Following this, several formations of bombers approached the British coast on a broad front, dispersing the defenders somewhat. Many broke through to attack targets as far apart as

Middle Wallop, Hullavington, Bristol, Netheravon, Colerne and Hawarden:

				Spitfires				
Unit	Dest	P.D.	Dam	MIA	Cat E	KIA	MIA	WIA
92 Sqn	7	1	0	0	0	0	0	0
234 Sqn	1	0	0	0	0	0	0	0
609 Sqn	3	0	0	1	0	0	1	0
				Hurricanes				
Unit	Dest	P.D.	Dam	MIA	Cat E	KIA	MIA	WIA
43 Sqn	1	0	0	1	0	0	1	0
87 Sqn	2	0	1	0	0	0	0	0
615 Sqn	0	0	1	0	0	0	0	0

Other, minor, actions during the day included a flight of Spitfires of 7 OTU, which caught a lone Ju88 near Chester and shot it down. Three 600 Sqn Blenheims were bombed and destroyed at Manston.

				Spitfires				
Unit	Dest	P.D.	Dam	MIA	Cat E	KIA	MIA	WIA
65 Sqn	0	0	0	0	1	0	0	0
7 OTU	1	0	0	0	0	0	0	0
				Hurricanes				
Unit	Dest	P.D.	Dam	MIA	Cat E	KIA	MIA	WIA
151 Sqn	0	0	0	0	1	0	0	0
213 Sqn	1	0	1	0	0	0	0	0
				Blenheims				
Unit	Dest	P.D.	Dam	MIA	Cat E	KIA	MIA	WIA
600 Sqn	0	0	0	0	3	0	0	0

15th August 1940

An interception of a reconnaissance Do215 brought 602 Squadron Spitfires a 'confirmed' victory in the early morning:

				Spitfires				
Unit	Dest	P.D.	Dam	MIA	Cat E	KIA	MIA	WIA
602 Sqn	1	0	0	0	0	0	0	0

Large-scale raids soon began to build up in the south and continued throughout the day. In the late morning a massive build-up of radar plots over the Pas de Calais heralded the first attacks, Ju87s escorted by Bf109s moving towards the forward airfields at Hawkinge and Lympne. Despite the intervention of RAF fighters, both were badly hit:

Spitfires								
Unit	Dest	P.D.	Dam	MIA	Cat E	KIA	MIA	WIA
54 Sqn	4	0	4	0	2	0	0	1

Hurricanes								
Unit	Dest	P.D.	Dam	MIA	Cat E	KIA	MIA	WIA
501 Sqn	10	1	3	0	2	0	0	0
615 Sqn	1	0	0	1	0	0	1	0

While fighter squadrons were engaged in the south, bombers from *Luftflotte 5* were crossing the North Sea to strike at targets in the northwest. (see inset). Total claims and casualties in the north were:

Hurricanes								
Unit	Dest	P.D.	Dam	MIA	Cat E	KIA	MIA	WIA
41 Sqn	8	4	1	0	0	0	0	0
72 Sqn	11	0	0	0	0	0	0	0
616 Sqn	8	3	1	0	0	0	0	0

Hurricanes								
Unit	Dest	P.D.	Dam	MIA	Cat E	KIA	MIA	WIA
73 Sqn	8	5	0	0	0	0	0	0
79 Sqn	7	0	1	0	0	0	0	0
605 Sqn	8	3	2	0	1	0	0	0
607 Sqn	9	5	5	0	0	0	0	0

Blenheims								
Unit	Dest	P.D.	Dam	MIA	Cat E	KIA	MIA	WIA
219 Sqn	1	0	0	0	0	0	0	0

Very soon a further large raid began building up over France and Belgium, preceded by 'Raid 22', an attack upon Martlesham Heath by Bf110s and 109s of *E.Gr.210*:

Hurricanes								
Unit	Dest	P.D.	Dam	MIA	Cat E	KIA	MIA	WIA
1 Sqn	2	0	1	2	1	0	2	1
32 Sqn	1	0	0	0	1	0	0	1

Then the main raid began to cross the Channel, heavily escorted Dorniers heading for Eastchurch and Rochester. British units engaged and there were several claims:

Spitfires								
Unit	Dest	P.D.	Dam	MIA	Cat E	KIA	MIA	WIA
64 Sqn	3	1	2	2	0	0	2	0

Hurricanes

Unit	Dest	P.D.	Dam	MIA	Cat E	KIA	MIA	WIA
111 Sqn	3	4	3	0	0	0	0	0
151 Sqn	3	1	0	0	0	0	0	0
501 Sqn	0	0	5	0	0	0	0	0

In the west The *Luftwaffe* continued the pressure by sending *Stukas* to hit Portland again, Ju88s crossed in east of the Isle of Wight to strike at Middle Wallop and Charmy Down, a massive air battle developing:

Spitfires

Unit	Dest	P.D.	Dam	MIA	Cat E	KIA	MIA	WIA
152 Sqn	0	0	0	0	1	0	0	0
234 Sqn	7	1	0	2	2	1	2	0
609 Sqn	4	3	0	0	0	0	0	0

Hurricanes

Unit	Dest	P.D.	Dam	MIA	Cat E	KIA	MIA	WIA
32 Sqn	3	2	0	0	0	0	0	0
43 Sqn	4	1	1	0	0	0	0	0
87 Sqn	13	1	1	1	2	0	1	1
111 Sqn	3	3	2	0	2	1	0	1
213 Sqn	19	3	0	1	0	0	1	0
249 Sqn	5	0	1	0	0	0	0	0
601 Sqn	4	2	2	0	1	0	0	1

Blenheims

Unit	Dest	P.D.	Dam	MIA	Cat E	KIA	MIA	WIA
604 Sqn	0	0	0	0	3[1]	0	0	1

1. Two were bombed and one was shot down by a *Spitfire*.

Further raids soon crossed the coast in the east and one of the targets was Kenley, chosen for *E.Gr.210*'s Bf110s and 109s. The German formation hit Croydon by accident, this and other raids were heavily engaged:

Spitfires

Unit	Dest	P.D.	Dam	MIA	Cat E	KIA	MIA	WIA
54 Sqn	2	2	4	0	1	0	0	1
266 Sqn	4	1	1	2	0	0	2	0
610 Sqn	0	2	2	0	0	0	0	0

Hurricanes

Unit	Dest	P.D.	Dam	MIA	Cat E	KIA	MIA	WIA
32 Sqn	3	5	0	0	0	0	0	0
111 Sqn	4	1	4	0	0	0	0	0
151 Sqn	1	0	0	0	0	0	0	0
501 Sqn	0	0	0	1	1	0	1	1

The Fighter Command War Diaries

15th August 1940 - The Raids in the North

In the mistaken belief that British losses had obliged Fighter Command to pull in reserves from the north, *Luftflotte 5* (Norway) despatched raids across the North Sea, timed to catch the RAF unawares.

At 1208 hours, a formation of 20+ was plotted far to the east of the Firth of Forth and, seven minutes later, the Spitfires of 72 Squadron were scrambled and ordered out to sea to patrol over Farne Island, while 605 Squadron were called down from Drem to patrol over the Acklington-Tyneside area. Further raids were plotted ten minutes later, in the same area as the first, apparently of smaller size, but all heading towards Blyth and Acklington. There was now no doubt that a considerable enemy force was tracking in. Thus during the next ten minutes 41 and 79 Squadrons were scrambled, the latter ordered to assist 72 Squadron, but in the event they were not to do so.

Three minutes later - at 1245 hours - 72 Squadron made contact, sighting a reported one hundred He111s (reported as both Heinkels and Ju88s), plus seventy-two Bf110 escorts in two stepped-up waves behind. Before the escorts could intervene, the Spitfires stormed in, bombers being claimed destroyed by Flying Officer Sheen (two), Flight Lieutenant Smith (two) and Pilot Officer Robson. Sheen and Flying Officer Pigg each claimed a Bf110 destroyed and Pilot Officer Winter claimed two, before the squadron retired without loss, leaving the phalanx of bombers and escort to carry on towards the English coast.

79 Squadron had barely cleared the coast when at 1300 hours they were given a radio warning of the approaching force and sighted the enemy almost at once, sixty Heinkels plus escorts crossing the coast at Blyth. The Hurricanes closed in fast, taking on the '110s. Pilot Officers Peters, Clift and Flying Officer Haysom claimed one apiece while Squadron Leader Heyworth, Flight Lieutenant Clerke and Pilot Officers Parker, Noble and Nelson-Edwards joined forces to claim two, one of which was reported as a 'Do17'. The squadron then reformed, and soon sighted the bombers again near Newcastle. They attacked again, Pilot Officer Millington reporting the destruction of two Heinkels and hits on a third. This attack took place almost certainly at the same time as 41 Squadrons, these pilots having seen the formation in the area Bishop Auckland-Durham-Seaham. The Spitfire pilots made the following claims:

The Battle of the Airfields

	41 Squadron		
P/O Lock	Bf110	destroyed
P/O Mackenzie	Ju88	probably destroyed
P/O Lock	Ju88	destroyed
P/O Wallens	Bf110	destroyed
P/O Bennions	Bf110	destroyed
P/O Shipman	Bf110	destroyed
P/O Bennions	He111	damaged
Sgt Usmar	He111	destroyed
P/O Morrogh-Ryan	Ju88	destroyed
F/O Lovell	Bf110	destroyed
F/L Ryder	Ju88	probably destroyed
F/O Lovell	Bf110	probably destroyed
P/O Boret	Ju88	probably destroyed

One 79 Squadron Hurricane was slightly damaged, the pilot believed unhurt.

As this fight was raging, 607 Squadron was scrambled and, a few minutes later, 605 Squadron came into action when 'B' Flight sighted and engaged eighty *Luftwaffe* aircraft near Newcastle. Flight Lieutenant McKellar claimed three He111s destroyed plus a 'probable', Pilot Officer Currant two and a 'probable', Pilot Officer Passy, Flying Officer Muirhead and Pilot Officer Jones, one apiece, Jones also claiming two 'probables'. Another He111 was claimed damaged by an unrecorded pilot. This engagement was followed, five minutes later, by 607 Squadron, whose pilots claimed seven Heinkels destroyed, four 'probables' and four 'damaged' plus a Bf110 probably destroyed and a second damaged. The pilots included Flight Lieutenant Blackadder, Pilot Officer Welford, Sergeant Cunningham, Flying Officer Gore, Sergeant Burnell-Phillips, Pilot Officer Drake, Flight Lieutenant Bazin, Pilot Officer Parnall, Sergeant Hewett, Flying Officer Craig, Pilot Officer Whitty, Pilot Officer Lenahan, Flying Officer Bowen and Pilot Officer Sulman. There were three casualties, all from 605 Squadron; Pilot Officer Passy force-landed near Usworth, unhurt but with his fighter 'written-off', Pilot Officer Law force-landed near Hart railway station, badly injured, while Flight Lieutenant McKellar's fighter was less seriously damaged.

While the above encounters were taking place in the north, a second formation of bombers - Ju88s from *KG 30* - were heading towards Scarborough, a plot of 30+ being reported at 1239 hours. It was almost twenty minutes before Fighter Command reacted, 616 Squadron being scrambled at 1300 hours to patrol Hornsea, followed during the next ten minutes by the Defiants of 264 Squadron, sent to protect a convoy in the Humber, 73 Squadron from Church Fenton - 'A' Flight on convoy patrol and 'B' Flight on base patrol and, finally, the Blenheims of 219 Squadron.

Five minutes later, at 1315 hours, the 616 Squadron Spitfire pilots saw a large formation of Ju88s approaching Flamborough Head and engaged them out to sea. 'A' Flight of 73 Squadron, having been sent north to assist, closed in as 616 disengaged, fighting the bombers as they crossed in over the coast near Scarborough at 1317 hours. Between them, the two units made the following claims:

616 Squadron

Sgt Hopewell	Ju88	destroyed
P/O Murray	Ju88	destroyed
P/O Murray	Ju88	destroyed
F/O Moberley	Ju88	destroyed
P/O Marples	Ju88	shared destroyed
P/O Dundas	Ju88	shared destroyed
S/L Robinson	Ju88	unconfirmed
P/O Casson	Ju88	unconfirmed
P/O Marples	Ju88	unconfirmed
F/L Gillam	Ju88	destroyed
P/O Smith	Ju88	shared destroyed
F/L Hellyer	Ju88	shared destroyed
P/O Dundas	Ju88	damaged

73 Squadron

Sgt McNay	Ju88	destroyed
Sgt McNay	Ju88	destroyed
Sgt Griffin	Ju88	destroyed
P/O Carter	Ju88	destroyed
P/O Carter	Ju88	destroyed
F/L Lovell	Ju88	destroyed
P/O Scott	Ju88	destroyed
S/L Robinson	Ju88	probably destroyed
F/L Lovell	Ju88	probably destroyed
P/O Carter	Ju88	probably destroyed
S/L Robinson	Ju88	damaged
S/L Robinson	Ju88	damaged

After crossing the coastline, the Junkers fanned out, attacking Tees, Tyneside, Wear and Driffield - where seven Whitleys were destroyed and five damaged. Blenheims from 219 Squadron were powerless to prevent the raids, for the Junkers were too fast to be caught. Flying

The Spitfire flown by Plt.Off. R.A.Hardy of 234 Sqn, who was taken prisoner on 15th August.
(Chris Goss)

Officer Goddard made the only claim, reporting a 'Do17' destroyed off Scarborough. Sergeant Dupee also managed to get within shooting distance, but was the recipient of a well-aimed burst of gunfire which severely damaged his Blenheim.

16th August 1940

It was not until the late morning that the first German attacks developed, the main targets being West Malling, Hornchurch Farnborough, Harwell, Brize Norton and Biggin Hill:

Spitfires								
Unit	Dest	P.D.	Dam	MIA	Cat E	KIA	MIA	WIA
54 Sqn	3	0	3	0	0	0	0	0
64 Sqn	2	2	1	0	0	0	0	0
266 Sqn	0	3	0	0	4	3	0	1

Hurricanes								
Unit	Dest	P.D.	Dam	MIA	Cat E	KIA	MIA	WIA
32 Sqn	3	0	0	0	0	0	0	0
56 Sqn	0	0	0	0	1	0	0	1
111 Sqn	6	0	3	0	2	1	0	1
213 Sqn	1	0	0	1	0	0	1	0

Meanwhile further raids were plotted to the west as German bombers headed for Tangmere, Lee-on-Solent and Gosport:

Spitfires								
Unit	Dest	P.D.	Dam	MIA	Cat E	KIA	MIA	WIA
152 Sqn	2	0	0	0	0	0	0	0
602 Sqn	1	0	0	0	0	0	0	0

Hurricanes

Unit	Dest	P.D.	Dam	MIA	Cat E	KIA	MIA	WIA
1 Sqn	0	0	0	0	1	0	0	1
43 Sqn	17	4	4	0	5[1]	0	0	1
249 Sqn	1	0	0	0	2	0	0	1
601 Sqn	9	2	4	0	1	0	0	1[2]

1. Four aircraft destroyed by bombing.
2. Pilot died of wounds

Lesser incursions took place in the early evening. Several engagements took place between Worthing and the Isle of Wight, mainly against fighters:

Spitfires

Unit	Dest	P.D.	Dam	MIA	Cat E	KIA	MIA	WIA
152 Sqn	0	1	0	0	0	0	0	0
234 Sqn	6	1	0	0	2	0	0	0
602 Sqn	2	0	0	0	0	0	0	0

Hurricanes

Unit	Dest	P.D.	Dam	MIA	Cat E	KIA	MIA	WIA
601 Sqn	1	0	0	0	0	0	0	0

The story was the same in the east:

Spitfires

Unit	Dest	P.D.	Dam	MIA	Cat E	KIA	MIA	WIA
19 Sqn	2	2	0	0	0	0	0	0
64 Sqn	1	1	3	0	1	0	0	0
65 Sqn	5	1	2	1	1[1]	0	1	0
610 Sqn	0	1	2	1	0	0	1	0

1. strafed on ground.

Hurricanes

Unit	Dest	P.D.	Dam	MIA	Cat E	KIA	MIA	WIA
1 Sqn	7	2	0	0	1	0	0	0
32 Sqn	3	5	1	0	0	0	0	0
56 Sqn	2	4	3	0	1	0	0	0
501 Sqn	0	1	3	0	0	0	0	0
615 Sqn	2	2	1	0	1	0	0	1

Blenheims

Unit	Dest	P.D.	Dam	MIA	Cat E	KIA	MIA	WIA
600 Sqn	0	0	0	0	1[1]	0	0	0

1. bombed on ground.

The Battle of the Airfields

16/17th August 1940

A 29 Squadron Blenheim pilot was successful when Pilot Officer R.A.Rhodes engaged an He111 off Spurn Head 03.00 hours, claiming it destroyed.

				Blenheims				
Unit	Dest	P.D.	Dam	MIA	Cat E	KIA	MIA	WIA
29 Sqn	1	0	0	0	0	0	0	0

17th August 1940

- nil -

18th August 1940

Two interceptions were made against reconnaissance aircraft during the morning, a Bf110 being claimed destroyed and a Do17 probably so.

				Spitfires				
Unit	Dest	P.D.	Dam	MIA	Cat E	KIA	MIA	WIA
54 Sqn	1	0	0	0	0	0	0	0

				Hurricanes				
Unit	Dest	P.D.	Dam	MIA	Cat E	KIA	MIA	WIA
257 Sqn	0	1	0	0	0	0	0	0

The main raids did not begin until the early afternoon and can be summarised as covering three distinct phases. The first, three separate fomations comprising three hundred-plus raiders, crossed into British airspace shortly after noon, heading for Biggin Hill, West Malling, Croydon and Kenley. More than eighty British fighters scrambled to engage them and the ensuing battle covered the whole of southeast England:

				Hurricanes				
Unit	Dest	P.D.	Dam	MIA	Cat E	KIA	MIA	WIA
1 Sqn	2	0	0	0	0	0	0	0
17 Sqn	1	0	1	1	1	0	1	0
32 Sqn	10	3	3	0	2	0	0	2
56 Sqn	5	0	0	0	0	0	0	0
111 Sqn	6	1	6	0	3	1	0	0
501 Sqn	1	0	0	0	4	0	0	3
615 Sqn	4	2	1	0	6 [1]	1	0	2

1. 3 bombed on ground

Spitfires

Unit	Dest	P.D.	Dam	MIA	Cat E	KIA	MIA	WIA
54 Sqn	3	3	4	0	0	0	0	0
64 Sqn	6	0	2	0	0	0	0	0
92 Sqn	1	0	0	0	1	0	0	1
266 Sqn	1	1	0	0	2	0	0	0
610 Sqn	10	1	4	0	0	0	0	0

1. bombed on ground

In the mid-afternoon action switched to the west where Ju87s and Ju88s under heavy escort were briefed to raid Gosport, Poling, Ford and Thorney Island. Six squadrons of fighters were scrambled and caused great destruction among the Ju87 units. (see inset):

Hurricanes

Unit	Dest	P.D.	Dam	MIA	Cat E	KIA	MIA	WIA
43 Sqn	9	1	0	0	1	0	0	1
152 Sqn	11	0	1	0	0	0	0	0
213 Sqn	1	0	0	0	0	0	0	0
234 Sqn	6	2	3	0	0	0	0	0
601 Sqn	8	0	1	1	1	0	1	0
602 Sqn	8	1	7	0	1	0	0	0

Blenheims

Unit	Dest	P.D.	Dam	MIA	Cat E	KIA	MIA	WIA
FIU	0	0	1	0	0	0	0	0

As these raiders retired, a third huge formation was building over the Pas de Calais. These formed into five separate formations, heading for Kent. Most passed the east coast and moved into the Thames estuary, where eight fighter squadrons, plus elements from six others, engaged:

Spitfires

Unit	Dest	P.D.	Dam	MIA	Cat E	KIA	MIA	WIA
54 Sqn	4	4	6	0	0	0	0	0
65 Sqn	0	3	0	0	0	0	0	0

Hurricanes

Unit	Dest	P.D.	Dam	MIA	Cat E	KIA	MIA	WIA
1 Sqn	1	0	0	0	0	0	0	0
32 Sqn	6	1	0	0	0	0	0	0
46 Sqn	1	1	3	0	0	0	0	0
56 Sqn	3	1	3	0	0	0	0	0

Unit	Dest	P.D.	Dam	MIA	Cat E	KIA	MIA	WIA
85 Sqn	13	2	7	1	1	0	1	0
151 Sqn	4	1	2	1	1	0	1	1
257 Sqn	1	1	2	0	1	0	0	1
501 Sqn	3	0	1	0	3	2	0	0

18th August 1940 - The Demise of the Stukas.

This day, one of the most heavily contested of the entire battle, was to see one of the hitherto most deadly weapons of the *Luftwaffe* not only blunted, but rendered totally useless in the skies above the Solent. The first indication of a heavy raid build-up came at 14.00 hours, when three formations totalling '100-plus' were plotted moving out from Cherbourg and Le Havre. Five squadrons were scrambled, joining one already airborne. Some twenty minutes later they met the enemy - *Stukas*, escorted by many fighters. 234 Squadron charged into one formation just off Ventnor, but failed to reach the bombers. Pilots claimed six Bf109s destroyed, two 'probables' and three damaged without loss. The dive-bombers slipped through to bomb Gosport.

Meanwhile a second formation of *Stukas*, flying a few miles to the east, split into three formations. One group of forty, with Bf109 escort was found near Thorney Island and attacked almost simultaneously by 43 and 601 Squadrons before the diving attacks commenced. The two squadrons claimed fourteen Ju87s shot down, and a 'probable' plus three Bf109s and a 'damaged' for the loss of three Hurricanes and two pilots, with another fighter badly shot-up. A second formation of dive-bombers made for Ford and was again intercepted, this time by 602 Squadron. The Spitfire pilots claimed six bombers destroyed, one 'probable' and seven damaged, plus two Bf109s shot down. One Spitfire was lost, with four more damaged, two pilots being wounded. Another *Stuka* was claimed damaged by a lone Blenheim pilot from the Fighter Interception Unit. The third part of the 'split' formation managed to reach Poling RDF station unopposed and caused heavy damage. Meanwhile the Gosport attackers, retreating south, were engaged by Spitfires of 152 Squadron off the Isle of Wight. Nine aircraft were claimed destroyed with one damaged, plus two Bf109s claimed shot down. Two Spitfires were damaged. Finally Hurricane pilots of 213 Squadron engaged the rear cover Bf109 screen some miles south of Ventnor, one being claimed shot down without loss.

The German dive-bomber force had sustained heavy losses. Thirteen failed to return, three were 'written-off' on return and several more were damaged. These, added to the sixteen casualties sustained two days earlier, were enough to force the *Luftwaffe* High Command to withdraw the *Stuka* units from the battle. They had proved their worth in the earlier 'campaigns of movement', but in the skies over England they had become a lumbering liability and with their absence, the *Luftwaffe* lost a major part of its precision bombing capability.

19th August 1940

Following the bitter fighting of the previous day, the only *Luftwaffe* presence around the British Isles consisted of reconnaissance aircraft and lone bombers. One bomber damaged four Spitfires during a hit and run attack upon Bibury. Several units reported engagements:

Spitfires								
Unit	Dest	P.D.	Dam	MIA	Cat E	KIA	MIA	WIA
19 Sqn	1	0	0	0	0	0	0	0
66 Sqn	0	1	0	1	0	0	1	0
92 Sqn	1	0	1	0	1	0	0	0
602 Sqn	2	0	0	0	1	0	0	1

Hurricanes								
Unit	Dest	P.D.	Dam	MIA	Cat E	KIA	MIA	WIA
213 Sqn	1	0	0	0	0	0	0	0

19/20th August 1940

There was one engagement, again involving 29 Squadron, when an unidentified bomber was attacked and claimed probably destroyed off Portland. A 1 Squadron Hurricane was lost after hitting the balloon barrage at Finsbury Park, the pilot baling out safely.

Hurricanes								
Unit	Dest	P.D.	Dam	MIA	Cat E	KIA	MIA	WIA
1 Sqn	0	0	0	0	1	0	0	0

Blenheims

Unit	Dest	P.D.	Dam	MIA	Cat E	KIA	MIA	WIA
29 Sqn	0	1	0	0	0	0	0	0

20th August 1940

Bad weather further reduced German activity. Apart from morning sorties by reconnaissance aircraft, just one raid by Do17s was reported, this turning back after being engaged over the Thames estuary:

Spitfires

Unit	Dest	P.D.	Dam	MIA	Cat E	KIA	MIA	WIA
65 Sqn	2	2	0	0	1	0	0	0
66 Sqn	1	1	0	0	0	0	0	0

Hurricanes

Unit	Dest	P.D.	Dam	MIA	Cat E	KIA	MIA	WIA
32 Sqn	0	0	1	0	0	0	0	0
213 Sqn	2	0	0	0	0	0	0	0
242 Sqn.	0	0	0	1	0	0	1	0
257 Sqn	0	0	1	0	0	0	0	0
302 Sqn	1	0	0	0	0	0	0	0
615 Sqn	3	0	0	0	0	0	0	0

21st August 1940

Again no major attacks took place, but there was a great deal of activity by lone German aircraft and small forces:

Spitfires

Unit	Dest	P.D.	Dam	MIA	Cat E	KIA	MIA	WIA
41 Sqn	1	0	0	0	0	0	0	0
66 Sqn	0	0	1	0	0	0	0	0
152 Sqn	1	0	0	0	0	0	0	0
234 Sqn	1	0	0	0	0	0	0	0
611 Sqn	2	1	2	0	0	0	0	0

Hurricanes

Unit	Dest	P.D.	Dam	MIA	Cat E	KIA	MIA	WIA
17 Sqn	2	0	0	0	0	0	0	0
56 Sqn	1	0	0	0	0	0	0	0
238 Sqn	2	0	0	0	0	0	0	0
242 Sqn	2	0	0	0	0	0	0	0
302 Sqn	1	2	0	0	0	0	0	0

Ace in a Day - Ronnie Hamlyn

Combat Report

24th August 1940

I was Yellow 2. I saw three waves of bombers approaching the S coast. I attacked one of these waves in which there were about 15-18 Junkers 88 at about 300 - 350 yards. I received a large amount of cross fire, but I didn't open fire until 250 yards. I gave a two second burst and saw one Ju88 dive away from the rest and I watched it crash into the sea. I did not break away, but throttling back an Me109 overshot me and pulled up right in front at about 150 yards. I opened fire and saw it starting to smoke. I followed it down and saw it also hit the sea.

- Sgt R.F.Hamlyn, Yellow Section, 610 Squadron.

Combat Report

24th August 1940

1135

I was Yellow 2. I was attacked while in formation over Dover. After a short dogfight I got onto the Me109's tail and he at once flew for France. I followed, and while I was chasing him I saw another dogfight between two Spitfires and one Me109. The Me109 went down smoking badly but carried on flying, eventually going into the sea off Cap Griz Nez. By this time I had got into range of the Me109 I was chasing but did not open fire until he had crossed over the coast into France, after about three more bursts I saw it go out of control with smoke pouring out and watched it crash in a field. I did not experience any AA fire while over France. The Me109 that I saw crash into the sea was the one destroyed by F/O Lamb, Yellow Section Leader.

- Sgt R.F.Hamlyn. 610 Squadron

The Battle of the Airfields

Combat Report

24th August 1940
1555

I was Yellow Leader, on taking off we started to fly towards Gravesend but on reaching 5,000 feet we saw AA fire over NE London, so we changed course. At about 12,000 feet I first sighted about 20 Junkers 88s heading in a westerly direction. I led my section towards them but I saw a bunch of Me109s just above me so I pulled up and attacked one, after two bursts smoke started pouring out and he fell away out of control. I was just about to break away when I saw tracer bullets passing me. I at once turned sharply and saw my number three being attacked by an Me109. So I attacked it and it started to pull up, I gave another burst and it started smoking after another burst it caught fire and went down with pieces falling off it. The last I saw of the Spitfire, my No.3, was that he was still diving and he looked out of control.

- Sgt R.F.Hamlyn, 610 Squadron

Squadron Leader Ronald Fairfax Hamlyn DFM, AFC

'Ronnie' Hamlyn was a sergeant pilot with No.610 Squadron in September 1939, flying throughtout the Battle of Britain. He was commissioned in February 1941 and transferred to No.242 squadron in June, becoming a Flight Commander a month later. He later commanded No.276 (Air-Sea Rescue) Squadron, remained with the RAF postwar and retired on 19th October 1957.

Victory List

3.7.40	Do17	shd damaged	24.8.40	Bf109	destroyed
29.7.40	Do17	shd damaged	26.8.40	Bf109	destroyed
14.8.40	Bf109	damaged	26.8.40	Bf109	prob destroyed
24.8.40	Bf109	destroyed	28.8.40	Bf109	destroyed
24.8.40	Ju88	destroyed	30.8.40	Bf109	destroyed
24.8.40	Bf109	destroyed	4.7.41	Bf109	destroyed
24.8.40	Bf109	destroyed	27.7.41	Bf109	destroyed

22nd August 1940

Day: The reduced activity was repeated. In the early afternoon a convoy was attacked by fighter-bombers off Deal:

Unit	Dest	P.D.	Dam	Spitfires MIA	Cat E	KIA	MIA	WIA
54 Sqn	2	1	0	1	0	0	1	0
610 Sqn	0	0	0	0	1	0	0	0

In the evening fighter-bombers again attacked long-sufering Manston:

Unit	Dest	P.D.	Dam	Spitfires MIA	Cat E	KIA	MIA	WIA
65 Sqn	1	1	0	1	0	0	1	0

Unit	Dest	P.D.	Dam	Hurricanes MIA	Cat E	KIA	MIA	WIA
32 Sqn	0	0	1	0	0	0	0	0

This was followed by large *Luftwaffe Freijagds*, one RAF unit being engaged. A 610 Squadron pilot claimed a Bf109 destroyed, but one pilot was shot down, baling out wounded. During the late afternoon and early evening several reconnaissance aircraft were engaged by RAF fighters:-

Unit	Dest	P.D.	Dam	Spitfires MIA	Cat E	KIA	MIA	WIA
152 Sqn	2	0	1	0	0	0	0	0
610 Sqn	1	0	0	0	1	0	0	1

Unit	Dest	P.D.	Dam	Hurricanes MIA	Cat E	KIA	MIA	WIA
213 Sqn	1	0	0	0	0	0	0	0

22/23rd August 1940

Many bombers were over Britain during the night. One 1 Sqn Hurricane pilot, Sergeant H.J.Merchant, chased three enemy aircraft without success. He then wrote his aircraft off when he crash-landed near Maidstone out of fuel.

Unit	Dest	P.D.	Dam	Hurricanes MIA	Cat E	KIA	MIA	WIA
1 Sqn	0	0	0	0	1	0	0	0

23rd August 1940

Bad weather. A few reconnaissance aircraft were plotted and a few minor raids took place. An He111 was claimed destroyed by Hurricanes near Sumburgh and a Ju88 by Spitfires off Bournemouth.

				Spitfires				
Unit	Dest	P.D.	Dam	MIA	Cat E	KIA	MIA	WIA
152 Sqn	1	0	0	0	0	0	0	0

				Hurricanes				
Unit	Dest	P.D.	Dam	MIA	Cat E	KIA	MIA	WIA
232 Sqn	1	0	0	0	0	0	0	0

24th August 1940

For the first time the hitherto highly efficient British reporting system broke down, some seven small formations crossing the British coast in the early morning and roaming at will over southern England and East Anglia largely undetected. Only two units engaged near Ramsgate:

				Spitfires				
Unit	Dest	P.D.	Dam	MIA	Cat E	KIA	MIA	WIA
610 Sqn	2	0	0	0	1	0	0	1.

				Hurricanes				
Unit	Dest	P.D.	Dam	MIA	Cat E	KIA	MIA	WIA
85 Sqn	1	0	0	0	1	0	0	1

The airspace was reported clear by 09.00 hours, but shortly thereafter came radar indications of a new build-up, the first of a series of 'rolling wave' assaults that were to continue throughout the day, thus it is not possible to resolve them into individual attacks:

				Hurricanes				
Unit	Dest	P.D.	Dam	MIA	Cat E	KIA	MIA	WIA
32 Sqn	3	1	1	0	5	0	0	3
56 Sqn	4	0	1	0	0	0	0	0
111 Sqn	1	0	2	0	0	0	0	0
151 Sqn	1	3	3	0	1	0	0	1
501 Sqn	9	0	6	1	1	0	1	1
615 Sqn	3	1	0	0	0	0	0	0

				Defiants				
Unit	Dest	P.D.	Dam	MIA	Cat E	KIA	MIA	WIA
264 Sqn	7	0	4	3	1	0	6	2[1.]

1. Pilot wounded, gunner died of wounds.

				Spitfires				
Unit	Dest	P.D.	Dam	MIA	Cat E	KIA	MIA	WIA
19 Sqn	3	0	0	0	0	0	0	0
54 Sqn	5	1	1	0	1	0	0	0
65 Sqn	0	2	0	0	1	0	0	0
610 Sqn	6	2	0	0	2	0	0	2

To the west, a large radar plot appeared, dispersing into seven formations, six of which proved to be fighters. The bombers, Ju88s, attacked Portsmouth while the Bf109 escorts held the RAF interceptors away:

				Spitfires				
Unit	Dest	P.D.	Dam	MIA	Cat E	KIA	MIA	WIA
234 Sqn	2	1	1	0	1	0	0	0

				Hurricanes				
Unit	Dest	P.D.	Dam	MIA	Cat E	KIA	MIA	WIA
17 Sqn	1	0	0	0	0	0	0	0
249 Sqn	3	0	0	0	0	0	0	0

24/25th August 1940

An estimated 350 German bombers were over the British Isles, two fighter pilots reporting successful engagements. Pilot Officer J.R.D.Braham of 29 Squadron claimed an He111 probably destroyed near The Humber, while Flight Lieutenant J.G.Sanders of 615 claimed a Ju88 destroyed and an He111 damaged during a patrol off Hastings. A 73 Squadron Hurricane was shot down, believed by AA gunfire. The pilot baled out unhurt.

				Hurricanees				
Unit	Dest	P.D.	Dam	MIA	Cat E	KIA	MIA	WIA
73 Sqn	0	0	0	0	1	0	0	0
615 Sqn	1	0	1	0	0	0	0	0

				Blenheims				
Unit	Dest	P.D.	Dam	MIA	Cat E	KIA	MIA	WIA
29 Sqn	0	1	0	0	0	0	0	0

25th August 1940

Apart from lone raiders and reconnaissance aircraft, no *Luftwaffe* attacks were mounted until the afternoon, when co-ordinated raids began in both east and west. The western attackers were first plotted at 16.40 hours, 'one hundred-plus bandits' moving north from St.Malo and heading towards Weymouth. It was in truth around three hundred strong, Ju88s, Bf109s and Bf110s, the formation splitting to attack Portland and Warmwell. Seven squadrons were scrambled and again the fighting was prolonged and vicious:

| Hurricanes ||||||||
Unit	Dest	P.D.	Dam	MIA	Cat E	KIA	MIA	WIA
17 Sqn	7	5	0	1	1	0	1	0
87 Sqn	10	1	5	0	1	0	0	0
213 Sqn	7	0	1	2	0	0	2	0

| Spitfires ||||||||
Unit	Dest	P.D.	Dam	MIA	Cat E	KIA	MIA	WIA
152 Sqn	3	1	0	2	0	0	2	0
602 Sqn	11	0	0	0	2	0	0	0
609 Sqn	8	1	2	0	0	0	0	0

Meanwhile a further heavy raid had moved out across the Dover Straits, four units scrambling to engage, the enemy aircraft turning back without delivering any attacks:

| Spitfires ||||||||
Unit	Dest	P.D.	Dam	MIA	Cat E	KIA	MIA	WIA
54 Sqn	2	1	0	0	0	0	0	0
610 Sqn	1	0	0	0	0	0	0	0
616 Sqn	2	1	0	2	0	0	2	0

| Hurricanes ||||||||
Unit	Dest	P.D.	Dam	MIA	Cat E	KIA	MIA	WIA
32 Sqn	3	0	1	1	1	0	1	0

Other engagements against single aircraft resulted in Hurricane pilots claiming an Hs126 shot down off Dungeness, while a Do17 was claimed destroyed by Spitfire pilots.

| Spitfires ||||||||
Unit	Dest	P.D.	Dam	MIA	Cat E	KIA	MIA	WIA
92 Sqn	1	0	0	0	0	0	0	0

| Hurricanes ||||||||
Unit	Dest	P.D.	Dam	MIA	Cat E	KIA	MIA	WIA
32 Sqn	1	0	0	0	0	0	0	0

25/26th August 1940

Interceptions cost Fighter Command two aircraft. A 29 Squadron Blenheim is believed to have been shot down by return fire off Wainfleet, crew lost, while another of 604 Squadron crashed at Witheridge again with both crew perishing.

Blenheims								
Unit	Dest	P.D.	Dam	MIA	Cat E	KIA	MIA	WIA
29 Sqn	0	0	0	1	0	0	2	0
604 Sqn	0	0	0	0	1	2	0	0

26th August 1940

Shortly before midday a large formation of escorted Heinkels and Dorniers moved into British airspace, crossing the coast near Dover and heading for Biggin Hill. They were engaged by several fighter units between the coast and the Canterbury/Maidstone area:

Spitfires								
Unit	Dest	P.D.	Dam	MIA	Cat E	KIA	MIA	WIA
54 Sqn	2	2	0	0	0	0	0	0
610 Sqn	4	2	0	0	3	1	0	1
616 Sqn	1	0	0	0	7	2	0	4

Hurricanes								
Unit	Dest	P.D.	Dam	MIA	Cat E	KIA	MIA	WIA
56 Sqn	3	0	0	0	2	0	0	0

Defiants								
Unit	Dest	P.D.	Dam	MIA	Cat E	KIA	MIA	WIA
264 Sqn	7	0	1	0	3	0	0	2

Some hours later further raids were plotted coming in, passing east of the Kent coast and moving into the Thames estuary. These were escorted Dorniers, their targets being Debden and Hornchurch. Many units intercepted:

Spitfires								
Unit	Dest	P.D.	Dam	MIA	Cat E	KIA	MIA	WIA
65 Sqn	2	1	2	0	0	0	0	0

Hurricanes								
Unit	Dest	P.D.	Dam	MIA	Cat E	KIA	MIA	WIA
85 Sqn	8	1	3	0	1	0	0	0
111 Sqn	3	0	0	0	0	0	0	0
257 Sqn	0	0	0	0	1[1.]	0	0	0
310 Sqn	3	0	0	0	2	0	0	1
615 Sqn	4	1	2	0	3	0	0	1
1 (RCAF)	3	0	3	0	1	0	0	0

1. Bombed at Debden

Dornier Do17Z-3 (U5+GK) of 2./KG 2 shot down near Eastchurch on 26th August (Chris Goss)

Shortly afterwards came the next raid in the west, where fifty He111s struck at Portsmouth:

Spitfires								
Unit	Dest	P.D.	Dam	MIA	Cat E	KIA	MIA	WIA
234 Sqn	6	0	0	0	0	0	0	0
602 Sqn	5	0	1	0	1	0	0	0

Hurricanes								
Unit	Dest	P.D.	Dam	MIA	Cat E	KIA	MIA	WIA
43 Sqn	5	1	1	0	3	0	0	3
615 Sqn	0	0	2	0	1	0	0	1

There were two further engagements, Hurricanes finding Bf110s near Colchester claiming 2:1:0 (possibly stragglers from the earlier raid), while Spitfire pilots discovered an He59 off the Isle of Wight and destroyed it.

Spitfires								
Unit	Dest	P.D.	Dam	MIA	Cat E	KIA	MIA	WIA
602 Sqn	1	0	0	0	0	0	0	0

Hurricanes								
Unit	Dest	P.D.	Dam	MIA	Cat E	KIA	MIA	WIA
56 Sqn	2	1	0	0	0	0	0	0

26/27th August 1940

An He111 was attacked and claimed damaged by a 145 Squadron Hurricane pilot off Scotland, but another Hurricane, of 1 Squadron, was lost when Pilot Officer Chetham baled out having been held in, and blinded by, searchlights.

				Hurricanes				
Unit	Dest	P.D.	Dam	MIA	Cat E	KIA	MIA	WIA
1 Sqn	0	0	0	0	1	1	0	0
145 Sqn	0	0	1	0	0	0	0	0

27th August 1940

The return of bad weather brought only isolated bombers and reconnaissance aircraft. Hurricane pilots from 238 Squadron claimed a Do215 shot down as did others from 56 Squadron, who 'shared' it with a pilot from 501. A Bf110 'probable' was claimed by 17 Squadron. Lone He111s were encountered by Spitfires. One each was claimed destroyed by 610 and 152 Squadrons the latter unit losing a Spitfire to return fire, the pilot of which was safe.

				Spitfires				
Unit	Dest	P.D.	Dam	MIA	Cat E	KIA	MIA	WIA
152 Sqn	1	0	0	0	1	0	0	0
610 Sqn	1	0	0	0	0	0	0	0

				Hurricanes				
Unit	Dest	P.D.	Dam	MIA	Cat E	KIA	MIA	WIA
17 Sqn	0	1	0	0	0	0	0	0
56 Sqn	0.5	0	0	0	0	0	0	0
238 Sqn	1	0	0	0	0	0	0	0
501 Sqn	0.5	0	0	0	0	0	0	0

27/28th August 1940

Two fighters were lost on patrols, a Spitfire near Bristol and a Gladiator.

				Spitfires				
Unit	Dest	P.D.	Dam	MIA	Cat E	KIA	MIA	WIA
92 Sqn	0	0	0	0	1	0	0	0

				Gladiators				
Unit	Dest	P.D.	Dam	MIA	Cat E	KIA	MIA	WIA
247 Sqn	0	0	0	0	1	1	0	0

28th August 1940

Two *Luftwaffe* raids were sent in in the morning, Dorniers targeted to Eastchurch and Heinkels to Rochford. Several squadrons made contact:-

The Battle of the Airfields

				Hurricanes				
Unit	Dest	P.D.	Dam	MIA	Cat E	KIA	MIA	WIA
79 Sqn	0	4	1	0	0	0	0	0
501 Sqn	3	0	1	0	0	0	0	0
615 Sqn	1	1	0	0	1	0	0	1

				Defiants				
Unit	Dest	P.D.	Dam	MIA	Cat E	KIA	MIA	WIA
264 Sqn	1	0	2	0	3	5	0	1

A brief pause followed, during which 79 Squadron found two He59s in the middle of the Channel and attacked them:

				Hurricanes				
Unit	Dest	P.D.	Dam	MIA	Cat E	KIA	MIA	WIA
79 Sqn	1	1	0	0	0	0	0	0

Then the next raid came in, more Dorniers, again heading for Rochford. Several units engaged over Kent and the Thames estuary:

Combat Report

30th August 1940

While patrolling with squadron over North Weald enemy sighted on left at 1705 (approx.). Enemy aircraft in vic formation stepped up from 12,000 - 18,000 feet. Attacked middle section of '110s and two enemy a/c broke off to attack. Succeeded in getting behind one enemy and opened fire at approx 100 yds. Enemy a/c burst into flames and dived towards ground. Next attacked He111 formation and carried out beam attack on nearest one opening fire at approx 150 - 200 yds. Port engine stopped and a/c rolled over on back, finally starting to smoke then burst into flames and crashed to earth. Lastly was attacked by Me110 but succeeded in getting behind and followed him from 10,000 ft to 1,000 ft. Enemy a/c used very steep turns for evasive action but finally straightened out. I opened fire from approx 30 yards, enemy's starboard engine stopped and port engine burst into flame. Enemy crashed in flames alongside large reservoir. No return fire noticed from first two enemy but last machine used large amount. Weather hazy with no cloud. Took off at Duxford 1626 hrs, landed at 1735 hrs.

- P/O W.L.McKnight Red 2, 242 Squadron

Flying Officer William Lidstone McKnight DFC

'Willie' McKnight, a Canadian, joined the RAF in 1939 and was posted to No.615 Squadron when the Battle of France began. He soon moved to No.242 Squadron, principally composed of his countrymen. 242 Squadron returned to England in a bad way, having lost many pilots, most of its aircraft and all its equipment. It was given a new lease of life by the arrival of Squadron Leader D.R.S.Bader and soon formed part of Bader's controversial '12 Group Wing'. McKnight went back into action on 30th August 1940, adding three Bf110s to his tally of ten. He survived the battle, but was killed in action on 12th February 1941, shot down off Calais by a Bf109 of *JG 3* while on an early 'Rhubarb' operation.

19.5.40	Bf109	destroyed	14.6.40	Bf109	destroyed
28.5.40	Bf109	destroyed	14.6.40	Bf109	destroyed
29.5.40	Do17	destroyed	30.8.40	Bf110	destroyed
29.5.40	Bf109	destroyed	30.8.40	Bf110	destroyed
31.5.40	Bf110	destroyed	30.8.40	Bf110	destroyed
31.5.40	Bf110	destroyed	9.9.40	Bf109	destroyed
1.6.40	Ju87	destroyed	9.9.40	Bf109	destroyed
1.6.40	Ju87	destroyed	18.9.40	Ju88	destroyed*
1.6.40	Ju87	prob destroyed	18.9.40	Do17	destroyed
1.6.40	Ju87	prob destroyed	5.11.40	Bf109	destroyed*

Note: * indicates shared claim

Spitfires

Unit	Dest	P.D.	Dam	MIA	Cat E	KIA	MIA	WIA
54 Sqn	2	2	0	0	1[1]	0	0	0
603 Sqn	0	1	0	0	0	0	0	0

1. Believed shot down by Spitfire.

Hurricanes

Unit	Dest	P.D.	Dam	MIA	Cat E	KIA	MIA	WIA
1 Sqn	2	0	1	0	0	0	0	0
56 Sqn	3	3	1	0	1	0	0	0
615 Sqn	1	0	0	0	0	0	0	0

Further incursions in the evening proved to be fighter sweeps, with which several British units - perhaps unwisely - came to grips:

Spitfires								
Unit	Dest	P.D.	Dam	MIA	Cat E	KIA	MIA	WIA
54 Sqn	1	0	1	0	1	0	0	0
603 Sqn	3	2	2	2	1	0	2	0
610 Sqn	2	1	0	0	1	0	0	0

Hurricanes								
Unit	Dest	P.D.	Dam	MIA	Cat E	KIA	MIA	WIA
56 Sqn	2	0	0	0	2	0	0	1
85 Sqn	6	0	1	0	0	0	0	0
151 Sqn	0	1	0	0	1	0	0	1

29th August 1940

Apart from a single skirmish in the morning when 501 Squadron claimed a Bf110 damaged, the sky was clear until the mid-afternoon, when the first enemy plots began to build up over France. This coalesced into a huge number of *Luftwaffe* fighters covering a small group of bombers, which approached the British coastline between Hastings and Beachy Head. Squadrons already airborne were ordered to intercept. These were joined by others, until thirteen squadrons were airborne, engaging over the coast:

Spitfires								
Unit	Dest	P.D.	Dam	MIA	Cat E	KIA	MIA	WIA
603 Sqn	2	2	1	0	1	0	0	1
610 Sqn	1	4	3	0	2	1	0	0
616 Sqn	1	0	0	0	0	0	0	0

Hurricanes								
Unit	Dest	P.D.	Dam	MIA	Cat E	KIA	MIA	WIA
85 Sqn	3	1	0	0	2	0	0	1

This attack, plainly designed to lure British fighters before the guns of the six hundred or more German fighters present, was followed by a large *Freijagd*, which was again opposed:

Spitfires								
Unit	Dest	P.D.	Dam	MIA	Cat E	KIA	MIA	WIA
603 Sqn	2	2	0	0	1	0	0	0
610 Sqn	1	1	0	0	0	0	0	0

Wing Commander Alan Christopher Deere, OBE, DSO, DFC* DFC(US), CdeG

'Al' Deere arrived in the UK from New Zealand in 1937 and was posted to 54 Squadron in 1938. He was involved in the defence of Dunkirk in May and June 1940 and fought throughout the Battle of Britain. On 28th August he fell victim to a Spitfire pilot, believed to have been from 603 Squadron and, on 31st August, was leading a section of three Spitfires down the Hornchurch runway when the airfield came under attack. The two other Spitfires were blown off the runway and Deere's aircraft was blown onto its back, skidding down the runway at 100 mph. Deere, survivor of many mishaps, walked away from the wreckage, as did the other two pilots.

In 1941 Deere moved to 602 Squadron first as a flight commander and then CO until 1942 when, after a trip to the USA, he returned to take command of 403 (RCAF) Squadron. In August he took up a staff posting, but returned to operations in 1943, first with 611 Squadron and then becoming Biggin Hill Wing Leader. He later commanded the CGS Fighter Wing and subsequently led 145 (Free French) Wing.

He remained in the RAF after the war and retired in 1967 as an Air Commodore. He has recently died.

Victory List

Date	Aircraft	Result	Date	Aircraft	Result
23.5.40	Bf109	destroyed	15.8.40	Bf109	damaged
	Bf109	destroyed		Bf109	destroyed
	Bf109	unconfirmed		Bf109	prob destroyed
24.5.40	Bf109	destroyed	28.8.40	Bf109	prob destroyed
25.5.40	Bf110	destroyed	30.8.40	Do17	prob destroyed
26.5.40	Bf110	destroyed	1.8.41	Bf109	destroyed
	Bf110	destroyed	9.8.41	Bf109	damaged
27.5.40	Ju88	destroyed		Bf109	damaged
	Ju88	destroyed*		Bf109	damaged
28.5.40	Do17	damaged*	13.10.41	Bf109	damaged
17.6.40	Ju88	unconfirmed*	18.11.41	Bf109	damaged
9.7.40	Bf109	destroyed	16.2.43	FW190	destroyed
	Bf109	unconfirmed	4.5.43	FW190	destroyed
24.7.40	Bf109	destroyed	10.6.43	FW190	damaged
12.8.40	Bf109	destroyed	23.6.43	FW190	destroyed
	Bf110	destroyed	14.7.43	FW190	prob destroyed
15.8.40	Bf109	destroyed			

Note: * indicates shared claim.

			Hurricanes				
Unit	Dest	P.D.	Dam	MIA	Cat E	KIA	MIA	WIA
85 Sqn	1	0	0	0	1	0	0	0
501 Sqn	2	0	0	0	2	0	0	1

29/30th August 1940

A confirmed success was achieved when Flying Officer Alan Wright of 92 Squadron claimed an He111 destroyed near Bristol.

			Spitfires				
Unit	Dest	P.D.	Dam	MIA	Cat E	KIA	MIA	WIA
92 Sqn	1	0	0	0	0	0	0	0

30th August 1940

The 30th was to see the steady escalation of *Luftwaffe* attacks emerge into a day-long running battle, during which the Germans, by sending wave after wave of bombers into the skies over southeast England, sought to exhaust the British forces. Although, for reasons of space, it is not possible to chronicle each wave, the attacks can be said to have covered two separate periods (a) mid-morning to shortly after noon (b) mid-afternoon to evening. Engagements during the first phase resulted in:

			Spitfires				
Unit	Dest	P.D.	Dam	MIA	Cat E	KIA	MIA	WIA
222 Sqn	0	0	0	0	1	0	0	0
603 Sqn	0	1	1	0	1	0	0	0
616 Sqn	1	0	0	0	1	0	0	0

			Hurricanes				
Unit	Dest	P.D.	Dam	MIA	Cat E	KIA	MIA	WIA
43 Sqn	0	1	0	0	1	1	0	0
79 Sqn	5	1	1	0	1	0	0	0
85 Sqn	8	2	4	0	1	0	0	0
253 Sqn	4	6	1	0	3	2	0	1
501 Sqn	2	1	1	0	0	0	0	0
601 Sqn	5	2	0	0	0	0	0	0

The afternoon attacks over the southeast brought claims and losses of:

			Spitfires				
Unit	Dest	P.D.	Dam	MIA	Cat E	KIA	MIA	WIA
54 Sqn	2	1	0	0	0	0	0	0

The Fighter Command War Diaries

Unit	Dest	P.D.	Dam	MIA	Cat E	KIA	MIA	WIA
66 Sqn	1	0	0	0	1	0	0	0
222 Sqn	1	2	1	0	5	1	0	2
603 Sqn	2	1	0	0	1	0	0	0
610 Sqn	1	0	0	0	0	0	0	0
616 Sqn	2	2	2	0	0	0	0	0

Hurricanes

Unit	Dest	P.D.	Dam	MIA	Cat E	KIA	MIA	WIA
1 Sqn	1	1	6	0	0	0	0	0
32 Sqn	0	0	0	0	1[1]	0	0	0
43 Sqn	0	0	1	0	1	0	0	1[2]
56 Sqn	4	1	1	0	2	0	0	1
79 Sqn	0	2	1	0	0	0	0	0
111 Sqn	0	0	3	0	0	0	0	0
151 Sqn	1	2	0	0	1	0	0	0
242 Sqn	13	1	1	0	0	0	0	0
253 Sqn	1	0	0	0	1	0	0	0
303 Sqn	1	0	0	0	0	0	0	0
501 Sqn	2	0	2	0	0	0	0	0
601 Sqn	1	0	0	0	0	0	0	0

1. Destroyed in raid.
2. Pilot died of wounds

Despite the efforts of British fighter pilots, a large group of He111s passed undetected through the defences and flew north to bomb the Vauxhall works at Luton, which was heavily damaged.

31st August 1940

The day's operations by the *Luftwaffe* maintained the dreadful pressure upon Fighter Command's pilots to an almost unbearable degree. Rolling wave attacks took place from the early morning until dusk, with no respite at all. Among the targets attacked were North Weald, Duxford, Debden, Eastchurch, Croydon, Biggin Hill (twice) and Hornchurch. The many interceptions again produced bitter combats:

Spitfires

Unit	Dest	P.D.	Dam	MIA	Cat E	KIA	MIA	WIA
19 Sqn	2	0	0	0	3	1	0	1
54 Sqn	2	2	0	0	3[1]	0	0	1
66 Sqn	1	0	0	0	0	0	0	0
72 Sqn	0	0	4	0	2	1	0	1

The Battle of the Airfields

Unit	Dest	P.D.	Dam	MIA	Cat E	KIA	MIA	WIA
222 Sqn	4	3	3	0	1	0	0	1
602 Sqn	2	2	0	0	0	0	0	0
603 Sqn	12	1	0	0	2	1	0	1
616 Sqn	1	0	0	0	0	0	0	0

1. Bombed on take-off from Hornchurch.

Hurricanes

Unit	Dest	P.D.	Dam	MIA	Cat E	KIA	MIA	WIA
1 Sqn	1	3	5	0	1	0	0	0
17 Sqn	2	1	0	0	0	0	0	0
56 Sqn	1	0	0	1	3	0	1	2
79 Sqn	6	5	4	0	4	1	0	3
85 Sqn	9	6	5	0	2	0	0	2
111 Sqn	2	3	3	0	1	0	0	1
151 Sqn	3	3	6	0	2 [3][1]	0	0	2
253 Sqn	1	1	1	0	2	1	0	1
257 Sqn	5	0	2	0	2	1	0	1
303 Sqn	6	0	0	0	0	0	0	0
310 Sqn	6	0	0	0	2	1	0	0
501 Sqn	6	0	2	0	1	0	0	1
601 Sqn	6	4	4	1	3	0	0	2
1 (RCAF)	3	0	2	0	4	0	0	3

1. Bracket figure indicates total Cat E losses as shown in AIR16/960.

A Ju88 being bombed-up before a sortie (S.Parry)

Summary - August 1940

Air Combat Claims:
>1,006 : 416 : 425

Missing/destroyed aircraft:
>113 Spitfires, 213 [214] Hurricanes,
>10 Defiants, 11 Blenheims and 1 Gladiator
>130 aircrew killed or missing and 100
>wounded, of which 7 subsequently died.

Notes:

247 Sqn	formed at Roborough with Gladiator IIs on 1st, ex-Sumburgh Fighter Flight.
306 Sqn	formed at Church Fenton with Hurricane Is.
312 Sqn	formed at Duxford with Hurricane Is.
611 Sqn	replaced Spitfire Is with Spitfire IIAs.

By late August fighter pilot casualties within Fighter Command were forcing new, barely trained, pilots into the squadrons to face Luftwaffe-veterans. Many were lost without ever seeing the '109 that killed them. Here fledgling pilots are introduced to the Spitfire at an Operational Training Unit.

(C.Ellis)

September 1940

1st September 1940

The first incoming raid was plotted coming across the Dover Straits in the mid-morning, crossing in at Dover and heading north. It split into several smaller formations, Heinkels and Dorniers with massive fighter escorts heading for Biggin Hill, Detling, Eastchurch and the London Docks. Although many RAF squadrons had been scrambled, few succeeded in getting through to the bombers:

Spitfires

Unit	Dest	P.D.	Dam	MIA	Cat E	KIA	MIA	WIA
54 Sqn	1	0	0	0	0	0	0	0
72 Sqn	2	1	0	0	2	1	0	1
222 Sqn	3	0	0	0	0	0	0	0
616 Sqn	1	3	6	0	0	0	0	0

Hurricanes

Unit	Dest	P.D.	Dam	MIA	Cat E	KIA	MIA	WIA
1 Sqn	4	0	0	0	1	0	0	0
85 Sqn	2	0	0	0	0	0	0	0

The fighter squadrons had but a brief respite until the early morning, when nearly 200 *Luftwaffe* aircraft crossed in over Kent, Biggin Hill again being one of the primary objectives:

Spitfires

Unit	Dest	P.D.	Dam	MIA	Cat E	KIA	MIA	WIA
54 Sqn	1	1	0	0	0	0	0	0
72 Sqn	2	2	4	0	0	0	0	0
603 Sqn	1	0	0	0	1	0	0	0
616 sqn	3	1	1	0	0	0	0	0

Hurricanes

Unit	Dest	P.D.	Dam	MIA	Cat E	KIA	MIA	WIA
79 Sqn	1	1	3	0	1	0	0	1
85 Sqn	5	0	1	1	3	1	1	2[1].
253 Sqn	0	1	3	0	1	0	0	0
501 Sqn	0	0	1	0	0	0	0	0
1 (RCAF)	1	0	4	0	2	0	0	1

1. One pilot died of wounds

A further raid in the early evening was believed to be composed solely of fighters and was not opposed. However a small group of Do17s sneaked through and hit Biggin Hill again.

2nd September 1940

(See inset) Total claims and casualties:-

Spitfires

Unit	Dest	P.D.	Dam	MIA	Cat E	KIA	MIA	WIA
54 Sqn	4	2	3	0	0	0	0	0
66 Sqn	1	0	0	0	0	0	0	0
72 Sqn	1	0	5	0	3	1	0	0
222 Sqn	1	1	2	0	0	0	0	0
603 Sqn	6	2	3	0	1	0	0	1
616 Sqn	2	0	0	0	1	0	0	0

Hurricanes

Unit	Dest	P.D.	Dam	MIA	Cat E	KIA	MIA	WIA
1 Sqn	0	1	1	0	0	0	0	0
43 Sqn	2	1	0	0	3	1	0	2
46 Sqn	2	2	3	0	1	0	0	0
111 Sqn	1	3	5	1	0	0	1	0
151 Sqn	1	2	0	0	0	0	0	0
249 Sqn	4	2	5	0	1	0	0	1
253 Sqn	0	0	1	0	2	0	0	2
257 Sqn	0	1	0	0	0	0	0	0
303 Sqn	2	1	1	0	0	0	0	0
501 Sqn	6	0	5	1	0	0	1	0

2nd September 1940
The Morning Raids.

Signs that the Germans were preparing for a strong attack were evident as early as 0715, and by 0730 two medium sized forces were over the middle of the Dover Straits, while a third was plotted off the North Foreland. They showed no sign of moving inland, but between 0725 and 0745 hours 249, 253, 603, 501, 54 and 72 Squadrons were scrambled to patrol the south coast, Maidstone and the Thames estuary. Five more units were ordered off to patrol airfields in the 11 Group area, but these latter were not subsequently engaged.

It was not until 0740 that the German forces crossed the coastline, the two southernmost formations coming in between Dover and Folkestone, and the third further north. All were heading towards Gravesend/Chatham, but due to the cloud and overcast, no precise details could be obtained from Observer Corps positions.

253 Squadron, patrolling north of Dover, were the first to engage. A formation of 20-30 bombers were sighted at 17,000 feet some ten miles south of the North Foreland, with a similar number of fighter escorts, and the squadron turned north, diving from 20,000 feet to attack. The Bf109 escorts - from *JG 51* - defended their charges successfully however, and a single claim for a Bf109 damaged was submitted. Sergeant J.Metham was shot down over Thanet, but escaped slightly injured.

This German force then continued to fly along the estuary, but were heavily engaged by A.A. gunsites at Chatham, and were forced to turn inland.

The A.A. fire had alerted the nine Spitfires of 54 Squadron, who at once attacked, but again the Bf109s held the RAF at bay. No casualties were sustained by this squadron, and Messerschmitts were claimed destroyed by Squadron Leader Leathart and Pilot Officer Gray, while Flying Officer Gribble and Pilot Officer McMullen each reported a 'probable' and Sergeant Robbins a 'damaged' before the Spitfires withdrew. It is believed that this force was responsible for attacking Rochester at 08.10 hours, but no industrial damage was done.

Meanwhile, the second German force - 20 Do17s with escorts of Bf109s and '110s - had crossed the coast at Folkestone, and was tracking northward across Kent towards the Thames. Interceptions were effected by 74, 249 and 501 Squadrons, which fought independently and engaged the enemy formation as far as the target area. 72 Squadron attacked north of Maidstone, and claimed five destroyed without loss, but the Hurricane squadrons fared less well due to the agressive escorts. 501 Squadron, intercepting over North Kent, claimed four Bf109s destroyed, a "probable' and a 'damaged'. One Dornier was claimed shot down and two 'damaged', but 501 suffered two casualties; Pilot Officer Skalski force-landed at Sellinge, whilst Sergeant Henn returned to base with a damaged aircraft, both pilots sustaining injuries.

249 Squadron engaged over Rochester, but claimed only one confirmed success when Flight Lieutenant Barton and Pilot Officer Meaker joined forces to despatch a Dornier, the latter pilot firing on another and claiming it damaged. Squadron Leader Grandy also reported hits on a Do17 in this encounter. Pilot Officer Burton claimed another Dornier probably destroyed, but was himself shot down by a Bf110 of *II./ZG 26* and crash-landed at Meopham unhurt.

The Fighter Command War Diaries

Pilot Officer Beazley, after attacking one of the big Messerschmitts and claiming it probably destroyed, was attacked in his turn, and baled out unhurt. Flight Lieutenant Parnall also attacked one of the '110s, claiming it damaged. The squadron sustained one casualty when the Hurricane flown by Pilot Officer Wynn was attacked by another Bf110, which severely the damaged the Hurricane and wounded the pilot.

It is clear that many of the Dorniers jettisoned their loads during the initial interceptions, for many bombs fell near Canterbury and Maidstone, but the attacks upon Gravesend airfield and Chatham were carried out nonetheless - albeit without significant damage.

As the force retired to the south, 603 Squadron engaged them near Canterbury, but again the actions were fought against the escorts.

Three Bf109s were claimed destroyed, and a Bf110 damaged, in exchange for damage to Sergeant Stokoe's Spitfire over Hawkinge.

While Fighter Command's attention was drawn to the main threats over Kent, the Germans launched a surprise attack upon Lympne shortly after 08.30 hours. Thirty bombs fell, but the attack was not concentrated, and most fell outside the airfield, which remained serviceable.

The Afternoon Raids

For three hours, there was peace, then at 12.00 hours a build-up of enemy forces was plotted over the Dover Straits. This force moved inland at 12.20 hours, crossing in at Hythe and making towards Ashford. Ten minutes later more than a hundred aircraft crossed in at Dover, making for Chatham, and simultaneously forty more approached the Thames estuary over the North Foreland, apparently heading for the Essex coast. Meanwhile, between 12.05 and 12.30 hours, eleven fighter squadrons were scrambled, six to patrol the sector stations north of the estuary while the remainder were ordered south to patrol Maidstone-Chatham-Rochford. This was followed by the despatch of six more squadrons bewteen 12.40 and 13.00 hours, by which time the northernmost enemy formation was near the Isle of Sheppey. Four squadrons remained on local airfield defence duties, but 501 and 43 Squadrons were ordered to fly towards Maidstone.

First to engage was 72 Squadron, which met 30 Dorniers with escorting fighters near Herne Bay - apparently the right wing of the formation that had flown in over Hythe. The Spitfires attacked in a steep dive, and the pilots claimed three Do17s and two Bf110s shot down. A further Bf110 was claimed as a 'probable' and one more damaged, but a third of the defending unit were shot down by the escorts. Sergeant Norfolk crashed near Bekesbourne without injury, and the Spitfires flown by Pilot Officer Douthwaite and Squadron Leader Collins were badly shot about, the latter pilot sustaining wounds. The squadron became badly dispersed during this initial engagement, and the German bomber formation maintained its course toward its target; Eastchurch. Shortly thereafter, 603 Squadron engaged this same force near Chatham, where two Bf109s and a Do17 were claimed destroyed, with one more of each type damaged. Pilot Officer Haig's aircraft was hit, and he was obliged to belly-land without injury.

Meanwhile, 111 and 46 Squadrons had made rendezvous over Rochford, and were ordered south. Twenty He111s were sighted over the estuary, escorted by Bf109s and with Bf110s (the latter at first hidden by cloud). Strangely enough, only 111 Squadron were able to engage. The Germans were heading west, and one section charged the bombers head-on, while the rest were engaged by the escorts. Flight Lieutenant Bruce claimed a Heinkel destroyed, Flying Officer Bowring claimed a 'probable', while Pilot Officers Ritchie and Brown jointly claimed another. Pilot Officer Simpson reported hits on a fourth. The remainder of the Hurricanes became embroiled with the escorts. Sergeant Hampshire claimed a Bf110 probably destroyed, whilst Flying Officer Bowring and Flight Lieutenant Bruce reported damage to others, and Pilot Officer Brown claimed a Bf109 damaged. The price was fairly high, for Sergeant Dymond was shot down by a Bf109 and failed to return. The aircraft flown by Pilot Officers Ritchie, Simpson and Flight Lieutenant Giddings all sustained battle damage.

By 1305 hours, the two German formations had escaped their opponents, and the way was clear to their targets. The first formation, from the south, bombed Eastchurch at 13.10 hours, causing great devastation and wrecking five aircraft. The formation that had so recently evaded 111 Squadron attacked Detling five minutes later - catching Flight Lieutenant Giddings of 111 Squadron who had just force-landed - and making the base unserviceable for three hours. Then the bombers headed for home. The Detling force apparently retraced their path along the estuary, while those bombing Eastchurch made their way south, towards Dungeness. Some of these were intercepted by 43 Squadron between Maidstone and the coast. Flight Lieutenant Reynell and Sergeant Jeffrey each claimed a Bf109 destroyed, the latter also claiming another damaged, but the unit sustained three losses. Pilot Officer Woods-Scawen baled out near Ivychurch, too low for his parachute to open, and was killed, Flying Officer Carswell baled out injured near Ashford, and Pilot Officer Du Vivier crash-landed wounded at Old Romney.

In the meantime, another force had crossed the coastline at Hythe at 13.10 hours, probably withdrawal cover for the Eastchurch attackers. This force was not engaged, neither was the force reported earlier off the North Foreland, since these aircraft remained off the coast, and reached as far as Foulness Island.

The Evening Raids

It was 15.45 hours before the next indications of German activity were received, and by 16.00 hours it was clear that a large attack was imminent. Between 15.55 and 16.15 hours, seven squadrons were scrambled, with orders either to patrol fighter bases or to proceed to Canterbury, Maidstone and Dungeness.

Three separate raids were plotted, coming in over the coast at Dungeness, Deal and the North Foreland. It was again 72 Squadron, patrolling over the former area, that first made contact. A formation of Do17s, escorted by Bf110s and Bf109s, were sighted some miles out into the Channel. The Spitfires formed line astern and dived on the Bf110s, claiming a Bf110 probably destroyed and two more damaged. Flight Lieutenant Graham was shot down near Lympne, and Wing Commander Lees crashed at Hawkinge with battle damage. Graham was unhurt, but Lees was wounded. The pilots reported that the enemy formation turned to starboard and headed for France, and indeed, some may have done so, but the main formation tracked northwards, passing Biggin Hill and Hornchurch and feinting towards North Weald before turning back to bomb Hornchurch. No interceptions were made against this force until it reached the target area, where 603 Squadron were patrolling. They were at 23,000 feet when a solid formation of about fifty bombers, escorted by a similar number of fighters were sighted, The Spitfires dived, but were held at bay by the fighters, and no successes were claimed or losses suffered. The bombing, although heavy, was inaccurate, and only six bombs hit the airfield, causing no serious damage. This force then retired. Some fled across Essex and out over the estuary, where 54 Squadron engaged them. Pilot Officer McMullen claimed a Do17 destroyed and Pilot Officer Edsall and Sgt Robbins reported hits on two more, the latter pilot also engaging a Bf109 and claiming this destroyed. No losses were sustained by the Spitfire unit.

The majority of this force headed south towards Maidstone, and at least three squadrons engaged before the *Luftwaffe* finally recrossed the British coastline. 616 Squadron intercepted near Maidstone, claiming a Dornier and a Bf110 destroyed, with another Bf110 damaged. One Spitfire was lost when Flight Lieutenant Gillam was shot down by one of the twin-engined fighters. He baled out near Capel. 501 Squadron entered the fray slightly further south, and fought the formation from Ashford to Dungeness, claiming a Bf109 destroyed, another damaged, and a Do17 damaged. Two Hurricanes were shot down. Sergeant Adams crash-landed after the initial pass, but Flying Officer Rose-Price failed to return from combat off Dungeness. Another engagement took place off Dungeness at around this time when 1 Squadron entered the fray, but reported engagements only with Bf109 escorts. Flight Lieutenant Hillcoat and Sergeant Chetham reported a 'probable' and a 'damaged' respectively.

The movements of the German force entering British airspace near Deal are uncertain, but it is believed that these aircraft were engaged near Manston by 151 Squadron. Flying Officer Blair claimed an He111 shot down, Pilot Officer Surma reported a 'probable' and Pilot Officer Pattulo a Dornier 'probable' for no loss. A number of places in North Kent were bombed, including the Short Works at Rochester. It is believed that these bombers also dropped bombs upon Maidstone and Ashford as they withdrew to the south.

The only interception against the most northerly German force was effected by 249 Squadron. Again the *Luftwaffe* escorts prevented the defenders from closing with the bombers - twelve in number - which slipped through and delivered another accurate attack upon already damaged Eastchurch. The Hurricane pilots claimed three Bf110s destroyed - by Flight Lieutenant Parnall, Pilot Officer Meaker and Sgt Davidson. Two more were reported damaged by Parnall and Pilot Officer Barclay. No losses were sustained.

While the engagements above were taking place, a patrol of three Spitfires from 66 Squadron patrolled near Smith's Knoll, where an He111 was engaged. It was claimed destroyed by Pilot Officers Bodie, Mildren and Sgt Hunt.

These *Luftwaffe* forces had barely cleared the British coastine when a further force of 'twenty plus' emerged from the Straits and headed for the North Foreland. At the same time several smaller forces crossed the Kent coast, but almost immediately turned back, one bombing the inner harbour at Folkestone at 1735 hours.

Several British squadrons were still in the air after the attacks above. 46 Squadron was patrolling between North Weald and the Thames, and 72 Squadron near Dover. Between 17.20 and 17.25 hours, 303 Squadron left Northolt to intercept over Chatham, 257 Squadron to East Mersea, and 85 Squadron, patrolled an unknown area. Four squadrons were ordered to intercept the German force. 72 Squadron made the first contact after sighting AA fire, which drew the pilots' attention to some fifty Do17s, with Bf109 and 110 escorts. Squadron Leader Collins, despite having been slightly wounded in combat earlier in day, led his Spitfires into a diving stern attack from the sun, but were unable to reach the bombers. One Bf109 was claimed as destroyed and two more damaged. The aircraft flown by Squadron Leader Collins was hit, and he was wounded for the second time. Despite this, he returned to base where the aircraft was classified as a 'write-off'.

Shortly thereafter, 46 Squadron came into action over Sheppey, where two Bf109s were claimed destroyed, one probably so, and two more damaged. Although the Hurricanes managed to penetrate the fighter screen and fire on the bombers - claiming two damaged - they were unable to prevent the German aircraft from reaching their target (Eastchurch) and sustained two aircraft casulties; Pilot Officer Bailey was shot down over the estuary and killed, while Flight Lieutenant Rabagliati force-landed near Sittingbourne, his fighter severely damaged.

Several squadrons engaged the retreating Germans, although it is doubtful whether all the engagements were made against this particular formation. 257 Squadron intercepted a Bf109 formation near Ramsgate, but delayed attacking in the belief that they were RAF aircraft. When they were identified as German an attack was delivered, and Sergeant Nutter reported one probably destroyed. 603 Squadron were engaged over Maidstone; a Bf109 and a Bf110 were claimed as 'probables', but Sergeant Stokoe's Spitfire was hit, and he baled out wounded. 222 Squadron would appear to have been involved against the Eastchurch formation when at 17.45 hours the unit entered combat between Maidstone and Gravesend. Flight Lieutenant Robinson claimed a Bf109 shot down, while Sergeant Baxter reported a Bf110 'probable' and hits on another and a Do17. Robinson's aircraft was hit during a head-on attack and he force-landed wounded at Hornchurch. A further two Spitfires received minor damage.

> 303 Squadron had been ordered to patrol Dover, but were bounced by '109s at 19,000 feet. Sergeant Rogowski saw them coming and turned into the attack, claiming one destroyed. Sergeant Frantisek claimed a second shot down. Flying Officer Henneberg, Pilot Officer Feric and Sergeants Rogowski and Frantisek chased the '109s back across the French coast, but disengaged due to intense *Flak* after Feric and Henneberg had claimed a 'probable' and a 'damaged' respectively. Feric subsequently force-landed due to battle damage.

3rd September 1940

An early morning 'feint' by *Luftwaffe* fighter units drew British fighter units away from the main attack on North Weald by Dorniers, who succeeded in heavily damaging the airfield. They were then hotly engaged by RAF units who had arrived too late to prevent the attack:

Spitfires

Unit	Dest	P.D.	Dam	MIA	Cat E	KIA	MIA	WIA
19 Sqn	2	1	0	0	0	0	0	0
54 Sqn	2	3	0	0	0	0	0	0
222 Sqn	5	2	3	0	0 [2]	0	0	0
603 Sqn	3	0	0	0	2	0	0	2

Hurricanes

Unit	Dest	P.D.	Dam	MIA	Cat E	KIA	MIA	WIA
1 Sqn	0	0	0	1	1	0	0	0
17 Sqn	5	2	0	0	1	0	0	1
46 Sqn	2	0	6	1	2	0	1	2
257 Sqn	0	1	1	0	2	1	0	1
302 Sqn	0	0	0	0	0 [1]	0	0	0
310 Sqn	7	1	0	0	1	0	0	0
501 Sqn	0	0	1	0	0	0	0	0
601 Sqn	0	0	1	0	0	0	0	0

Blenheims

Unit	Dest	P.D.	Dam	MIA	Cat E	KIA	MIA	WIA
25 Sqn	0	0	0	0	1	1	0	0

Shot down by Hurricane, pilot killed, gunner safe.

Later patrols over the Channel met German fighters:

Spitfires

Unit	Dest	P.D.	Dam	MIA	Cat E	KIA	MIA	WIA
222 Sqn	1	0	0	0	0	0	0	0

Hurricanes

Unit	Dest	P.D.	Dam	MIA	Cat E	KIA	MIA	WIA
303 Sqn	1	0	0	0	0	0	0	0

3/4th September 1940

A bomber was claimed damaged by a Hurricane pilot near Wells.

Hurricanes

Unit	Dest	P.D.	Dam	MIA	Cat E	KIA	MIA	WIA
87 Sqn	0	0	1	0	0	0	0	0

4th September 1940

Early sweeps by Bf109s across the south coast and over east Kent drew fighters into unnecessary engagements:

Spitfires

Unit	Dest	P.D.	Dam	MIA	Cat E	KIA	MIA	WIA
19 Sqn	0	1	0	0	0	0	0	0
66 Sqn	1	1	0	0	2	0	0	21.

1. One pilot died of wounds.

Hurricanes

Unit	Dest	P.D.	Dam	MIA	Cat E	KIA	MIA	WIA
111 Sqn	5	0	4	2	0	0	2	0
253 Sqn	0	0	0	0	1	0	0	0

In the early afternoon '250-plus bandits' crossed the south coast to attack Canterbury, Reigate, Redhill, Eastchurch and Faversham, while a small formation aircraft fsuccessfully bombed the Vickers Works at Brooklands:

Spitfires

Unit	Dest	P.D.	Dam	MIA	Cat E	KIA	MIA	WIA
66 Sqn	1	5	0	0	1	0	0	1
72 Sqn	7	1	2	0	2	0	0	0
152 Sqn	0	0	0	1	0	0	1	0
222 Sqn	2	3	1	0	2	1	0	1
234 Sqn	15	0	6	0	0	0	0	0
602 Sqn	4	1	2	0	0	0	0	0

4th September 1940 - The Brooklands Raid

Since the battle had begun, the big Messerschmitt Bf110 two-seat, twin-engined fighter had not proved as successful as it had in France. Like virtually all day fighters of this configuration, it had shown itself to be less manoeuvreable than opposing single-engined fighters. Its armament was concentrated and heavy, yet to deliver decisive attacks it had to be able to stay with its opponent. Since the convoy battles of early August the Bf110 crews had developed the defensive circle, where each fighter covered the tail of the aircraft in front. There would in theory be no 'tail-ender' to be picked off by a Hurricane or Spitfire. The only unit to have gained real success was the crack *Erprobungsgruppe 210*, equipped with both the Bf109 and the '110, operating in the low-level fighter-bomber rôle. On 4th September 1940, this unit was briefed to attack the Vickers and Hawker aircraft factories at Brooklands, near Weybridge, in Surrey.

The first indications of forthcoming raids came at 08.30 hours, when 'twenty-plus bandits' were reported assembling south of Griz Nez, soon to be joined by more formations plotted near Calais and Crecy. 111 Squadron, already airborne, were the first RAF fighters to engage. They met Do17s escorted by Bf109s of *I.* and *II./JG 2 'Richthofen'* and *I.* and *III./JG 54 'Grünherz'* to the southeast of Dungeness. The RAF claimed five and three damaged for the loss of two Hurricanes with two more damaged. The Germans reported nine kills, lost three from *II./JG 2* and *I./JG 54*, and swept on northwards towards Tunbridge Wells. Meanwhile the Spitfires of 66 Squadron met other Bf109 sweeps approaching the Thames estuary near Ramsgate and claimed one and a 'probable', but lost three aircraft. One pilot force-landed slightly wounded while the other two baled out both wounded. Sergeant A.D.Smith later succumbed to his injuries.

This raid caused slight damage to RAF Bradwell Bay and several other places in south Essex.

The Gravesend attack

There were smaller plots reported during the later part of the morning, but no interceptions resulted. Thus it was not until shortly after noon that further radar plots indicated that more raids were afoot, particularly one of '100-plus' over Norrent-Fontes, another of '50-plus' heading out across the Channel from Boulogne and two smaller plots near Calais.

Six Spitfire and five Hurricane squadrons were scrambled at 12.30 hours, being deployed in a defensive line along the south coast and further north to protect their airfields. As these units began to reach their designated patrol lines, a fifth *Luftwaffe* formation was plotted a few miles south of Dungeness. The latter proved to be He111s with a fifty-strong Bf109 escort, which crossed in near Hastings. The Spitfires from 66 Squadron caught them near Tunbridge Wells, but the '109s, believed to have been from *JG 51*, held them off as the bombers tracked northward to be again engaged, this time by 222 Squadron Spitfire pilots before the target at Gravesend was bombed. Hurricanes from 46 Squadron had also scrambled, but made no claims. They sustained four casualties; Flying Officer Plummer and Pilot Officer Ambrose baled out, Plummer, severely wounded, died ten days later. Pilot Officer Barber crash-landed at Heybridge, wounded, while Flying Officer Austin crashed landing at Stapleford. In total, pilots from *I.* and *III./JG 51* and *I./JG 77* claimed fifteen Spitfires destroyed and actually shot down ten RAF fighters - three each from the two Spitfire units plus four Hurricanes. The British pilots claimed three '109s shot down, eight probables and a 'damaged'. They actually shot down one machine of *I./JG 77* that went into the sea, from which the pilot was rescued, and damaged a fighter from *I./JG 51*. It is believed that the reported 'Heinkels' were actually Ju88s from *I./LG 1*, one of which returned to Dinard where it was belly-landed.

The Diversion

Meanwhile the larger force was heading west along the Channel, composed of Bf110s from *ZG 2*, *ZG 76*, *V./LG 1* and *E.Gr.210*. Near Hastings the *II./ZG 76* aircraft swung away towards the coast, heading north. These were a diversion for the main attack and, between Tenterden and Tunbridge Wells, were engaged by nine Spitfires from 72 Squadron that had been scrambled at 12.55 hours. As the three 'vics' of Spitfires engaged, the Bf110s turned into their defensive circle but, before the circle had closed, the leading '110 came under attack from Red Section; Flying Officer Elsdon and Pilot Officer Holland forcing this aircraft out of formation with one engine smoking. Holland had attacked it head-on, closing until he almost collided before breaking away. Flying Officer 'Pancho' Villa, leading Yellow Section, came under attack, broke hard away, and then saw a detached '110 which he attacked until it caught fire and began to go down. Blue Section, acting as cover, then joined the fray. Pilot Officer Elliot and Sergeant Gilders attacked another Messerschmitt, Elliot seeing a large piece of wing break away and one engine burst in flames. M8+CP went down and crashed near Cowden, killing

Oberleutnant Günther Piduhn and his gunner *Unteroffizier* Rudolf Condé. Sergeant Bill Rolls and Flying Officer Desmond Sheen attacked another, a tail-ender curiously identified by Rolls as a 'Ju86', Rolls chasing this machine down to ground level, where *Leutnant* Hermann Weeber crash-landed M8+AC on the lawn of Little Butts Farm, Causley Wood. His gunner, *Unteroffizier* Max Michael was badly wounded. Villa and Elsdon, high above, saw four Bf110s heading for the coast and chased one over Bexhill, finally shooting M8+JM down into the sea twenty miles off the coast. *Oberleutnant* Ernst Hartmann von Schlotheim and *Unteroffizier* Georg Hommel were picked up by the British Air-Sea Rescue Service and captured unhurt. In total, 72 Squadron pilots were credited with seven 'confirmed', one 'probable' and two 'damaged' and actually brought down three, with a fourth crash-landing near Boulogne with the gunner, *Unteroffizier* Paul Neumann, wounded. Three Spitfires were hit; Pilot Officer Males baled out before his aircraft crashed at Culvers Farm, Hartfield, Pilot Officer Elliot crashed at Tenterden, believed unhurt, and Pilot Officer Holland's Spitfire was badly damaged in a head-on attack.

These German fighters then headed northeast to attack targets around Chatham, including the Pobjoy engine works at Rochester, before making their escape out across the Thames estuary.

The Main Attack

Mainwhile the main force had been heading west, 'A' Flight of 602 Squadron, plus Green Section, finding them near Beachy Head and claiming three shot down, two 'probables' and a 'damaged' between there and Arundel, where a Bf109 was also claimed destroyed. The Hurricanes of 'A' Flight, 79 Squadron were also in the Beachy Head area, meeting fifteen Bf110s and claiming one destroyed. Two 602 Squadron Spitfires were shot-up in this encounter, one seriously so.

Then the Germans were away, speeding westwards towards Worthing, where several further RAF units awaited them; 234 Squadron (Spitfires), 43 Squadron and 'B' Flight 79 Squadron (Hurricanes) all engaged. The RAF overclaimed heavily in this battle, which turned inland as the '110s headed north. One Bf110 went down, apparently even before this action began, when *Hauptmann* Hans von Boltenstern, the somewhat inexperienced *Kommandeur* of *E.Gr.210* simply dived into the sea before a shot had been fired, killing himself and his gunner *Feldwebel* Fritz Schneider. Then Flight Lieutenant Pat Hughes led Blue Section of 234 Squadron in a head-on attack against the leading '110s, which were already across the coast and beginning to form a defensive circle. He and Flight Lieutenant Morgan shot down the leader, 2N+DP of *III./ZG 76*, near Washington, Sussex. *Oberleutnant* Herbert Florenz and *Gefreiter* Rudolf Herbert both perished. Hughes then attacked another '110, claiming to have shot it down ten miles northeast of Tangmere. Pat Hughes was then engaged by three more, out-manoeuvred them and took on one of these assailants, seeing its engines catch fire as he ran out of ammunition. At the same time Sergeant van den Hove d'Ertsenrijk of 43 Squadron fired on this aircraft and so, it is believed, did Pilot Officer Bob Doe of 234. The Messerschmitt went into the sea seven miles off Worthing. Then d'Ertsensenrijk himself came under fire and he nursed his crippled Hurricane back to Ford.

Meanwhile Pilot Officer Upton of 43 Squadron joined with Sergeant Boddington's Spitfire of 234 to attack another Messerschmitt; their combined gunfire blew the tail unit off and 2N+BM crashed near High Salvington, Worthing after *Oberleutnant* Walter Schiller and *Feldwebel* Helmut Winkler had parachuted. Boddington then pursued another, claiming to have shot it down into the sea. Pilot Officer Horton of 234 Squadron also claimed one, reporting that it went down to bellyland at Black Patch Hill, near Patching, where 2N+CN caught fire and burned out. *Oberleutnant* Hans Münich and *Unteroffizier* Adolf Käser were both captured unhurt. Then the '110s were through the first line of defence, streaking northward to where just one further fighter squadron awaited them.

The last line of defence before London were the Canadians of 1 (RCAF) Squadron, airborne from Northolt, who engaged elements of *II./ZG 26* west of Horsham. Flight Lieutenant McGregor led the squadron in a diving attack from the eye of the sun. He saw his opponent go down apparently out of control, Flying Officer Nesbitt fired a long burst at another and watched it burst into flames and others were claimed hard hit by Nesbitt and Flying Officer Smither.

A second Messerschmitt was also shot down, 2N+KP of *III./ZG 76* in which both *Oberleutnant* Kurt Raetsch and *Gefreiter* Werner Hempel were killed.

Then the Messerschmitts were speeding northward, with a pack of Hurricanes chasing them. There was now nothing between them and their targets. At 13.00 hours, 253 Squadron were scrambled from Kenley to patrol Croydon and arrived on the scene to find that Brooklands was already being dive-bombed. They dived from 18,000 feet to engage the Bf110s, one of the German fighters from *V./LG 1* being pursued by Flight Lieutenant Cambridge and Pilot Officer Corkett across the village of Ockham. The gunner, *Unteroffizier* Joachim Jäckel, baled out wounded, but *Feldwebel* Karl Röhring stayed with L1+BK until it crashed, killing him. One further Messerschmitt had fallen. L1+FK of *V./LG 1* crashed and burned at Upper Common, Netley, near Dorking, killing *Oberleutnant* Michael Junge and *Unteroffizier* Karl Bremser. This was the second German fighter to be brought down by 253 Squadron.

Then the '110s were speeding south again, low down and flat-out. More fighters had been scrambled to catch them over Worthing; 601 Squadron, 43 Squadron and Blue Section of 602, the latter having lost contact with the squadron during the earlier encounter. In the fight that followed two Bf110s crashed on land. *Unteroffizier* Wilhelm Schultis put 2N+HM of III./ZG 76 down at Portway, Steyning, where he and his gunner *Unteroffizier* Richard Bilek were captured. The second aircraft was from *Stab./ZG 2* and was attacked off the coast by Pilot Officer Gilbert of 601 Squadron in a head-on pass that forced *Oberleutnant* Wilhelm Schäfer to turn back. Sergeant Jeffrey 0f 43 Squadron also attacked this aircraft as did Flight Lieutenant Morgan of 234 and, when his engines finally failed, Schäfer belly-landed 3M+AA at Mill Hill, on Shoreham Downs. Schäfer, the *Geschwader Adjutant*, and his gunner *Unteroffizier* Heinz Bendjus were captured.

Three more Bf110s failed to return. Two were from *V./LG 1*; *Leutnant* Hans Braukemeier and *Obergefreiter* Josef Krischewski were lost in L1+CK, while *Unteroffiziers* Wilhelm Neumann and Walter Speier failed to return in L1+FL. The third was from *III./ZG 76*, 2N+AC crewed by *Oberfeldwebel* Konrad Daum and Unteroffizier Ferdinand Mayer. All three are believed to have fallen into the sea during the opening battle between Beachy Head and Worthing or on the way out. Another '110 from *V./LG 1* was damaged in combat and force-landed at Abbeville with the gunner wounded.

During the running fight with the main formation the following claims were submitted.

43 Squadron

F/L T.F.Dalton-Morgan	2 Bf110s destroyed
P/O H.C.Upton	Bf110 destroyed
Sgt J.W.Jeffrey	Bf110 destroyed
S/L C.B.Hull	2 Bf110s probably destroyed
P/O Van Den Hove	Bf110 probably destroyed

79 Squadron

P/O G.C.B.Peters	Bf110 destroyed
P/O D.W.A.Stones	Bf110 probably destroyed
P/O T.C.Parker	2 Bf110s damaged

234 Squadron

P/O R.F.T.Doe	3 Bf110s destroyed
F/L P.C.Hughes	3 Bf110s destroyed
Sgt M.C.B.Boddington	2 Bf110s destroyed
Sgt J.Olenski	Bf110 destroyed
Sgt A.S.Harker	Bf110 destroyed
Sgt Z.Klein	Bf110 destroyed
P/O P.W.Horton	Bf110 destroyed & 1 damaged
Sgt W.H.Hornby	Bf110 destroyed & 3 damaged
Sgt J.Szlagowski	Bf110 destroyed, Do17 destroyed
Sgt G.T.Bailey	2 Bf110s damaged

253 Squadron

F/L W.P.Cambridge	Bf110 destroyed
P/O A.H.Corkett	Bf110 destroyed
Sgt A.S.Dredge	Bf110 destroyed
P/O T.Nowak	Bf110 destroyed
P/O W.M.C.Samolinski	Bf110 destroyed
F/L J.H.Wedgwood	Bf110 destroyed
Sgt R.D.H.Watts	Bf110 damaged
Sgt R.A.Innes	Bf110 damaged
Sgt E.H.C.Kee	Bf110 damaged

601 Squadron

F/L C.R.Davis	Bf110 destroyed
P/O H.T.Gilbert	Bf110 destroyed
P/O H.C.Mayers	Do215 destroyed, Bf110 shared probably destroyed
F/L P.B.Robinson	Bf110 shared probably destroyed
F/O J.S.Jankiewicz	Bf110 probably destroyed
F/O C.J.Riddle	Do17 shared destroyed with Spitfire
F/O W.H.Rhodes-Moorhouse	Do17 destroyed

602 Squadron

S/L A.V.R.Johnstone	Bf110 destroyed
F/O P.J.Ferguson	Bf110 probably destroyed
F/O P.C.Webb	Bf110 damaged
F/L R.F.Boyd	Bf109 destroyed & Do17 destroyed
P/O H.M.Moody	Do17 destroyed and Do17 probably destroyed

1 (RCAF) Squadron

F/O A.D.Nesbitt	Bf110 destroyed
F/O R.Smither	Bf110 destroyed & 1 damaged
F/O B.D.Russell	Bf110 probably destroyed and Ju88 damaged
F/L G.R.McGregor	Bf110 damaged
F/O O.J.Peterson	Bf110 damaged
F/O H.de M.Molson	2 Bf110s damaged

Apart from the three Spitfires hit during the diversionary raid to the east, 43 Squadron had one Hurricane severely damaged as did 601, the latter returning with the pilot, Flying Officer J.S.Jankiewicz wounded. Another Hurricane, of 79 Squadron, crashed at Surbiton after combat, injuring the pilot Sergeant J. Wright. Another Spitfire, of 234 Squadron, was also badly hit. In total the Bf110 crews had claimed thirteen victories; six each were claimed by crews from *II* and *III./ZG 76* and a lone Hurricane was reported shot down by *Unteroffizier* Bechtold of *V./LG 1*

Group Captain Francis Victor Beamish DSO* DFC

Victor Beamish, a fiercely aggressive Irishman, was the Commanding Officer of No.504 Squadron when war broke out. In January 1940, he was promoted to Wing Commander and Station Command of North Weald, from where he flew Hurricanes during the battles over Dunkirk and during the Battle of Britain. In August 1941 he reached the rank of Group Captain and later in the year moved to assume command of Kenley, still flying combat sorties. On 28th March 1942 he failed to return from a Rodeo off French coast, one of six Spitfire pilots lost, subsequently being posted as missing in action.

Victory List

30.6.40	Bf109	destroyed	25.10.40	Bf109	prob destroyed
30.6.40	Bf109	destroyed	25.10.40	Bf109	damaged
9.7.40	Bf110	shd damaged	30.10.40	Bf109	prob destroyed
12.7.40	Do17	shd destroyed	11.11.40	CR42	prob destroyed
18.8.40	Ju88	damaged	13.11.40	Bf109	damaged
24.8.40	Do215	damaged	10.1.41	Bf109	destroyed
30.8.40	Bf110	prob destroyed	10.1.41	Bf109	damaged
6.9.40	Ju87	destroyed	9.8.41	Bf109	damaged
6.9.40	Ju87	prob destroyed	9.8.41	Bf109	damaged
11.9.40	He111	prob destroyed	27.1.42	He115	destroyed
18.9.40	Bf109	destroyed	13.2.42	He114	shd destroyed
18.9.40	Bf109	prob destroyed	9.3.42	FW190	destroyed
27.9.40	Bf109	prob destroyed	26.3.42	Bf109	destroyed
12.10.40	Bf109	damaged	26.3.42	FW190	destroyed

Hurricanes

Unit	Dest	P.D.	Dam	MIA	Cat E	KIA	MIA	WIA
43 Sqn	4	3	0	0	0	0	0	0
46 Sqn	0	0	0	0	2	1	0	0
79 Sqn	1	1	2	0	1	0	0	1
253 Sqn	6	0	3	0	0	0	0	0
601 Sqn	5	2	0	0	0	0	0	0
1 (RCAF)	2	1	6	0	0	0	0	0

4/5th September 1940

Interceptions were effected over Bristol and East Anglia. In the west 85 Squadron pilots claimed three 'damaged', while others from 87 Sqronn claimed three more. The 'star' of the night was Pilot Officer M.J.Herrick of 25 Squadron, who claimed to have destroyed a He111 and a Do17 near Martlesham.

Hurricanes

Unit	Dest	P.D.	Dam	MIA	Cat E	KIA	MIA	WIA
85 Sqn	0	0	3	0	0	0	0	0
87 Sqn	0	0	3	0	0	0	0	0

Blenheims

Unit	Dest	P.D.	Dam	MIA	Cat E	KIA	MIA	WIA
25 Sqn	2	0	0	0	0	0	0	0

5th September 1940

Rolling attacks in the southeast began in the mid-morning and continued throughout the day, the main targets still being the airfields, particularly Biggin Hill:

Spitfires

Unit	Dest	P.D.	Dam	MIA	Cat E	KIA	MIA	WIA
19 Sqn	3	3	1	0	1	0	0	0
41 Sqn	9	4	5	1	1	0	0	0
66 Sqn	0	0	0	0	2	1	0	1
72 Sqn	1	0	1	0	3	2	0	1
222 Sqn	0	3	0	0	1	0	0	1
234 Sqn	5	0	0	0	0	0	0	0
603 Sqn	1	1	1	0	2	1	0	1

Hurricanes

Unit	Dest	P.D.	Dam	MIA	Cat E	KIA	MIA	WIA
17 Sqn	3	3	0	0	0	0	0	0
43 Sqn	1	0	0	0	0	0	0	0
46 Sqn	3	0	0	0	0 [1]	0	0	0
73 Sqn	0	1	1	0	3	1	0	1
79 Sqn	0	1	0	0	0	0	0	0
111 Sqn	1	2	2	0	0	0	0	0
249 Sqn	0	3	2	0	1	0	0	0
253 Sqn	0	0	0	0	1	0	0	0
303 Sqn	8	1	0	0	1	0	0	1
501 Sqn	3	2	1	0	1	0	0	1

Fighter Command Combat Report

5th September 1940

No.234 Squadron

234 Squadron were ordered to patrol Kenley at Angels 20. When over Kenley they sighted AA fire in the direction of Gravesend and went to investigate. It is now clear that they arrived in the region of the Thames estuary when the enemy raid was already going back. When near Gravesend, Blue Section were suddenly attacked out of the sun by Me109s.

Blue 1 [F/Lt Hughes] turned to attack and saw 12 Me109s, in two vics of five and seven, coming up the Thames estuary. Blue 1 turned and dived and was joined by two Hurricanes. A dogfight ensued over Eastchurch. Blue 1 fired a full deflection shot at one Me109 and hit his ammunition tanks. The e/a blew up and spun down. Blue 1 then attacked a vic of Me109s and chased one; he subsequently attacked it from dead astern. Blue 1 considers that he must have shot away the oil tank of the e/a, since the wings of his own aircraft were covered with oil up to the tops. The Me109 finally forcelanded in a field 15 miles south of Manston.

Blue 2 [P/O Zurakowski] meanwhile, flying at Angels 22, went down to investigate two machines and saw an Me109 flying south at Angels 14. Blue 2 approached from astern and, as the Me109 turned, Blue 2 gave him a short burst from 100 yards. The Me109 rolled and dived and flew low due south. Blue 2 stayed on his tail, fired a short burst at 120 yards, and closed to spend the rest of his ammunition. The e/a crossed the coast near Hastings and landed on the sea. The pilot got out and, two minutes later, the a/c sank.

Blue 3 [Sgt Boddington] then attacked an Me109 going away southeast over Sheppy. Blue 3 chased him all the way to Ramsgate

6th September 1940

The first of three major attacks was against airfields in the south:

Spitfires

Unit	Dest	P.D.	Dam	MIA	Cat E	KIA	MIA	WIA
41 Sqn	2	0	0	0	0	0	0	0
234 Sqn	8	3	3	0	2	1	0	1

Hurricanes

Unit	Dest	P.D.	Dam	MIA	Cat E	KIA	MIA	WIA
1 Sqn	2	1	1	0	1	0	0	1
43 Sqn	7	1	2	0	0	0	0	0
73 Sqn	0	1	0	0	1	0	0	1
79 Sqn	0	3	1	0	0	0	0	0
111 Sqn	1	0	3	0	0	0	0	0
249 Sqn	5	3	1	0	1	0	0	1
303 Sqn	7	2	1	0	2	0	0	2
501 Sqn	1	0	0	0	3 [5]	0	0	0
601 Sqn	6	1	1	0	4	2	0	2

The second raid commenced in the early afternoon and again the objectives were airfields in the south:

Spitfires

Unit	Dest	P.D.	Dam	MIA	Cat E	KIA	MIA	WIA
66 Sqn	0	2	1	0	0	0	0	0
72 Sqn	1	0	0	0	1	0	0	0
234 Sqn	0	0	0	0	1	0	0	1
602 Sqn	2	1	2	0	1	0	0	0
603 Sqn	0	1	0	1[1]	0	0	1	0

1. Pilot captured.

Hurricanes

Unit	Dest	P.D.	Dam	MIA	Cat E	KIA	MIA	WIA
1 Sqn	0	0	1	0	0	0	0	0
43 Sqn	0	1	0	0	0	0	0	0

The final attack came in the early early evening and, while airfields were still a priority, a heavy raid reached the Thames estuary to attack the oil storage complex at Thameshaven:

Spitfires

Unit	Dest	P.D.	Dam	MIA	Cat E	KIA	MIA	WIA
41 Sqn	4	3	0	0	0	0	0	0
222 Sqn	1	0	1	0	0	0	0	0

Hurricanes

Unit	Dest	P.D.	Dam	MIA	Cat E	KIA	MIA	WIA
249 Sqn	1	1	0	0	0	90	0	0

An unusual combat took place over Wales, where a 7 OTU cannon-armed Spitfire flown by Sergeant L.S.Pilkington, a Battle of France veteran, engaged and destroyed a Ju88 near Rhyll.

Spitfires

Unit	Dest	P.D.	Dam	MIA	Cat E	KIA	MIA	WIA
7 OTU	1	0	0	0	0	0	0	0

Summary 1st - 6th September 1940

Air Combat Claims:
230 : 105 : 140

Missing/Destroyed Aircraft
25 [27] Spitfires, 49 [53] Hurricanes
24 pilots killed or missing, 38 wounded of which 2 subsequently died.

Summary 3rd September 1939 - 6th September 1940

Air Combat Claims:
2,626 : 933 : 892

Missing/Destroyed Aircraft:
636 [637] Hurricanes, 241 [243] Spitfires,
19 Gladiators, 26 Defiants
and 20 Blenheims.
432 aircrew killed/missing and
207 wounded, of which 9 died of wounds

Summary

The Phoney War

In the late 1930s, a manual of air fighting had been drawn up by the Air Ministry, which laid down neat methods for fighters to deal with bombers. These were known as Fighter Command Area Attacks and were based on the premise that fighter aircraft were now too fast for the old 'dogfights' between fighters to take place. The combats by Fighter Command aircraft between September 1939 and April 1940 had proved relatively succesful, since the *Luftwaffe* aircraft had been necessarily bombers, minelayers and reconnaissance aircraft and the RAF always had the assistance of RDF to locate them. With this type of engagement the infamous 'Fighter Command Area Attacks', laid down in the air fighting manuals, had shown no great deficiencies. On the Western Front however, the Germans had introduced a new factor, which made 'the book' obsolete; the Messerschmitt Bf109. The Germans had sent an expeditionary force to Spain in 1936 and here they re-wrote fighter tactics when the Messerschmitt Bf109B arrived to equip *Jagdstaffel 88*, under command of *Hauptmann* Werner Mölders. This dynamic young officer quickly realised the potential of the fighter and its limitations when used in the traditional way - close formations of three aircraft. He developed the pair as the basic fighting element and, when Bf109s faced Hurricanes for the first time on the Western Front, the superiority of those tactics were proven. The Germans also realised that the British fighters could out-manouevre the Messerschmitts in combat and that the RAF pilots had been taught to fight on the horizontal plane as in World War One. Thus were developed the 'climb and dive' tactics, where '109 pilots used their superior rate of climb to initiate diving passes and refused to engage the Hurricanes in dogfights, thus negating the British superior manouevrability.

The Battle of France

The German ground assault, though expected, shocked the Allies with its speed and power. The BEF Hurricane squadrons were immediately thrust into a war of movement, with units forced to move and move again, with no time to consolidate and with the resulting lack of fuel and spares to keep their aircraft fully serviceable and with no time to organise airfield defences as the the *Luftwaffe* systematically strafed and destroyed the makeshift airfields. In this situation, no cohesive defence was possible and it was apparent from the moment of the Sedan break-through that the situation was irretrieveable. The RAF squadrons rapidly became isolated, relying on local intelligence rather than an overall battle plan and the air defence became fragmented, with small groups of RAF fighters attempting to stem the unstoppable air assault and being forced by events back towards the coast or deeper into western France. Even when it was clear that the battle was lost units were still being thrown in piecemeal and shot to pieces on the ground and in the air until Hugh Dowding, looking ahead, intervened to prevent further destruction.

For the historian, the Battle of France is a nightmare; so many units destroyed their records and those that remain are at best sketchy. The known figures for the Hurricane casualties are 386 aircraft lost, 178 having been abandoned and in most cases destroyed by the RAF units. From these figures, it is clear that other losses took place in combat or in accidents that have never been recorded and will not appear in the body of this text. Between 1st and 24th June a further 67 Spitfires were also lost. These figures represented the total loss of twenty-four fighter squadrons in just over a month. However, the loss of aircraft was never really a great problem; the real worry was the loss of trained fighter pilots. At least two hundred and fifty fighter pilots were killed or captured, either in action or due to

Summary

accidents, losses that Dowding could ill-afford in the battle that he knew would surely come.

The Battle of the Channel

For several weeks the *Luftwaffe* allowed the RAF to reform and prepare - mainly because the battle in France had cost the Germans a good deal of their strength and they too needed a breathing space. During this time the RAF operated bombers on escorted daylight raids but the situation changed on 4th July when, for the first time, the Germans struck at shipping in the Channel and port facilities at Portland, ushering in the first phase of what was to become known as the Battle of Britain. For the Germans, the ultimate goal was the invasion and occupation of Britain and to achieve this goal two factors were necessary;

(1) the total denial of the English Channel to British shipping, without which a seaborne landing would be impossible.

(2) Air superiority over the Channel between the Isle of Wight and the North Sea and over southern and southeast England as

The RAF had one main advantage during the Battle of Britain, that of operating over home territory. Many shot-down pilots would survive to fight again, like Sergeant H.J.Marsh of 238 Squadron, who crash-landed safely on 19th July. For the Luftwaffe pilots any such event meant capture.

(Chris Goss via Earnshaw)

far as the River Thames to protect both the projected seaborne landings and the planned paratroop assault.

Therefore, for over a month, medium and dive-bombers sought to clear the Channel and indeed succeeded by sinking sufficient ships to force the Admiralty to halt coastal convoys completely.

This period, while not as hectic as the Battle of France, was one of considerable concern to Hugh Dowding, since the air battles were being fought over the sea where the RAF was at a distinct disadvantage. The RAF pilots were ill-equipped with suvival gear and the Air-Sea Rescue service was, at best, rudimentary. Shot-down RAF pilots possibly stood a better chance of being rescued and captured by the Germans than the British, even though, from early on, German rescue floatplanes were attacked and shot down. This was ostensibly since they were believed to be armed and acting as reconnaissance aircraft - although there is no evidence to support this. The Channel raids reached their climax on 8th August, when rolling attacks took place against convoy CW9 and major air battles developed, proving costly to the RAF with fourteen aircraft and twelve pilots lost, while Bf109 sweeps cost two more aircraft and one more pilot.

Officially, the Battle of Britain began on 10th July, the date applied by the Air Ministry for the award of of the Battle of Britain clasp to patricipating aircrews, but the Germans consider this a nonsense. From their point of view, the battle proper began when the first major attacks were carried out against the British mainland on the night of 18th June 1940. German historians say, quite logically, that a battle begins and ends when the attackers commence and finally stop; since they were the attackers, who can deny this logic?

The Battle of the Airfields

The assault proper began on 12th August, with co-ordinated attacks on the south coast radar (RDF) stations, although these were, generally speaking, unsuccessful and did not seriously interrupt the radar coverage. Indeed, the Germans soon realised that the coverage was still operating effectively, but took the view that, 'If they can't find us, we can't shoot them down', for this was essentially the object; an air force must be destroyed in the air to kill or incapacitate its pilots. The destruction of aeroplanes on the ground is not enough. So for three weeks of almost constant action, the Germans struck at targets that they considered could not be left undefended; the Southampton Spitfire factory, the Kingston Hurricane factory, Vickers at Weybridge, Short Brothers at Rochester and, constantly, the airfields. It was perfectly possible for Fighter Command to operate without airfields, as the BEF had in France. Indeed, any large field and a handful of tents would suffice, However, the Sector Stations each contained its own operations room, which is curious, because there was absolutely no reason for this. It would have been tactically safer for the Ops Rooms to have been at some distance away and linked by land-line. However, the circumstances required that Biggin Hill, Hornchurch, Kenley and the other Sector Stations be defended rigorously, thus falling in with the German master-plan. And in those three weeks the radar reporting system failed only once, on 24th August, when large formations of German aircraft wandered unreported across southern England and the hazy conditions prevented the Royal Observer Corps from giving any but the most rudimentary reports.

It has often been said that, as a purely tactical air force, the *Luftwaffe* was attempting a task that it was fundamentally incapable of achieving. However, it is the belief of this author that, for a period of about a week, the *Luftwaffe* fighter force achieved sufficient air superiority over southern England for an invasion to have been carried out. This period was the opening days of September, when the airfields were only just functioning and the pilots were mentally and physically exhausted. The whole complexion of the battle would, on 7th September, change dramatically.

Index

Personnel - British and Allied

Adams, Sgt H.C. 501 Sqn 187
Allen, P/O J.A. 54 Sqn 67-9, 110
Allen, F/O J.H.L. 151 Sqn 101
Ambrose, P/O C.F. 46 Sqn 192
Appleby, P/O M.J. 609 Sqn 147
Ashfield, F/L G. FIU 90, 120
Atkinson, P/O H.D. 213 Sqn 148
Austin, F/O F. 46 Sqn 192
Bader, S/L D.R.S.
  222, 242 Sqns 70, 174
Badger, S/L J.V.C. 43 Sqn 144
Bailey, Sgt G.T. 234 Sqn 196
Bailey, P/O J.C.I.D. 46 Sqn 188
Baker, Sgt. 152 Sqn 148
Baker, Sgt R.D. 56 Sqn 112, 113
Ball, F/O G.E. 19 Sqn 88
Barber, P/O R.H. 46 Sqn 192
Barclay, P/O R.G.A. 249 Sqn 187
Barnwell, F/O J.S. 29 Sqn 88
Barton, F/L R.A. 249 Sqn 183
Barwell, P/O E.G. 264 Sqn 79
Batt, Sgt L.G.. 238 Sqn 145
Baxter, Sgt S. 603 Sqn 188
Bazin, F/L J.M. 607 Sqn 155
Beamish, W/C F.V.
  151 Sqn 94, 101, 198
Beazley, P/O H.J.S.
  249 Sqn 184
Bennions, P/O G.H. 41 Sqn 128, 155
Blackadder, F/L W.F.
  607 Sqn 155
Blair, F/O K.H. 151 Sqn 187
Boddington, Sgt M.C.B.
  234 Sqn 194, 196, 200
Bodie, P/O C.A.W. 66 Sqn 187

Boitel-Gill, F/L D.F.A.
  152 Sqn 148
Boret, P/O R.J. 41 Sqn 155
Bowen, F/O C.E. 607 Sqn 155
Bowring, F/O B.H. 111 Sqn 185
Boyd, F/L R.F. 602 Sqn 197
Braham, P/O J.R.D. 29 Sqn 168
Broadhurst, W/C H. 60 Wg 66
Brooker, F/O R.P. 56 Sqn 112, 150
Brothers, AC P.M. 32 Sqn 118
Brown, P/O R.J.W. 111 Sqn 185
Bruce, F/L D.C. 111 Sqn 185
Brzezina, F/L S. 74 Sqn 142
Burnell-Phillips, Sgt P.A.
  607 Sqn 155
Burton, P/O P.R.F. 249 Sqn 183
Bushell, Sgt G.D. 213 Sqn 149
Cambridge, F/L W.P.
  253 Sqn 195, 196
Camm, Sir Sydney 21
Capon, P/O C.A. 257 Sqn 149
Carey, P/O F.R. 43 Sqn 144
Carswell, F/O M.K. 43 Sqn 37, 186
Carter, P/O P.E.G. 73 Sqn 156
Casson, P/O L.H. 616 Sqn 156
Chamberlain, Neville 108
Chetham, Sgt C.A.G. 1 Sqn 171, 187
Churchill, Winston 61, 72, 85, 93
Cleaver, F/O G.N.S.
  601 Sqn 148
Clerke, F/L R.F.H. 79 Sqn 154
Clift, P/O D.G. 79 Sqn 154
Close, Sgt. 23 Sqn 88
Clouston, F/L W.G. 19 Sqn 133
Clyde, F/O. 601 Sqn 144, 145, 148

209

Cock, P/O J.R. 87 Sqn	52-3, 125	Eden, Anthony		74
Coghlan, F/L J.H. 56 Sqn	112, 113	Edsall, P/O E.F. 54 Sqn		186
Collins, S/L A.R. 72 Sqn	185, 188	Edwards, F/O J.D. 43 Sqn		37
Cooke, S/L D. 65 Sqn	108	Elliot, P/O R.D. 72 Sqn		192, 193
Cooke, F/L N.G. 264 Sqn	51, 79	Elsdon, F/O T.A.F. 72 Sqn		192, 193
Coope, S/L W.E. 87 Sqn	23	Falkson, P/O J. 152 Sqn		37
Corkett, P/O A.H. 253 Sqn	195, 196	Farquhar, S/L A.D. 602 Sqn		18
Cowsill, Sgt J.H. 56 Sqn.	112, 113	Fenton, S/L H.A. 238 Sqn		135
Craig, F/O G.D. 607 Sqn	155	Feary, Sgt A.N. 609 Sqn		147
Craig, Sgt J.T. 111 Sqn	143	Ferguson, F/O P.J. 602 Sqn		197
Crisp, Sgt J.L. 43 Sqn	144	Feric, P/O M. 303 Sqn		189
Crook, P/O D.M. 609 Sqn	147	Ferris, F/O H.M. 111 Sqn		111, 143
Crossley, F/L M.N. 32 Sqn	82	Finlay, S/L D. 41 Sqn		41
Cunningham, Sgt W.G. 607 Sqn	155	Fiske, P/O W.L.M.. 601 Sqn		144, 145
Currant, P/O C.F. 605 Sqn	155	Fokes, Sgt R.H. 92 Sqn		105
Dalton-Morgan, F/L T.F. 43 Sqn	144, 196	Folkes, F/O. 43 Sqn		37
David, P/O W.D. 87 Sqn	149	Forward, Sgt R.V. 257 Sqn		127
Davidson, Sgt H.J. 249 Sqn	187	Franklin, F/Sgt W.H. 65 Sqn		125
Davies, F/O P.F McD. 56 Sqn	150	Frantisek, Sgt J. 303 Sqn		189
Davis, F/L C.R. 601 Sqn	144, 145, 148, 197	Fredman, F/O L. 615 Sqn		52
Davis, P/O C.T. 238 Sqn	146	Freeborn, F/L J.C. 74 Sqn		127, 28, 142
Deere, P/O A.C. 54 Sqn	67-9, 110, 176	George VI, HM		38, 69
Deller, Sgt A.L.M. 43 Sqn	144	Giddings, F/L H.S. 615, 111 Sqns		101, 185
De Mancha, P/O R.A. 43 Sqn	120	Gifford, F/L A. 603 Sqn		18, 20
Dewar, W/C J.S. 87 Sqn	145	Gilbert, F/Sgt E.G. 64 Sqn		143
Dredge, Sgt A.S. 253 Sqn	196	Gilbert, P/O H.T. 601 Sqn		195, 197
Doe, P/O R.F.T.. 234 Sqn	194, 196	Gilders, Sgt J.S. 72 Sqn		92
Donaldson, S/L E.M. 151 Sqn	101	Gillam, F/L D.E. 616 Sqn		156, 187
Doulton, F/O M.D. 601 Sqn	144, 145	Gilroy, P/O G. 603 Sqn		20
Douthwaite, P/O B. 72 Sqn	185	Gleed, W/C I.R. 87 Sqn		63
Dowding, AM H.T.	13, 14, 60, 61, 123, 204-5, 206	Glyde, F/O R.L. 87 Sqn		23, 145
Drake, P/O G.J. 607 Sqn	155	Goddard, F/O H.G. 219 Sqn		156-7
Duke-Woolley, F/L R.M.B.D. 23 Sqn	87	Goodwin, F/O H. McD. 609 Sqn		147
Dundas, P/O H.S.L. 616 Sqn	156	Gore, F/O W.E. 607 Sqn		155
Dundas, F/O J.C. 609 Sqn	147, 148	Gracie, F/L E.J. 56 Sqn		150
Dupee, Sgt G.A. 219 Sqn	157	Graham, F/L E. 72 Sqn		103, 186
Dutton, AC R.G. 145 Sqn	34	Grandy, S/L J. 249 Sqn		183
Du Vivier, P/O D.A.R.G. LeR. 43 Sqn	186	Gray, P/O C.F. 54 Sqn		140, 183
Dymond, Sgt W.L. 111 Sqn	143, 185	Gray, F/O C.K. 43 Sqn		144
		Gribble, F/O G.D. 54 Sqn		183
		Grier, P/O T. 601 Sqn		144, 145, 148
		Griffin, Sgt J.J. 73 Sqn		156
		Gunn, P/O H.R. 74 Sqn		127
		Guy, Sgt L.N. 601 Sqn		148

Index

Haig, P/O J.G.E. 603 Sqn — 185
Hallowes, Sgt J.H. 43 Sqn — 37, 144, 149
Hamlyn, Sgt R.F. 610 Sqn — 164-5
Hampshire, Sgt C.W. 111 Sqn — 185
Hanks, W/C P.P. 1 Sqn — 83
Hardy, P/O R.A. 234 Sqn — 157
Harker, Sgt A.S. 234 Sqn — 196
Hastings, P/O D. 74 Sqn — 142
Havercroft, F/Sgt R.E. 92 Sqn — 149
Hawkings, Sgt R.P. 601 Sqn — 144
Hayes, F/O T.N. 600 Sqn — 51
Haysom, F/O G.D.L. 79 Sqn — 154
Hellyer, F/L R.G. 616 Sqn — 156
Henn, Sgt W.B. 501 Sqn — 183
Henneberg, F/O Z. 303 Sqn — 189
Herrick, P/O M.J. 25 Sqn — 199
Hewett, Sgt G.A. 607 Sqn — 155
Heyworth, S/L J.H. 79 Sqn — 154
Higgs, F/O T.P. 111 Sqn — 111
Hillcoat, F/L H.B.L. 1 Sqn — 187
Hillwood, Sgt P. 56 Sqn — 101, 112, 150
Holland, P/O D.F. 72 Sqn — 192, 193
Hood, S/L H.R.L. 41 Sqn — 80
Hope, S/L Sir A, Bt. 601 Sqn — 144, 145, 148
Hopewell, Sgt J. 616 Sqn — 156
Hornby, Sgt W.H. 234 Sqn — 196
Horton, P/O P.W. 234 Sqn — 194, 196
Howell, F/L F.J. 609 Sqn — 147
Hughes, F/L D.P. 238 Sqn — 146
Hughes, F/L P.C. 234 Sqn — 194, 196, 200
Hulbert, Sgt D.J. 257 Sqn — 143
Hull, S/L C.B. 43 Sqn — 37, 196
Hulton-Harrop, P/O 56 Sqn — 17
Humphreys, P/O J.D. 29 Sqn — 87
Hunt, Sgt D.A.C. 66 Sqn — 187
Hunter, F/O A.S. 604 Sqn — 65, 79
Hunter, S/L P.A. 264 Sqn — 59
Innes, Sgt R.H. — 196
Inness, P/O R.F. 152 Sqn — 148
Jankiewicz, F/O J.S. 601 Sqn — 197
Jay, P/O D.T. 87 Sqn — 145
Jeffrey, Sgt J.W. 43 Sqn — 185, 195, 196
Jeffries, P/O C.G. St.D. 3 Sqn — 55
Johnstone, S/L A.V.R. 602 Sqn — 100, 197
Joll, P/O I.K.S. 604 Sqn — 51
Jones, P/O R.L. 64 Sqn — 143
Jones, P/O R.E. 605 Sqn — 155
Jones, LAC. 264 Sqn — 79
Joubert, P/O C.C.O. 56 Sqn — 150
Kain, F/O E.J. 73 Sqn — 25, 40, 41, 86
Karasek, LAC L.R. 23 Sqn — 88
Kay, P/O D.M.S. 264 Sqn — 79
Kayll, S/L J.R. 615 Sqn — 96, 125-6
Kee, Sgt E.H.C. 253 Sqn — 196
Kells, P/O L.H.G. 29 Sqn — 87
Kelly, F/L D.P.D.G. 74 Sqn — 127
Kilner, Sgt J.R. 65 Sqn — 150
King-Clark, P/O. 23 Sqn — 87
Klein, Sgt Z. 234 Sqn — 196
Lane, P/O R. 43 Sqn — 144
Larichliere, P/O J.E.P. 213 Sqn — 146, 148
Law, P/O K.S. 605 Sqn — 155
Laws, F/Sgt A.F. 64 Sqn — 143
Leathart, S/L J.A. 54 Sqn — 67-9, 183
Leather, F/L W.J. 611 Sqn — 104
Lee, F/O R.H.A. 85 Sqn — 25, 26
Lees, W/C R.B. 72 Sqn — 186
Lenahan, P/O J.D. 607 Sqn — 155
Little, Sgt R.A. 238 Sqn — 147
Little, Cpl. 23 Sqn — 87
Llewellyn, Sgt R.T. 213 Sqn — 146
Lock, P/O E.S. 41 Sqn — 155
Long, Sgt K.L. 29 Sqn — 88
Lott, S/L C.G. 43 Sqn — 110
Lovell, F/O A.J.D. 41 Sqn — 128, 155
Lovell, F/L. 73 Sqn — 156
Lyne, P/O M. 19 Sqn — 70-71
MacDonald, Sgt A.S. 601 Sqn — 148
Malan, S/L A.G. 74 Sqn — 69, 87, 127, 128, 130-1, 142
Males, P/O E.E. 72 Sqn — 193
Manton, S/L G.A.L. 56 Sqn — 112
Marples, P/O R. 616 Sqn — 156
Marrs, P/O E.S. 152 Sqn — 148

Marsh, Sgt H.J. 238 Sqn	146, 147, 205	Mungo-Park, F/L J.C. 74 Sqn	142
Martin, P/O R.E. 73 Sqn	23	Murray, P/O T.B. 616 Sqn	156
Mawhood, P/O. 85 Sqn	51	Nelson, F/O W.H. 74 Sqn	142
Mayers, P/O H.C. 601 Sqn	144, 145, 197	Nelson-Edwards, P/O. 79 Sqn	154
McArthur, F/L J.H.G. 609 Sqn	147	Nesbitt, F/O A.D. 1 (RCAF) Sqn	194, 197
McDowall, Sgt A. 602 Sqn	121	Newall, ACM Sir Cyril	60
McGrath, F/O J.K.U.B. 601 Sqn	144, 148	Noble, P/O B.R. 79 Sqn	154
McGregor, F/L G.R. 1 (RCAF) Sqn	194, 197	Noble, Sgt D. 43 Sqn	144
McIntyre, P/O A.G. 111 Sqn	143	Norfolk, Sgt N.R. 72 Sqn	185
McKellar, F/L A.A. 602 Sqn	20, 24, 155	North, P/O H.L. 43 Sqn	37
MacKenzie, P/O. 41 Sqn	155	Nowak, P/O T. 253 Sqn	196
McKnight, P/O W.L. 242 Sqn	173, 174	Nowell, Sgt G.L. 87 Sqn	52
McMullen, P/O D.A.P. 54 Sqn	183, 186	Nowierski, F/O T. 609 Sqn	147
McNay, Sgt A. 73 Sqn	156	Nutter, Sgt R.C. 257 Sqn	188
Meaker, P/O J.R.B. 249 Sqn	183, 187	O'Brien, S/L J.S. 23 Sqn	87-8
Measures, F/L W.E.G. 74 Sqn	67	Olenski, Sgt J. 234 Sqn	196
Merchant, Sgt H.J. 1 Sqn	166	Olive, F/L C.G.C. 65 Sqn	150
Metham, Sgt J. 253 Sqn	183	Orton, F/O N. 73 Sqn	41, 51
Mildren, P/O P.R. 66 Sqn	187	Osmond, P/O A.G. 213 Sqn	148
Miller, P/O R.F.G. 609 Sqn	147	Ostaczewski, F/O P. 609 Sqn	147
Millington, P/O W.H. 79 Sqn	154	Overton, P/O C.N. 609 Sqn	147
Mills, Sgt J.P. 43 Sqn	144	Page, P/O A.G. 56 Sqn	112
Milne, F/O R.M. 151 Sqn	143	Parker, P/O T.C. 79 Sqn	154, 196
Mitchell, F/O L.R.G. 257 Sqn	143	Parnall, F/L D.G. 249 Sqn	184, 187
Mitchell, P/O H.T. 87 Sqn	54	Parnall, P/O S.B. 607 Sqn	155
Mitchell, R.J.	122	Passy, P/O C.W. 605 Sqn	155
Moberley, F/O G.E. 616 Sqn	156	Pattulo, P/O W.B. 151 Sqn	187
Molson, P/O H.de M. 1 (RCAF) Sqn	197	Perry, Sgt R.M. 73 Sqn	29
Moody, P/O H.M. 602 Sqn	197	Peters, P/O G.C. 79 Sqn	154, 196
More, S/L J.W.C. 73 Sqn	52	Peterson, F/O O.J. 1 (RCAF) Sqn	197
Morgan, F/L. 234 Sqn	194, 195	Petre, F/O G.W. 19 Sqn	87-8
Morris, Sgt P.P. 213 Sqn	148	Pigg, F/O O.St.J. 72 Sqn	154
Morrogh-Ryan, P/O G.B. 41 Sqn	155	Pilkington, Sgt L.S. 7 OTU	202
Mould, Sgt E.A. 74 Sqn	108, 127	Pinkerton, F/L G. 602 Sqn	18
Mould, P/O P.W.O. 1 Sqn	19	Plummer, F/O R.P. 46 Sqn	192
Mounsden, F/O M.H. 56 Sqn	150	Pond, F/Sgt A.H.D. 601 Sqn	145, 148
Muirhead, F/O I.J. 605 Sqn	155	Rabagliati, F/L A.C. 46 Sqn	188
		Ramsay, Adm, RN	84
		Reynaud, M Paul	61
		Reynell, F/L R.C. 43 Sqn	185
		Rhodes, P/O R.A. 29 Sqn	159

Index

Rhodes-Moorhouse,
F/O W.H. 601 Sqn 197
Riddle, F/O C.J. 601 Sqn 144, 148, 197
Ritchie, P/O J.R. 111 Sqn 185
Robbins, Sgt R.H. 54 Sqn 183, 186
Roberts, P/O R. 64 Sqn 143
Robertson, P/O C. 603 Sqn 20
Robinson, F/L A.I. 222 Sqn 188
Robinson, Sgt D.N. 152 Sqn 148
Robinson, S/L M. 616 Sqn 156
Robinson, F/L P.B. 601 Sqn 197
Robson, P/O N.C.H. 72 Sqn 154
Rogowski, Sgt J. 303 Sqn 189
Rolls, Sgt W.T.E. 72 Sqn 193
Rose, P/O. 56 Sqn 17
Rose-Price, F/O A.T.
501 Sqn 187
Rothermere, Lord 89
Russell, F/O B.D.
1 (RCAF) Sqn 197
Ryder, F/L E.N. 41 Sqn 42, 141, 155
Salmond, AM Sir John 12
Samolinski, P/O W.M.C.
253 Sqn 196
Sanders, F/L J.G. 615 Sqn 101, 168
Saunders, P/O C.H.
92 Sqn 105
Saville, Sgt J.E. 151 Sqn 143
Scott, P/O D.H. 73 Sqn 156
Seabourne, Sgt. 238 Sqn 145, 146
Sheen, F/O D.F.B. 72 Sqn 154, 193
Shipman, P/O E.A. 41 Sqn 155
Shute, S/L F.W.C. 152 Sqn 37, 38
Simmonds, P/O V.C.
238 Sqn 146
Simpson, F/O J.W.C.
43 Sqn 37
Simpson, P/O P.J.
64, 111 Sqns 143, 185
Sing, F/L J.E.J. 213 Sqn 149
Skalski, P/O S. 501 Sqn 183
Skinner, Sgt W.M. 74 Sqn 142
Smart, F/L T. 65 Sqn 150
Smith, Sgt A.D. 66 Sqn 191
Smith, F/L R.L. 151 Sqn 101, 115, 143
Smith, P/O D.S. 616 Sqn 156
Smith, F/L F.M. 72 Sqn 154
Smither, F/O R.
1 (RCAF) Sqn 194, 197

Smythe, Sgt G. 56 Sqn 101, 112
Staples, P/O M.E. 609 Sqn 147
Steere, F/S H. 72 Sqn 103
Stephen, P/O H.M. 74 Sqn 127, 142
Stephens, F/L M.M. 3 Sqn 55
Stevenson, S/L G. 19 Sqn 70-71
Stevenson, P/O P.C.F.
74 Sqn 127, 128
St.John, P/O P.C.B. 74 Sqn 127
Stokes, P/O R.W. 264 Sqn 79
Stokoe, Sgt J. 603 Sqn 184, 188
Stones, P/O D.W.A. 79 Sqn 196
Studd, P/O J.A.P. 66 Sqn 88
Sulman, P/O J.E. 607 Sqn 155
Summers, Capt J. 123
Surma, P/O F. 151 Sqn 187
Sutton, P/O F.B. 56 Sqn 150
Szczesny, P/O H. 74 Sqn 142
Szlagowski, Sgt J. 234 Sqn 196
Thompson, S/L J.M.
111 Sqn 111, 143
Thorne, Sgt R. 264 Sqn 79
Townsend, F/L P.W.
43 Sqn 37, 38
Trenchard, ACM Hugh 11
Tuck, F/L R.R.S. 92 Sqn 69, 149
Upton, P/O H.C.. 43 Sqn 144, 194, 196
Urwin-Mann, P/O J.R.
238 Sqn 146
Usmar, Sgt F. 41 Sqn 155
Van den Hove d'Ertsenrijk,
Sgt. 43 Sqn, 194, 196
Villa, F/O J.W. 72 Sqn 192, 193
Walch, F/L S.C. 238 Sqn 125
Walker, P/O J.A. 111 Sqn 143
Wallens, P/O R.W. 41 Sqn 155
Waller, P/O. 73 Sqn 29
Watling, P/O W.C. 92 Sqn 149
Watson, P/O P.V. 19 Sqn 70-71
Watts, Sgt R.D.H. 253 Sqn 196
Weaver, F/O P.S. 56 Sqn 150
Webb, F/O P.C. 602 Sqn 18, 197
Webster, F/L J.T. 41 Sqn 80, 128
Wedgwood, F/L J.H.
253 Sqn 196
Welford, P/O G.H.E.
607 Sqn 155
Wells, F/O E.P. 41 Sqn 141

The Fighter Command War Diary

Welsh, P/O T.D. 264 Sqn	79	
Weygand, Gen	85, 93	
White, S/L F.L. 74 Sqn	67-9	
Whitfield, Sgt J.J. 56 Sqn	112, 113	
Whitley, P/O D. 264 Sqn	79	
Whitty, P/O W.H.R. 607 Sqn	155	
Wigglesworth, P/O J.S. 238 Sqn	146	
Wilcox, F/O E.J. 72 Sqn	103	
Winn, Sgt J. 73 Sqn	29	
Winter, P/O D.C. 72 Sqn	154	
Woods-Scawen P/O C.A. 43 Sqn	133, 144, 186	
Woodward, F/O H.J. 64 Sqn	143	
Wright, Sgt J. 79 Sqn	197	
Wynne, P/O R.E.N.E. 249 Sqn	184	
Young, P/O B.P. 615 Sqn	101	
Young, P/O J.H.R. 74 Sqn	127	
Zurakowski, P/O J. 234 Sqn	200	

Personnel - German

v.Arnim, Oblt J. KG 4	87
Bachaus, Lt. KG 4	88
Bechtold, Uffz, LG 1	197
Bendjus, Uffz H. ZG 2	195
Bilek, Uffz R. ZG 76	195
Böhm, Lt J. JG 51	107, 108, 109
v.Boltenstern, Hptm H. E.Gr.210	193
v.Boremski, Uffz E. JG 3	101
Braukemeier, Lt H. LG 1	195
Bremser, Uffz K. LG 1	195
Brügelmann, Gfr. JG 26	127
Büder, Uffz. JG 51	112, 113
Condé, Uffz R. ZG 26	193
Corpus, Oblt. KG 4	87
Daum, Ofw K. ZG 76	195
Dobislav, Oblt M. JG 27	125
Florenz, Oblt H. ZG 76	194
Fözö, Hptm J. JG 51	107, 112
Framm, Lt G. JG 27	125
Galland, Maj A. JG 26	127, 128, 129
Gebhardt, Gfr. JG 51	128
Gildner, Uffz P. ZG 1	51
Goering, Hermann	13, 73, 74
Groten, Lt. JG 53	55
Guderian, Gen H.	61
Hafele, Obstlt, KG 26	42
v.Hahn, Oblt H. JG 53	29
Heitmann, Ofw. JG 3	101
Hempel, Gfr W. ZG 76	194
Herbert, Gfr R. ZG 76	194
Hitler, Adolf	12, 13, 73-4
Höhnisch, Uffz JG 53	55
Hommel, Uffz G. ZG 76	193
Illner, Fw H. JG 51	109, 110
Ihlefeld, Hptm H. LG 2	101
Jäckel, Uffz J. LG 1	195
John, Fw H. JG 51	112
Junge, Oblt M. LG 1	195
Käser, Uffz A. ZG 76	194
Kesselring, Gen A.	73
Kirchheiss, Oblt. JG 51	127
v.Kleist, Gen	74
Klotz, Fw. JG 20	101
Knacke, Lt R. ZG 1	51
Kolbow, Lt H. JG 20	101
Kriker, Lt. JG 27	120
Krischewski, Ogfr J.LG 1	195
Kroll, Uffz. JG 20	101
Kupka, Oblt. JG 3	101
Lelsen, Uffz.	103
Leppla, Oblt R. JG 51	127-8
v.Massenbach, Maj D Fhr, KG 4	87
Mayer, Uffz F. ZG 76	195
Mayer, Oblt H-K, JG 53	55
Messerschmitt, Prof W.	13
Michael, Uffz M. ZG 76	193
Mölders, Hptm W. JG 53	29, 80, 127-8, 129, 203
Müncheberg, Oblt J. JG 26	127, 129
Munich, Oblt H. ZG 76	194
Neumann, Uffz P. ZG 76	193
Neumann, Uffz W. LG 1	195
Niehoff, Lt R. KG 26	20
Pfeiffer, Gfr. JG 3	101
Piduhn, Oblt G. ZG 76	193
Prochnow, Hptm. KG 4	87

214

Index

Raetsch, Oblt K. ZG 76	194
Rauhaut, Uffz. LG 2	101
Röhring, Fw K. LG 1	195
v.Runstedt, FeldM.	73
Schäfer, Oblt W. ZG 2	195
Schenk, Lt W. ZG 1	51
Schiller, Oblt W. ZG 76	194
v.Schlotheim, E.H. ZG 76	193
Schmid, Ofw. JG 51	128
Schneider, Fw F. E.Gr.210	194
Schultis, Uffz W. ZG 76	195
Speier, Uffz W. LG 1	195
Streib, Olt W. ZG 1	51
Tietzen, Hptm H. JG 51	112
Tornow, Fw. JG 51	112
Trautloft, Hptm H. JG 51	59, 117
Weeber, Lt H. ZG 76	193
Wessling, Gfr. JG 3	101
Wilms, Fw H. KG 26	37
Winkler, Fw H. ZG 76	194

Units - Royal Air Force

Fighter Command

1 Squadron	14, 18, 19, 25, 31,37, 40, 41, 44, 46, 52, 53, 55, 56, 57,60, 61, 62, 65, 66,73, 75, 86, 93, 94, 102, 117, 124,132, 137, 149, 152, 158, 158, 160, 162, 166, 171, 172, 174,178, 179, 181, 182, 187,189, 201
3 Squadron	14, 31, 53, 55, 56,57, 60, 61, 62, 65, 66, 95, 124
17 Squadron	14, 31, 55, 64, 64,65, 72, 75, 76, 78, 80, 82, 84, 86, 90,92, 102, 109, 113, 130, 138, 142, 149, 159, 163, 168, 169, 172, 179, 189
19 Squadron	14, 31, 34, 55, 70,75, 77, 84, 87, 88, 95, 102, 123, 133, 149, 158, 162, 168, 178, 189, 190, 199
23 Squadron	14, 31, 87, 88, 95,100
25 Squadron	14, 26, 31, 117, 118,189, 199
29 Squadron	4, 32, 87, 88, 95,159, 163, 168, 170
32 Squadron	14, 32, 64, 65, 66, 72, 73, 75, 85, 90, 91, 92, 104, 105, 109, 111, 117, 118, 119, 123, 130, 137, 141, 150, 152, 153, 157, 158, 159, 160, 163, 166, 167, 169, 178
41 Squadron	14, 19, 32, 42, 44, 80, 81, 84, 95, 125, 126, 134, 135, 138, 141, 152, 154, 155, 163, 199, 200
43 Squadron	14, 32, 35, 36, 37, 38, 41, 44, 46, 50, 84, 90, 104, 106, 110, 114, 117, 119, 120, 133, 135, 140, 141, 142, 144, 146, 148, 149, 151, 153, 158, 160, 161, 171, 177, 178, 182, 184, 185-6, 193, 194, 195, 196, 197, 198, 199, 201
46 Squadron	15, 19, 28, 36, 50, 62, 63, 75, 76, 77, 78, 80, 83, 84, 90, 91, 102, 120, 160, 182, 185, 188, 189, 192, 198, 199
54 Squadron	15, 32, 36, 55, 67, 72, 73, 74, 75, 77, 94, 106, 107, 110, 114, 119, 124, 139, 140, 152, 153, 157, 159, 160, 166, 168, 169, 170, 174, 175, 176, 177, 178, 181, 182, 183, 186, 189
56 Squadron	15, 17, 23, 32, 62, 64, 65, 72, 73, 76, 77, 91, 101, 102, 104, 111, 112, 114, 115, 119, 124, 128, 138, 141, 149, 150, 157, 158, 159, 160, 163, 167, 170, 171, 172, 174, 175, 178, 179
64 Squadron	15, 32, 49, 78, 81, 84, 92, 104, 105, 106, 111, 114, 117, 121, 124, 126, 134, 136, 137, 138, 140, 141, 143, 149, 152, 157, 158, 160

215

The Fighter Command War Diary

Squadron	Pages
65 Squadron	15, 32, 62, 72, 74, 75, 77, 98, 105, 106, 107, 108, 109, 119, 121, 123, 125, 134, 136, 139, 140, 141, 149, 150, 151, 158, 160, 163, 168
66 Squadron	15, 32, 33, 56, 84, 88, 95, 110, 130, 162, 163, 163, 178, 182, 187, 190, 191, 199, 201
72 Squadron	15, 19, 28, 32, 43, 84, 99, 100, 103, 104, 152, 154, 178, 181, 182, 183, 184-5, 186, 188, 190, 192-3, 199, 201
73 Squadron	15, 18, 23, 25, 28, 29, 32, 40, 41, 44, 46, 47, 51, 52, 53, 55, 56, 57, 60, 61, 62, 66, 73, 74, 75, 76, 77, 84, 85, 86, 92, 93, 94, 102, 152, 156, 168, 199, 201
74 Squadron	15, 17, 24, 32, 67, 72, 73, 74, 75, 77, 87, 92, 95, 102, 105, 106, 107, 108, 111, 114, 117, 121, 124, 126, 127, 130, 132, 137, 138, 141, 142
79 Squadron	15, 24, 32, 55, 56, 60, 62, 65, 66, 76, 83, 91, 95, 99, 105, 106, 109, 110, 136, 152, 154, 155, 173, 177, 178, 179, 181, 193, 196, 197, 198, 199, 201
80 Squadron	80
85 Squadron	15, 18, 25, 32, 38, 51, 52, 53, 55, 56, 57, 60, 61, 62, 65, 66, 83, 107, 113, 130, 131, 134, 138, 142, 161, 167, 170, 175, 177, 179, 181, 188, 199
87 Squadron	15, 18, 23, 32, 46, 50, 52, 53, 54, 55, 56, 57, 60, 61, 62, 63, 65, 66, 83, 93, 113, 116, 124, 125, 137, 141, 145, 148, 149, 151, 153, 169, 190, 199
92 Squadron	22, 32, 43, 73, 74, 75, 85, 105, 110, 111, 115, 116, 121, 124, 125, 141, 146, 148, 149, 151, 160, 162, 169, 172, 177
98 Squadron	102
111 Squadron	15, 27, 32, 34, 35, 40, 44, 46, 64, 65, 82, 84, 85, 86, 91, 92, 93, 101, 111, 116, 117, 124, 126, 132, 138, 141, 142, 143, 153, 157, 159, 167, 170, 178, 179, 182, 185, 190, 191, 199, 201
141 Squadron	22, 27, 32, 34, 49, 59, 117
145 Squadron	22, 32, 34, 43, 64, 65, 72, 73, 75, 76, 82, 84, 92, 104, 106, 110, 113, 115, 116, 117, 120, 125, 126, 128, 132, 133, 135, 137, 140, 171, 172
151 Squadron	15, 32, 64, 64, 65, 72, 75, 78, 84, 85, 91, 94, 99, 101, 102, 110, 113, 115, 130, 134, 139, 141, 142, 143, 150, 151, 153, 161, 167, 175, 178, 179, 182, 187
152 Squadron	22, 32, 36, 37, 38, 114, 119, 124, 135, 137, 139, 141, 146, 147, 148, 153, 157, 158, 160, 161, 163, 166, 167, 169, 172, 190
213 Squadron	15, 32, 63, 64, 65, 66, 72, 76, 77, 78, 80, 82, 115, 135, 137, 140, 141, 145, 146, 147, 148, 149, 151, 153, 157, 160, 162, 162, 163, 166, 169
219 Squadron	22, 32, 152, 156
222 Squadron	32, 81, 84, 95, 99, 124, 177, 178, 179, 181, 182, 188, 189, 190, 192, 199, 201
229 Squadron	22, 32, 43, 64, 72, 78, 84
232 Squadron	132, 167
234 Squadron	22, 32, 43, 106, 114, 125, 126, 136, 151, 153, 158, 160, 161, 163, 168, 171, 190, 193, 194-5, 196, 197, 199, 200, 201

216

Index

238 Squadron	32, 83, 102, 113, 114, 119, 120, 125, 126, 135, 137, 141, 142, 145, 146, 147, 163, 172, 203
242 Squadron	22, 33, 39, 63, 65, 72, 73, 74, 75, 77, 78, 82, 84, 92, 93, 110, 113, 121, 133, 163, 165, 173, 174, 178
245 Squadron	22, 33, 39, 43, 63, 80, 82, 84, 93, 95, 96
247 Squadron	172, 180
249 Squadron	83, 107, 134, 153, 158, 168, 182, 183-4, 187, 199, 201, 202
253 Squadron	22, 33, 39, 64, 65, 72, 73, 140, 177, 178, 179, 181, 182, 183, 190, 195, 196, 198, 199
257 Squadron	83, 117, 118, 126, 127, 135, 141, 142, 148, 149, 159, 161, 163, 170, 179, 182, 188, 189
263 Squadron	22, 33, 46, 47, 50, 62, 72, 73, 74, 75, 76, 77, 78, 84, 90, 102, 132
264 Squadron	22, 33, 51, 53, 56, 59, 74, 76, 77, 79, 82, 156, 170, 173
266 Squadron	22, 33, 35, 63, 85, 139, 142, 153, 157, 160
302 Squadron	132, 163, 189
303 Squadron	132, 178, 179, 182, 188, 189, 190, 199, 201
306 Squadron	180
310 Squadron	132, 170, 179, 189
312 Squadron	180
403 Squadron	176
452 Squadron	34
457 Squadron	118
501 Squadron	15, 33, 53, 55, 56, 57, 60, 61, 66, 75, 77, 85, 86, 91, 111, 113, 114, 119, 125, 128, 132, 139, 140, 141, 152, 153, 158, 159, 161,167, 172, 173, 177, 178, 179, 181, 182, 183, 184, 187, 189, 199, 201
504 Squadron	15, 33, 44, 60, 61, 62, 63, 65, 66, 125, 126, 198
600 Squadron	15, 27, 33, 51, 53, 102, 136, 151, 158
601 Squadron	15, 26, 33, 39, 63, 64, 65, 72, 76, 91, 99, 106, 113, 115, 119, 125, 135, 137, 141, 142, 144, 145, 146, 148, 153, 158, 160, 161, 177, 178, 179, 189, 195, 197, 198, 201
602 Squadron	15, 18, 19, 20, 28, 33, 34, 35, 36, 99, 104, 106, 109, 118, 121, 151, 157, 158, 160, 161, 162, 169, 171, 176, 179, 190, 193, 195, 197, 201
603 Squadron	15, 18, 19, 20, 28, 33, 35, 40, 99, 102, 104, 106, 114, 115, 116, 118, 119, 121, 130, 131, 174, 175, 176, 177, 178, 179, 181, 182, 184, 185, 186, 188, 189, 199, 201
604 Squadron	15, 33, 51, 53, 65, 72, 83, 94, 137, 138, 153, 170
605 Squadron	15, 24, 27, 33, 38, 41, 46, 50, 72, 75, 76, 136, 152, 155
607 Squadron	15, 19, 33, 41, 43, 51, 52, 53, 55, 56, 57, 60, 61, 62, 63, 65, 66, 102, 152, 155
609 Squadron	15, 33, 38, 81, 84, 110, 113, 114, 115, 125, 126, 135, 137, 139, 141, 146, 147, 148, 151, 153, 169
610 Squadron	15, 33, 77, 78, 81, 91, 92, 104, 107, 109, 111, 115, 116, 119, 121, 124, 128, 130, 137, 139, 150, 153, 158, 160, 163, 164-5, 166, 167, 168, 169, 170, 172, 175, 178
611 Squadron	15, 33, 38, 85, 104, 163, 176, 180
615 Squadron	15, 22, 33, 49, 52, 53, 56, 57, 60, 61, 62, 63, 66, 92,

217

	96, 101, 102, 115, 116, 119,	60 Wing	66
	123, 126, 140, 150, 151,	82 Squadron	62
	152, 158, 159, 163, 167,	107 Squadron	101
	168, 170, 171, 173, 174	110 Squadron	101
616 Squadron	15, 22, 27, 33, 36, 77, 84,	276 Squadron	165
	86, 95, 99, 100, 104, 134,	512 Squadron	34
	152, 155, 156, 169, 170,	515 Squadron	59
	175, 177, 178, 179, 181,	608 Squadron	19
	182, 187	1423 Flt	102
1 (RCAF)		PDU	
Squadron	170, 179, 181, 194, 197, 198	40	
F.I.U	90, 120, 160, 161	**Wings**	
Scapa Def. Flt	19	145 Wg	130, 176
Spec Duties Flt	56	244 Wg	63
Sullom Voe		Biggin Hill Wg	130, 176
Fighter Flt.	33	Culmhead Wg	118
Sumburgh		Detling Wg	82
Fighter Flt.	42	Ibsley Wg	63
Miscellaneous		Kenley Wg	42
4 CFF	65	Middle	
7 OTU	151	Wallop Wg	63
44 Squadron	28	Milfield Wg	118
53 Squadron	142, 147, 150	Tangmere Wg	118

Units - Luftwaffe

Erprbungsruppe 210	137, 139, 149,15	III./JG 27	120, 125, 129
	3, 191, 192,	Jagdgeschwader 51	97, 110, 183,
	193-4		192
FAG./O.b.d.L.	36	St./JG51	127, 129
Fliegerkorps II	76	I./JG51	127, 128, 192,
Jagdgeschwader 2			192
I./JG 2	191	2./JG 51	128
II./JG 2	110, 191	II./JG 51	99, 105, 107,
Jagdgeschwader 3	97, 174		109, 112
I./JG 3	62	III./JG 51	59, 117, 129,
III./JG 3	101		192
9./JG 3	101	Jagdgeschwader 53	
Jagdgeschwader 20		1./JG 53	55
I./JG 20	101	III./JG 53	29, 129
Jagdgeschwader 26		Jagdgeschwader 54	
St./JG 26	129	I./JG 54	191
III./JG 26	121, 127, 128,	III./JG 54	191
	129	Jagdgeschwader 77	
7./JG 26	129	St./JG 77	129
8./JG 26	93	I./JG 77	192
Jagdgeschwader 27	24, 97	1./JG 77	192

218

Index

Jagdgruppe 88	203	*Kampfgeschwader 55*	
Jagdverbande 44	129	*III./KG 55*	57
Kampfgeschwader 1		*Küstenflieger Gruppe 606*	19
5./KG 1	94	*Kampfgruppe 100*	36
Kampfgeschwader 2	111, 142, 143	Kampfgruppe 126	
Kampfgeschwader 3		*2./K.Gr.126*	93
III./KG 3	134	Lehrgeschwader 1	146
Kampfgeschwader 4	94	*I./LG 1*	192
St./KG 4	87	*IV./LG 1*	112
II./KG 4	87	*V./LG 1*	192, 195, 197
4./KG 4	87	*Lehrgeschwader 2*	
5./KG 4	88	*I(J)./LG 2*	101
Kampfgeschwader 26	19, 28	*Luftflotte 5*	152
St./KG 26	20, 27	*Zerstorergeschwader 1*	
I./KG 26	37	*I./ZG 1*	51
II./KG 26	42	*Zerstorergeschwader 2*	192
4./KG26	35, 37	*St./ZG 2*	195
6./KG 26	44	*Zerstorergeschwader 26*	149
Kampfgeschwader 30	155	*II./ZG 26*	183
I./KG 30	18	*Zerstorergeschwader 76*	192
Kampfgeschwader 54		*II./ZG 76*	192-3, 197
I./KG 54	144	*III./ZG 76*	194, 195, 197
4./KG 54	105	*1(F)./123*	25
II./KG 54	144		

Places

Abbeville, Fr	33, 66, 86, 94, 98, 195		157, 159, 170, 178, 181, 186, 207
Abbotsinch AD, UK	15		
Aberdeen, UK	106	Bishop Auckland, UK	154
Acklington AD, UK	22, 32, 37, 154	Bishop's Waltham, UK	147
Amiens, Fr	66, 95, 142	Black Patch Hill, UK	194
Andover AD, UK	147	Blyth, UK	154
Arras, Fr	66, 67	Bognor Regis, UK	145
Arundel, UK	142, 143, 193	Boos AD, Fr	95
Ashford, UK	184, 186, 187	Bordeaux, Fr	92
Banniel Flat Farm, UK	37	Borkum, Ger	26
Bardufoss, Nor	67, 76	Botleigh, UK	148
Beachy Head, UK	175, 193, 195	Boulogne, Fr	72, 74, 99, 191, 193
Bekesbourne, UK	185		
Bembridge, UK	146, 148	Bournemouth, UK	167
Benson AD, UK	147	Bouzonville, Fr	41
Berry-au-Bac AD, Fr	52	Bradwell Bay AD, UK	191
Bexhill, UK	193	Breda, NL	56
Bibury AD, UK	162	Brighton, UK	120
Biggin Hill AD, UK	14, 15, 24, 32,	Bristol, UK	151, 172, 177

219

Brize Norton AD, UK	157	Dieppe, Fr	142
Brooklands, UK	190, 191, 195	Digby AD, UK	15, 22, 32, 33, 102
Brussels, Bel	54, 62		
Burton Bradstock, UK	147	Dinard, Fr	192
Calais, Fr	67, 70, 72, 74, 75, 96, 99, 137, 151, 160, 191	Dorking, UK	195
		Dover, UK	106, 107, 108, 114, 116, 117, 121, 124, 125, 126, 127, 137, 138, 140, 149, 150, 164, 170, 181, 182, 183, 184, 188, 189
Cambrai, Fr	65		
Cambridge, UK	87, 94		
Canterbury, UK	142, 170, 184, 186, 190		
Canvey Is, UK	87, 94		
Capel, UK	187		
Castle Camps AD, UK	83	Dover Straits UK	106, 107, 110, 112, 117, 121, 126, 133, 137, 139, 149, 169, 181, 182, 184, 187
Catfoss, UK	130		
Catterick AD, UK	14, 15, 22, 32		
Causley Wood, UK	193		
Charmy Down AD, UK	153		
Chatham, UK	182, 183, 184, 185, 188		
		Drem AD, UK	32, 33, 154
Chelmsford, UK	87	Driffield AD, UK	156
Cherbourg, Fr	94, 145, 161	Druridge Bay, UK	37
Chester, UK	151	Dungeness, UK	143, 169, 185, 186, 187, 191, 192
Chilbolton AD, UK	32		
Church Fenton AD, UK	15, 22, 32, 33, 83, 102, 156, 180		
		Dunkirk, Fr	65, 70, 73, 74, 75, 76, 77, 78, 79, 80-1, 84, 85, 92, 97, 176, 198
Clacton, UK	149		
Cley-next-the Sea, UK	87		
Colchester, UK	171	Dunnet Head, UK	50
Colerne AD, UK	151	Durham, UK	154
Condé, Fr	51	Duxford AD, UK	14, 15, 31, 32, 132, 173, 178, 180
Cowden, UK	192		
Crail, UK	28		
Crecy, Fr	191	Eartham, UK	145
Cromer, UK	33	Eastbourne, UK	114
Croydon AD, UK	14, 15, 22, 31, 32, 153, 159, 178, 195	Eastchurch AD, UK	142, 152, 171, 172, 178, 181, 185, 186, 187, 188, 190
Culmhead	118		
Culvers Farm, UK	193	East Mersea, UK	188
Deal, UK	71, 149, 166, 186, 187	Eban Emael, Bel	50
		Evanton AD, UK	32
Debden AD, UK	14, 15, 32, 33, 83, 170, 178	Farnborough AD, UK	157
		Farne Is, UK	35, 37, 38, 154
Detling AD, UK	82, 150, 181, 185	Faversham, UK	190
		Felixstowe, UK	87

Index

Filton AD, UK	15, 22, 33, 105	Ibsley AD, UK	63
Finsbury Park, UK	162	Ivychurch, UK	186
Flamborough Head, UK	134, 156	Kaldadarnes AD, Ice	102
Folkestone, UK	105, 111, 117, 125, 132, 182, 183, 187	Kenley AD, UK	31, 32, 42, 153, 159, 195, 198, 200, 207
Forbach, Ger	40	Kidlaw, UK	19
Ford AD, UK	160, 161, 194	Kingston, UK	207
Forth, Firth of. UK	18, 28, 35, 154	Kinloss AD, UK	33
Foulness Is, UK	186	Kinnaird Head, UK	44
Gatwick AD, UK	32	Land's End, UK	106, 125
Goodwin Sands, UK	127	Leconfield AD, UK	15, 22, 32, 33, 83, 132
Gosport, UK	157, 160, 161		
Grangemouth AD, UK	32	Leeming AD, UK	32
Gravesend AD, UK	134, 165, 182, 184, 188, 191, 192, 200	Lee-on-Solent AD(RN), UK	157
		Le Havre, Fr	92, 116, 161
		Le Mans, Fr	93
Great Yarmouth, UK	133	Lesjaskog, Nor	47
Griz Nez, Cap, Fr	25, 46, 140, 142, 149, 164, 191	Le Touquet, Fr	32, 105
		Le Treport, Fr	101
Guernsey, CI	142, 143	Leysdown AD, UK	142
Hague, The, NL	51	Lille, Fr	32, 50, 52
Hart, UK	155	Linton, UK	121
Hartfield, UK	193	Lipezk, USSR	12
Harwell AD, UK	157	Little Butts Farm, UK	193
Harwich, UK	128, 137, 149	Littlehampton, UK	142, 143
Hastings, UK	168, 175, 192, 200	London, UK	165, 181, 194
		Louvain, Bel	59
Hawarden AD, UK	151	Lowestoft, UK	134
Hawkinge AD, UK	127, 139, 142, 150, 151, 184, 186	Lubey, Fr	25
		Luton, UK	178
		Lympne AD, UK	139, 140, 151, 184, 186
Hazebrouck, Fr	23		
Hendon AD, UK	83	Maastricht, Bel	54, 56
Herne Bay, UK	143, 184	Maidstone, UK	166, 170, 182, 183, 184, 185, 186, 187, 188
Heybridge, UK	192		
High Salvington, UK	194		
Hooten Park AD, UK	15	Manston AD, UK	22, 32, 33, 36, 128, 142, 149, 150, 151, 187
Hornchurch AD, UK	15, 32, 157, 170, 176, 178, 186, 188, 207		
		Marck AD (Calais), Fr	67, 73
Hornsea, UK	36, 155	Margate, UK	88, 121, 139
Horsham, UK	194	Marseilles, Fr	91
Hove, UK	133	Martlesham Heath AD, UK	15, 31, 32, 33, 83, 88, 142, 149, 152, 199
Hullavington AD, UK	151		
Humber, the UK	19, 156, 168		
Hythe, UK	184, 186	May Is, UK	100, 109

221

Meopham, UK	183		146, 147, 148,
Merville, Fr	101		153, 162, 169,
Metz, Fr	40, 91		205
Meuse R, Bel	54, 56, 59	Portland Bill, UK	148
Midhurst, UK	144	Portsmouth, UK	168, 171
Middle Wallop AD, UK	63, 147, 151, 153	Prestwick AD, UK	33
		Ramsgate, UK	110, 167, 188, 191, 200
Milfield AD, UK	118		
Mon Robert, Fr	101	Redhill AD, UK	32, 190
Mons, Bel	51	Reigate, UK	190
Montrose, UK	130	Rheims, Fr	91
Netheravon AD, UK	151	Rhyl, UK	202
Netley, UK	195	Roborough AD, UK	180
Newcastle, UK	38, 136, 154, 155	Rochester, UK	152, 183, 187, 193, 207
Norrent-Fontes, Fr	191	Rochford AD, UK	32, 150, 172, 173, 184, 185
North Benfleet, UK	80		
North Coates AD, UK	33	Ronaldsay Is, UK	46
North Foreland, UK	126, 142, 143, 182, 183, 184, 186, 187	Rotterdam, NL	50, 51, 56, 59
		Rouen, Fr	91
		Rouvres AD, Fr	31, 32, 50, 51
Northolt AD, UK	14, 15, 31, 32, 102, 132, 188, 194	Saarlautern, Ger	41
		St. Abb's Head, UK	38
		St. Alban's Head, UK	146
North Weald AD, UK	15, 32, 33, 173, 178, 186, 188, 189, 198	St. Avold, Fr	44
		St. Catherine's Pt, UK	145, 146
		St. Inglevert AD, Fr	32, 33
Norwich, UK	100	St. Omer, Fr	101
Ockham, UK	195	St. Quentin, Fr	52, 62, 64
Oise R, Fr	62	St. Valery-en-Caux, Fr	92, 99
Old Romney, UK	186	Saltwood, UK	132
Old Sarum AD, UK	120	Sandwich, UK	149
Orfordness, UK	109	Scapa Flow, UK	19, 33, 40, 46
Orkney Is, UK	38, 40, 41	Scarborough, UK	155, 156, 157
Ostend, Bel	60, 94	Scilly Is, UK	63
Paris, Fr	86, 91, 94	Scorton AD, UK	32
Patching, UK	194	Seclin (Lille), Fr	32, 51
Pembroke, UK	125	Sedan, Fr	50, 55, 56, 59, 60, 61
Peronne, Fr	65		
Peterhead, UK	42, 102	Seaham, UK	154
Petworth, UK	142, 144	Seine R, Fr	91
Plymouth, UK	106	Sellinge, UK	183
Poling, UK	160, 161	Selsey, UK	115, 148
Portishead, UK	125	Selsey Bill, UK	148
Portland, UK	105, 112, 113, 114, 116, 124, 125, 137, 145,	Senon, Fr	52
		Sheerness, UK	149, 150
		Sheppey, Isle of, UK	142, 150, 184,

Index

	188, 200	Thirsk, UK	138
Sherburn-in-Elmet AD, UK	102	Thorney Island AD, UK	147, 160, 161
Shetland Is, UK	33, 41	Toul, Fr	19
Shoreham Downs, UK	195	Tours, Fr	91
Sittingbourne, UK	188	Tunbridge Wells, UK	191, 192
Six-Mile Bottom, UK	87	Turnhouse AD, UK	15, 22
Skaanland, Nor	75, 76	Tyneside, UK	95, 154, 156
Skegness, UK	120	Usworth AD, UK	15, 155
Smith's Knoll, UK	187	Vassincourt AD, Fr	31
Solent, The, UK	147, 161	Ventnor, UK	161, 161
Southampton, UK	110, 147, 148, 207	Verdun, Fr	50
		Vignacourt, Fr	101
South Downs, UK	143	Vitry-en-Artois AD, Fr	33, 51
Southend, UK	24, 87, 94, 150	Wainfleet, UK	170
Southwold, UK	130	Walton-on-the-Naze, UK	117
Spithead, UK	142	Warmwell AD, UK	146, 169
Spurn Head, UK	159	Washington, UK	194
Stapleford AD, UK	192	Wear, UK	156
Steyning, UK	195	Wells, UK	190
Stockbridge, UK	120, 147	Westgate, UK	136
Sullom Voe AD, UK	23, 33	West Malling AD, UK	142, 157, 159
Sumburgh, UK	32, 167	Weston-Super-Mare, UK	105
Sunderland, UK	103	Weybridge, UK	191
Sutton Bridge AD, UK	22, 33	Weymouth, UK	125, 145, 146, 169
Swanage, UK	125, 145		
Tangmere AD, UK	15, 22, 33, 118, 120, 143, 144, 157, 194	Whitby, UK	37, 42, 44
		Whitchurch, UK	143
		Whitnose, UK	146
Teeside, UK	95, 156	Wick AD, UK	44, 50
Tenterden, UK	192, 193	Wight, Isle of, UK	111, 124, 125, 134, 139, 145, 146, 153, 158, 161, 171, 205
Ternhill AD, UK	33		
Thames estuary, R, UK	109, 113, 115, 121, 138, 142, 143, 149, 150, 160, 163, 170, 173, 182, 183, 184, 185, 186, 188, 191, 200, 201, 206		
		Winchester, UK	148
		Witheridge, UK	170
		Wittering AD, UK	14, 15, 31, 32, 33
		Worthing, UK	128, 143, 158, 193, 194, 195
Thameshaven, UK	201	Wroughton AD, UK	147
Thanet, UK	183	Yarmouth, UK	120
Thionville, Fr	44		

223

Miscellaneous

Fighter Command Aircraft
Hurricane I	20-1
Gladiator I/II	48-9
Defiant I/II	58-9
Blenheim If	89-90
Spitfire I	122-3

Ships
East Dudgeon LV	38
Gneisenau	90
HMS Acasta	90
HMS Ardent	90
HMS Basset	135
HMS Furious	62
HMS Glorious	90, 102
HMS Hood	18
Scharnhorst	90
South Knock LV	44

Various
23-Squadron Plan	11
51st Highland Div.	92
52-Squadron Plan	12
'Bacon' convoy	125
Battle of Britain Clasp	206
'Bosom' convoy	119
'Britain First'	89
Condor Legion	129
CW9 convoy	see 'Peewit'
Dyle Line	60
Dynamo, Operation	75, 81, 84, 86
Ftr Cmmd Area Attacks	203
Hawker Works, UK	191
London Docks	181
Lufthansa	11
'Mae West'	97
Maginot Line, Fr	50, 52
Munich Agreement	14
Paula, Operation	86
'Peewit' convoy	134-5, 206
Pobjoy Works, UK	193
Rapallo Treaty	12
RDF	13-14, 17, 203, 206
Rodeo operation	198
Russo-Finnish War	45
Scheme L	14
Scheme M	14
Short Works, UK	187, 207
Vauxhall Works, UK	178
Versailles Treaty	11
Vickers Works, UK	190, 191